HOLY HOMICIDE

An Encyclopedia of Those Who Go With *Their* God... And *Kill!*

by Michael Newton

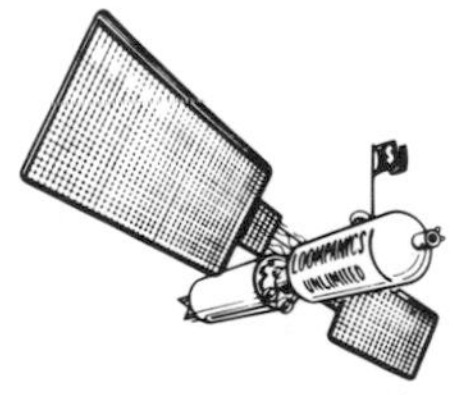

Loompanics Unlimited
Port Townsend, Washington

This book is sold for informational purposes only. Neither the author nor the publisher will be held accountable for the use or misuse of the information contained in this book.

Holy Homicide: An Encyclopedia of Those Who Go With *Their* God—And *Kill!*

Published by:
Loompanics Unlimited
PO Box 1197
Port Townsend, WA 98368
Loompanics Unlimited is a division of Loompanics Enterprises, Inc.
1-360-385-2230
E-mail: loompanx@olympus.net
Web site: www.loompanics.com

ISBN 1-55950-164-2
Library of Congress Card Catalog 98-65683

Contents

Author's Note

I have long since given up on trying to remember how I wrote nonfiction in the dim, dark days before I met Dave Frasier, trusted friend, fellow author, and researcher *par excellence*. To say this book would not exist without his help is an exaggeration only of degree. I owe you several, bro'.

Entries in the text include general topics (e.g., **Human Sacrifice**), specific individuals (e.g., **John Chivington**), recognized churches or groups (e.g., **Nation of Islam**), and broader religious "movements" or philosophies (e.g., **"Christian Identity"**). All relate in some way to the topic of religion-motivated homicide. Individuals named herein as killers are so identified on the basis of published confessions, criminal convictions, or — in the case of fugitives at large and subjects deceased prior to trial — from evidence released by law enforcement agencies. With respect to specific organizations, no general guilt is implied, nor should it be inferred, concerning homicides committed by individual members of a larger, presumably legitimate group. Where public spokesmen for such groups openly advocate murder, those statements speak for themselves. Disciples who choose to act upon those urgings are, both legally and morally, responsible for their own actions. Names which appear in **bold type** in the body of text are those of subjects with their own discrete entries. Where appropriate, entries are also cross-referenced to subjects of related interest.

Dedication

For Chase, a new player in the game of life.
Ante up, my man, and God keep.

Introduction

Philip Wylie, in *Generation of Vipers*, describes human history as "a black and gory business, with more scoundrels than wise men at the lead, and more louts than both put together to cheer and follow." The same could easily be said of organized religion, as this volume amply illustrates.

***Holy Homicide: An Encyclopedia of Those Who Go With* Their *God... And* Kill!** deals with holy homicides, whether committed by unstable loners or by armies, acting under orders from a pope, prime minister, or king. As demonstrated here, religion is among the oldest, most persistent motives for murder throughout human history. Millions — perhaps billions — of victims have suffered and died through the ages, in the name of one god or another.

We hear much today about the grisly homicides committed by Satanists, in pursuit of communion with their dark lord, but those cases are not included here. Readers with an interest in such crimes are referred to my previous works, *Raising Hell* (Avon, 1993) and "Written in Blood: A History of Human Sacrifice" (*The Journal of Psychohistory*, Fall 1996 issue). These pages, rather, catalog the crimes committed by devotees of other gods — be they Allah or Yahweh, Kali or Buddha, Jesus Christ or Damballah. On balance, it is evident that followers of "righteousness" have been responsible for far more bloodshed than the diabolists who seek a shortcut into Hell.

Holy Homicide: An Encyclopedia Of Those Who Go With *Their* God... And *Kill!*

2

It is impossible, in any book this size, to offer an exhaustive view of homicides committed in God's name. Still, it *is* possible to provide a broad overview of the problem, with pointers for serious students who wish to pursue a more intensive study. The entries collected here include case histories of 40 individual killers, 18 groups or churches involved in religion-motivated slayings, and half a dozen general topics — "gay bashing," holy wars, terrorism, and so forth. The section on religious wars alone includes details of more than 100 bloody conflicts spanning some 2,000 years, all fueled by contention between opposing faiths.

Holy Homicide should not be regarded as an effort to disparage faith in God or to discredit a specific church. The author's private view of certain racist teachings, violent exorcism and the like will be apparent in the text, but spokesmen for religious creeds that deal in violence are their own worst enemies. Their doctrines are presented here without apology, for all to see. And where those teachings have resulted in the loss of life, guilt lies with those who pull the trigger, wield the sword, or plant the bomb.

It is a sad fact that religion of all kinds, despite its influence on charity, good deeds, and such, has also been responsible for more concerted mayhem than all other social or political philosophies combined. One need only consider the record of the Christian Church during the Crusades and Inquisition, spanning some 500 years of torture, rape, and genocide. The love of God in Heaven has too often translated into hatred of men on earth, pursued with bloody zeal by those who would eradicate selected unbelievers, heretics, or "infidels." When enemies outside the faith are lacking, true believers often turn upon their own, annihilating relatives and loved ones in bizarre, sadistic ceremonies meant to "save" their souls.

3

"Think not that I am come to send peace on earth," Christ told his followers, in *Matthew* 10:34. "I came not to send peace, but a sword." For centuries on end, that sword has stained the pages of our history with blood from countless victims, and the slaughter still goes on — in Bosnia, in Northern Ireland, in the Middle East, and in America. Before a problem can be solved, it must be recognized and understood. The time is now, before new tools of mass destruction and a fresh wave of religious carnage take the world by storm.

A

Abraham, Patricia

A resident of Harlem, 25-year-old Patricia Abraham believed that her infant son Leon was possessed by Satan. On January 2, 1980, she endeavored to "cleanse him of the devil" by dousing the child with scalding water, then placing him inside a heated oven. Neighbors intervened at the sound of screams, and tiny Leon was hospitalized with second- and third-degree burns over 95 percent of his body. When he died, four days later, charges against Patricia were elevated from first-degree assault to murder. Eleven months later, in November 1980, Abraham was found incompetent for trial and confined to a hospital for treatment.

Aldrete, Sara: See Constanzo, Adolfo

Alt, Erns: See Michel, Josef and Anna

American Christian Movement for Life

There has seldom been an odder couple in religious history than the co-founders of the American Christian Movement for Life. One half of the team, Donald J. Glassey, was a white academic in his mid-twenties, teaching at the University of Pennsylvania while he polished off a master's degree in social work; the other, Vincent Leaphart, was a black, middle-aged grade-school dropout whose criminal record included convictions for auto theft and armed robbery. The unlikely duo met sometime in the early 1970s, at a fair-housing protest in Powelton Village, bordering the UPA campus, and they seemed to hit it off at once. By 1972, they were pushing a weird brand of communal religion on the streets of Philadelphia, Leaphart was sporting dreadlocks and railing against "The System," boarding disciples at Glassey's crumbling Victorian mansion on North 33rd Street. Three years later, there were 35 adults and children living in the house, with a roughly equal number of stray dogs and cats. The human residents included several junkies and ex-convicts, lured to the cult — called "Move," for short — by Leaphart's rousing rap.

By that time, Vincent had renamed himself "John Africa," with his disciples adopting the "Africa" surname. Glassey was the lone exception, clinging to his identity while he transcribed the "deep" thoughts of his colleague, producing a 300-page collection of wisdom entitled *The Teachings of John Africa* (later simply retitled *The Book.*) In practice, members of the cult obeyed their leader's every whim. Move women were expected to bear children for the cult, instructed by "expert" John Africa in the fine points of biting through the umbilical cord and licking their newborns clean. Cultists were also driven to relentless bouts of exercise, as many as 300 pushups at a time. While dissent was swiftly punished, those who played along were now and then rewarded with "distortion days," with junk-food binges as a special treat.

As Move began to grow, its members made their presence felt in Philly, courting media exposure through a series of noisy, pointless demonstrations. Pickets armed with signs and bullhorns, screaming insults and profanity, staked out the city zoo and college campuses, hospitals, even veterinary clinics. They began to pile up an impressive record of misdemeanor arrests and civil complaints, mostly for public nuisance, zoning, and sanitation violations around their squalid headquarters. In one seven-month period of 1974 alone, Move members were arrested 150 times, always representing themselves in court, with a rowdy cheering section in the gallery. The *Philadelphia Inquirer* described Move's performance at a governor's conference, held in a downtown restaurant: "It was this night that Move members demonstrated their most baffling ability: How can they talk continuously, punctuating each phrase with an obscenity, without ever saying anything comprehensible?"

Don Glassey bailed out of the cult in 1975, complaining that Leaphart/Africa "wanted absolute control over everyone," telling anyone who would listen that he feared violence in the offing. Move headquarters was the object of frequent complaints about animals running at large, nude toddlers roaming the neighborhood unsupervised, continuous racket and threats, garbage and human waste flung from windows to rot in the street. The cult responded by erecting a stockade around the house, with a wooden stage out front, complete with loudspeakers that bellowed threats and challenges around the clock. One tirade warned the neighborhood that Move was working on an A-bomb. In 1976, following a sidewalk scuffle with police, Move's amplifiers blared a charge that cops had stormed the house and killed infant "Life Africa." Reporters and city councilmen who investigated the case were shown a baby's rotting corpse, lying on a bed of dirt and garbage in a cardboard box. A female cult defector subsequently told authorities that the child had died of natural causes, a victim of John Africa's ban on medical treatment.

It was May 1977 before city authorities got an eviction order for Move, but the cultists were not prepared to go quietly. Half a dozen members brandished guns and clubs outside the house, while their P.A. system warned police, "The only way you will come in is over our dead bodies." Lawmen mounted 24-hour surveillance on Move headquarters and turned to Don Glassey, locked up on a drug rap, for more information on the cult. Glassey described a stockpile of illegal arms, including bombs allegedly planted in cars outside the compound, and federal firearms charges were filed against John Africa. Mayor Frank Rizzo told the press that "Move has had its day," but the zealots were still holed up in their stockade the following March, when Rizzo ordered a full blockade of the compound. In early August 1978, denouncing the cultists as "a bunch of complete idiots," Rizzo prepared to storm the makeshift fort.

Move's troops were waiting when police launched their assault at dawn, on August 8. Loudspeakers blared, "If you want us out, you'll have to bring us out dead!" When police used their battering ram on a window, squealing rats poured out and scattered in the unaccustomed daylight. Moments later, shots rang out, killing Officer James Ramp, wounding three other police officers and four firemen before raiders breached the cult's ramparts, dragging the defenders off in chains. Mayor Rizzo had their compound bulldozed the same day, and while nine Movers were finally sentenced to life for their part in the shootout, John Africa was nowhere to be found. He had slipped through the net and vanished while authorities delayed their raid for 15 months.

It should have been the end for Move, but such was not to be. Surviving members of the cult dispersed across the landscape, some to an affiliated chapter in Richmond, Virginia, others to a house in Rochester, New York, where they were shortly reunited with their leader. Feds and local officers descended on the house in 1981, arresting John Africa as a fugitive on weapons charges, but he was acquitted at trial and dropped out of sight once again. Before the year was out, his loyal disciples had returned to Philadelphia, setting up shop in a row house owned by Leaphart's sister, on Osage Avenue. Within a year, the sister — Louise James — bailed out, compelled by fear to leave her home as Movers started setting up their loudspeakers, collecting animals, living in filth. By early 1984, they were engaged in new construction on the house, boarding the windows up, building a bunker on the roof. Their all-night tirades were accompanied by the display of weapons, punctuated by threats to "take care of you people" on the August anniversary of the 1978 shootout.

Pugnacious Frank Rizzo had been replaced by black mayor Wilson Goode, but his successor had no love for Move's terrorist tactics. By April 1984, the cult compound was once more under siege, Mayor Goode and his police department laying strategy for an eventual attack, plotting their moves with the aid of aerial surveillance. In the absence of overt criminal acts, Goode felt obliged to watch and wait. A year elapsed before his lookouts spotted cultists dumping boxes filled with dirt outside the house, inspiring rumors of a tunnel network spreading underneath the neighborhood. The press joined in demands for action, while Mayor Goode procrastinated, finally handing "Operation Move" over to his police commissioner on May 7. Search and arrest warrants were issued on charges including riot, firearms violations, and terrorist threats, but cult members refused to budge unless their cronies were released from prison. One of the tribe, Ramona Africa, sent out a letter warning Mayor Goode, "If Move goes down, not only will everybody in this block go down ... we will burn this house and burn you up with us."

On Mother's Day, May 12, police began evacuating houses in a six-block area around Move headquarters, clearing some 300 homes by midnight. By dawn, the cult's loudspeakers were blasting a typical challenge: "Cops, come in and get this thing started. We're going to kill you motherfuckers. We're going to turn this city into a ghost town!" Police Commissioner Gregory Sambor issued a final ultimatum, to which cultists replied, "We ain't got a motherfucking thing to lose. Come in and get us!"

The battle was joined as water cannons opened up on the roof-top bunker, trying in vain to bring it down. Tear gas followed, and automatic weapons cut loose from the windows of Move headquarters, authorities responding with fire hoses and gunfire of their own. Ten thousand bullets had been fired into the house before Commissioner Sambor called a cease-fire, at 7:20 A.M., with television cameras beaming the action nationwide. The bunker still stood, despite 650,000 gallons of water poured into the fortress, and when police tried to flatten the house with a crane, they were stymied by lack of room to maneuver. By 2:00 P.M., it was decided that tear gas should be dropped from helicopters, but an opening would be required. To that end, a bomb was constructed out of Tovex, which generates heat up to 7,000° F. It might have been expected that such heat would start a fire, but no one in the raiding party seems to have considered it. The bombing went ahead at 5:30 P.M., flames leaping from the Move headquarters moments later, spreading rapidly throughout the neighborhood. By half-past midnight, when the fire was finally controlled, some 60 homes had been destroyed. Two members of the cult escaped, leaving John Africa and ten others to burn in the wreckage. Five of the dead were children, the youngest barely six years old.

"Ant Hill Kids": See Theriault, Roch

Anti-Catholicism: See Ku Klux Klan and "Nativist" Movement

Aryan Nations: See "Christian Identity"

Asahara, Shoko: See Aum Shinrikyo

Aum Shinrikyo

Japan is world-renowned as a haven for bizarre alternative religions, but none in recent memory has sparked more controversy — or spawned more lethal violence — than the sect known as Aum Shinrikyo ("Supreme Truth"). Organized in 1989, the cult was later linked to a triple murder commmitted in its first year of operation; six years later, its leaders were jailed for a mass-murder plan designed to bring about the ultimate apocalypse.

Aum Shinrikyo's founder, Shoko Asahara, was born in 1955 with poor eyesight and attended a school for the blind before moving to Tokyo in 1976. Early acquaintances recall his childhood obsession with money and power. Years later, in Tokyo, he founded a yoga school and was jailed on charges of selling phony medicine. That rap behind him, he shifted to religion in 1989, starting with a group of ten disciples who regarded the myopic messiah as their "venerated master."

Before the year was out, Aum Shinrikyo was already drawing complaints from the parents of youthful recruits. Several families pooled resources and retained attorney Tsutsumi Sakamoto to sue the cult. Weeks later, in November, Sakamoto, his wife and their 14-month-old son disappeared without a trace. It would be six years later, in September 1995, before their remains were discovered, resulting in murder charges against Asahara and company.

By then, however, the "venerable master" of Aum Shinrikyo had more pressing problems on his hands. After years of preaching imminent apocalypse, most recently a forecast that 90 percent of the world's urban population would die in poison gas attacks by 1997, Asahara had decided to give prophecy a helping hand.

In June 1994, seven residents of Matsumoto were killed and over 200 injured, when deadly sarin nerve gas was released in a residential neighborhood. Developed by German scientists in the 1930s, sarin is among the world's deadliest chemical weapons, all the more dangerous for its easy preparation from basic chemical compounds. Authorities investigating the attack found evidence of sarin byproducts near Aum Shinrikyo's headquarters in Kamikuishiki, 100 miles southwest of Tokyo, but there was insufficient evidence for any charges, and the case remained officially unsolved.

Nine months later, on March 20, 1995, persons unknown released another blast of sarin on the Tokyo subway, during morning rush hour. This time, 12 persons were killed, with over 5,500 treated for nonfatal injuries. Two days later, police raided cult headquarters in Kamikuishiki, but Asahara and his chief lieutenants had already fled. Four cultists were arrested, but the real surprise was in the evidence retrieved: two tons of chemicals required for making sarin — enough, in fact, to kill at least four million people; $7 million in cash; gas masks; and cult publications including Asahara's predictions of impending gas attacks throughout the world. Another 50 cultists were in residence, most of them severely malnourished, but none was detained by police.

Shoko Asahara was still at large on March 24, when he showed up on national television, denying any role in the Tokyo gas attack. His sincerity was questioned, three days later, when police found a chemical lab concealed at an Aum

Shinrikyo shrine, near Mt. Fuji. On March 29, his cultists were suspected in the near-fatal shooting of Takaji Kunimatsu, Japan's top law enforcement officer, and two more cultists were jailed on March 31, for carrying explosive chemicals. On April 7, illegal firearms were seized from a vehicle owned by the sect.

Asahara, for all his protestations of innocence, was still predicting disaster — most recently mass death for Tokyo, expected to occur on April 15. That date passed without incident, but four days later, in Yokohama, 300 persons were injured when poisonous phosgene gas was released in the city's main railroad terminal. On April 21, two dozen more were hospitalized by a gas attack in a Yokohama shopping center. The following week, Japanese authorities announced that two army sergeants, both members of Aum Shinrikyo, had forewarned Asahara of the police raids in March.

The dragnets and the terror went on. On May 4, police arrested cult attorney Yoshinebu Aoyama as a suspect in the gas attacks. Days later, an alert cleaning woman for the Tokyo subway discovered new gas bombs with sophisticated trigger mechanisms — enough gas, police said, to kill 10,000 people. On July 4, cyanide canisters were found at another Tokyo train station, but the devices were successfully disarmed. Australian police reported that cult members had apparently tested their gas on Aussie sheep, at a remote farm in the outback.

By that time, more than a dozen cultists were in custody, facing various charges related to the gas attacks. Shoko Asahara himself had been captured on May 15, indicted with six others on murder charges stemming from the March subway attack. On June 20, one of his disciples still at large hijacked an airliner with 350 persons aboard, demanding the immediate release of "venerable master" Asahara, but police stormed the plane and disarmed him without loss of life.

On October 5, 1995, Japanese news sources reported that Shoko Asahara had confessed involvement in the Tokyo subway attack and various other crimes. One of his aides, Masahiro Tominaga, surrendered to police three days later, facing charges of attempting to murder Tokyo's governor. On October 30, a Japanese court officially ordered the disbandment of Aum Shinrikyo, but murder trials are still pending as this is written. Asahara has recanted his alleged confession to describe himself as a victim of government persecution.

Auriol, Joseph

Father Joseph Auriol had worked long and hard to become a priest in the French Pyrenees, rising to the post of abbé at Prats-de-Mollo, but rude gossip surrounded his nocturnal visits to the young, attractive women of his parish. After five years in Prats-de-Mollo, Father Auriol moved on to the small village of Nohédes, where he was cared for by the elderly Fonda sisters, Rose and Marie. On the side, Auriol was conducting a clandestine love affair with a 22-year-old schoolteacher from a nearby village, sneaking out to meet her at night in the garb of a smuggler, complete with false beard.

By 1870, Father Auriol was fed up with the church, so desperate to leave that he asked a wealthy uncle for sufficient cash to let him make his way across the Spanish border, there to build a new life and career with his lover at his side. The self-righteous uncle angrily refused, informing Auriol that he could remain with the church or go out on his own as a beggar. The choice was his.

But it was not the only choice.

In July 1870, Auriol poisoned Marie Fonda with hellebore root from the nearby forest, her death ascribed to anemia. Marie left all her worldly goods to sister Rose, but Father Auriol at once began persuading Rose to put him in *her* will. His later story was that she agreed, in private conversation, but the formal will was never changed. When Auriol poisoned Rose's tea, on August 30, her death was initially blamed on a longstanding heart condition ... but her will contained no provision for the hopeful priest.

That didn't stop Auriol from grabbing the cash, however — some 11,000 francs in all — and he still had the money with him, along with a vial of deadly prussic acid, when police came to arrest him, tipped off by an anonymous letter. Exhumation confirmed the presence of prussic acid in Rose Fonda's body, and Auriol confessed both murders after 37 days in jail. At that, it took almost a year before his trial began, by which time he had recanted his statements of guilt, but it didn't help his case. Jurors convicted him of double murder, but considered his attempts to leave the church as an extenuating circumstance. It saved him from the guillotine, and Father Auriol was sentenced to spend the rest of his life in prison.

Bashir, Mohammed

Kousar Bashir had the makings of a modern young woman, despite her religion. A child of fundamentalist Muslim parents living in Lancashire, England, she aspired to the western concepts of education, affluence, and mobility. Still, there were setbacks. When Kousar failed her first driver's test at age 21, in the spring of 1990, she was visibly depressed — so much, in fact, that she considered suicide. Kousar was hospitalized for psychiatric care in April, but it failed to do the trick. When she returned home, more depressed than ever, relatives decided that she was possessed. An evil *djinn* had slipped into her body, somehow, and the only way to drive it out was with the help of a veteran exorcist.

Learned elders of the Muslim community referred Kousar's family to 55-year-old Mohammed Bashir (no relation), who in turn sought help from Sayeed Nourani. A recognized "healer," the 63-year-old Nourani had performed more than 200 exorcisms, convinced that possession by *djinn* was the root of most mental and physical ills. Nourani's brand of exorcism was straightforward and brutal: victims of possession needed beating, which would drive the evil spirits from their bodies and finally leave them in peace.

The "cleansing" of Kousar Bashir began on June 10, 1991, and lasted into the predawn hours of June 18. The girl was slapped, whipped, kicked, and beaten with various objects, including a walking stick and a heavy glass ashtray. During respites from the clubbing, hot chili powder was poured down her throat, to further discomfit the demons inside. When she finally stopped breathing, Mohammed Bashir warned her family, "If anyone asks, say that the demon pushed her down the stairs and that the fall killed her."

It was worth a try, but autopsy results quickly disproved the lie. Kousar Bashir had suffered sixteen broken ribs, together with a fractured sternum and more bruises than a simple fall downstairs could ever cause. Her relatives grudgingly described the exorcism they had witnessed, and indictments were filed: Mohammed Bashir faced murder charges, while Sayeed Nourani stood accused of conspiring to cause grievous bodily harm. Both men were convicted in a nine-day trial, Bashir receiving a life sentence, while Nourani was jailed for five years.

Bear, Michael: See Carson, Michael and Susan

Bestiality: See Capital Punishment

"Bible John"

Scotland's most elusive serial killer was a man with a mission, preaching to the women he selected from a Glasgow dance hall prior to strangling them and dumping their bodies like so much cast-off rubbish. Glib and handsome, a natural charmer, he carried a Bible in his pocket and referred to it often, quoting scripture from memory to make his point, fanning the pages to impress a captive audience with his knowledge of holy writ. Manhunters called him "Bible John," because he never gave another name. He killed at least three times, then vanished into mystery. He is, unfortunately, one of those who got away.

Bible John claimed his first victim on Friday, February 23, 1968. His hunting ground, then and always, was the popular Barrowland Ballroom, where he made a point of chatting up the ladies, mingling flirtation with good-natured lectures on the perils of fornication, making it clear that he was a godly man who still knew how to have a good time. Several women recalled their conversations with the dashing redhead, but he left with 25-year-old Patricia Docker. She never made it home that night, her nude body found on a street near the ballroom. Patricia had been strangled with her own tights; the rest of her clothes were missing from the scene.

Police staked out the dancehall, but in vain. Bible John apparently recalled that patience is the virtue of the saints, and he would wait another 18 months to claim his second victim.

The heat was off by August 16, 1969, when he returned to Barrowland and met Jemima MacDonald, afterward dumping her lifeless body in an abandoned house nearby.

Victim number three was 29-year-old Helen Puttock, visiting the ballroom with her sister on October 30, 1969. Both women met the Bible-quoting redhead that night, but he encouraged Helen's sister to make herself scarce. Later that night, when Helen failed to make it home, her sister would go searching through the streets. Two hundred yards from home, she would find Helen's body, stretched out like a broken mannequin, discarded by her murderer.

Glasgow police did everything within their power to identify the strangler, placing decoys in the dancehall, running sketches of their suspect in the local newspapers, but nothing did the trick. Bible John had retired, moved on, dropped dead — whatever. He remains anonymous today, and while a second string of unsolved murders vaguely echoed his technique, in 1977-78, no positive connection to the first three murders has been found. Suggestions that the Glasgow stranglings may have represented early work by "Yorkshire Ripper" **Peter Sutcliffe** likewise came to nothing, since England's self-styled "street-cleaner" habitually mutilated his victims. The case of Bible John remains as it began: unsolved.

Biblical Bloodshed

Biblical history is problematical at best. Some items are clearly fictional — there never was an Assyrian king named Pul, as described in 2 *Kings* 18:1 — and other items remain controversial. The first independent evidence of King David's existence was not discovered by archaeologists until 1993, and to this day there is no trustworthy reference to Jesus Christ in any document outside of the New Testament. Likewise, in the endless list of massacres and wars detailed by the Old Testament, many remain unsupported by any historical evidence, but it hardly matters for our purposes, since Biblical *attitude* has inspired so much real-life bloodshed throughout history.

The Old Testament, in fact, is a blueprint for genocide, beginning with Israel's flight from Egypt and proceeding through her subjugation of the "promised land." God Himself set the tone in *Joshua* 1:3, promising His chosen people "every place that the sole of your foot shall tread upon." Of course, that land was occupied, but not to worry: any predecessors of the Israelites would simply be annihilated, man, woman, and child. What follows — if, indeed, it ever happened — is a bloody land-grab dwarfing anything that befell the American Indian.

It began with the familiar battle of Jericho, wherein the sound of trumpets allegedly brought the walls tumbling down, but childhood versions of the tale omit mention of the fact that Jericho's population was "utterly destroyed... both man and woman, young and old," with the city burned around them. (*Joshua* 6:20-21) A short time later (*Joshua* Chapter 8), the Israelites slaughtered 12,000 residents of A'i, "both men and women," while hanging their king from a tree. There follows another massacre at Azekah, "a very great slaughter" at Makkedah, and a one-sided battle at Libnach, where the Israelites killed "all the souls that were within." Rolling on, Joshua and his troops slaughtered the entire population of Lachish; "none remained" when they were finished smiting the King of Gezer and his people; the residents of Eglon and Debir were "utterly destroyed"; while the raid on Hebron "left none remaining." In fact, we are told that the Israelites, acting on orders from God, "utterly destroyed all that breathed" in the territory "from Kardesh-barnea even unto Gaza, and all the country of Goshen, even unto Gibeon." (*Joshua*, Chapter

10) If this were not enough, the slaughter continues in Chapter 11, with further massacres at Hazor, Madon, Shimron and Achshaph, "from Mount Halak...even unto Ba'al-gad in the valley of Lebanon under Mount Hermon." In a classic understatement, we are told that "Joshua made war for a long time"; Chapter 12 of *Joshua* lists another 19 kings whose people were butchered by the rampaging Israelites.

Nor did the killing end with Joshua's reign. The book of *Judges* is a bit more specific on body counts, listing 10,000 Canaanites and Perizzites killed in Chapter 1; another 10,000 at Moab (Chapter 3); 600 Philistines massacred by one man (Chapter 3); all the soldiers of King Jabin slain (Chapter 4); the men of Penuel massacred in Chapter 8; about 1,000 men and women killed at Shechem (Chapter 9); 1,000 Philistines wiped out by Samson in one brawl (Chapter 15); 40,000 Israelites and 45,000 Benjamites killed in pitched battles against each other at Gibeah (Chapter 20).

And the beat goes on. King David butchered 80,700 Syrians in various battles (2 *Samuel* 8:5-13; 10:6-18), while his enemies retaliated in kind, raiding the city of Nob, among others, where they killed "both men and women, children and sucklings." (1 *Samuel* 22:18-19) Years later, King Amaziah reportedly slaughtered 20,000 "children of Seir" (2 *Chronicles* 25:11-12), while angry Jews massacred 75,000 of their enemies over two days' time, in the territory ruled by King Ahasuerus. (*Esther* 9:5-16)

Nor did God leave all His killing to mortal hands. In *Exodus*, He drowned Pharaoh's army (Chapter 12), and later crushed His enemies with stones from heaven at Gibeon. (*Joshua* 10:10-12) Ever irritable, He killed 57,070 men for peeking into the Ark of the Covenant (1 *Samuel* 6:19), and sent fire to consume another 102 at Elijah's request. (2 *Kings* 1:10-12) A short time later, when 42 children made fun of

Elisha's bald head, God sent two bears to kill them. (2 *Kings* 2:23-24) Overall, there is no arguing with the judgment of *Exodus* 15:3 that "The Lord is a man of war." Indeed, most of the Biblical wars were His fault, since He went out of His way to "harden the hearts" of Israel's enemies, from Egypt to Lebanon. (*Exodus* 7:3, 9:12, 10:20, etc.; *Joshua* 11:20)

True or not, the Old Testament example of kill-thy-neighbor is calculated to evoke belligerence against nonbelievers, and millions of zealots worldwide still pursue that intractable course, waging bloody war against the faithful of other religions and "heretics" within their own denominations. There appears to be no likelihood of a cessation in the mayhem caused by faith. **[See also: Crusades; Inquisition; Religious Wars; Terrorism]**

Black Hundreds

Local massacres (pogroms) of Russian Jews became a grim but predictable, fact of life after the 1881 assassination of Tsar Alexander II, but true organization of the atrocities was lacking until the rise of an anti-Semitic organization, the League of the Russian People, better known to its friends and enemies alike as the Black Hundreds. Secretly founded during the Russian Revolution of 1905 and unofficially sanctioned by the Tsarist government, the League drew its membership primarily from Russia's "upper crust": landowners, bureaucrats, police, and wealthy peasants. Between 1906 and 1911, the Black Hundreds murdered revolutionaries in the Russian provinces, but Jews remained the primary target, chosen as a scapegoat for Russia's many social and economic problems. In six years of active fighting, the Black Hundreds organized pogroms in more than 100 Russian cities; the lethal riots in Odessa lasted four days before order was restored.

Aside from brawling in the streets, the Black Hundreds also promoted circulation of a weird document, titled *The Protocols of the Learned Elders of Zion*, which pretends to be a blueprint for Jewish domination of the world. (In fact, it was a clumsy fraud, probably produced by agents of the Russian secret police to inflame public opinion against Jews, but countless bigots still accept the *Protocols* as authentic.) As hoped by the Tsar, sweeping violence against Jews gave the Russian autocracy a perfect excuse to delay enactment of the new constitution prepared in 1905. Sadly, there have been reports of a new racist group, also called the Black Hundreds, active in Russia since the 1991 collapse of Soviet communism. **[See also: Terrorism]**

Black Muslims: See Nation of Islam

"Bleeding Kansas": See Brown, John and **Religious Wars**

"Blood Atonement": See Mormons

Boudes, Abbé

Abbé Boudes was the kind of clergyman who gives religion a bad name. Expelled from the seminary at Perigueux, France, for stealing a cassock and candlesticks in 1855, he went on to ecclesiastical college, and got the boot there, a year later, on charges of immorality. Undeterred, the 26-year-old "holy man" made his way to Italy, where he was subsequently consecrated as a priest. That left the French church with no choice but to accept him, but formal ordination did nothing to improve Boudes's behavior. In fact, he was soon up to his old tricks, stealing from the church, procuring abortions for parishioners, loaning out money at extortionate rates, and in general disgracing himself.

Such antics are difficult to conceal over time, and Boudes was soon convinced that his supervising priest had evidence against him. Rather than confess his sins and hope for mercy, Boudes poisoned the wine his superior was supposed to drink at Mass, but an altar boy observed him in the act and blew the whistle. At that, the church was merciful, and Boudes got off with a transfer to Viviers, where he soon lapsed back into a life of venal crime. Transferred again — this time to Taurinos, with a promotion — Boudes lost all restraint, fatally stabbing another priest, Abbé Alvar, during a church burglary. Charged with murder in that case, he pled mental instability and was sent to an asylum, where he spent ten years before escaping with the help of a corrupt guard.

Free once more, Boudes resurfaced in Tarn, posing as an Alsatian priest called "Father Jean Marie." He was soon promoted again, this time to serve as professor of religion at the Ste. Marie School in Albi, but his luck was running out. A member of his former parish recognized Boudes one day and turned him in to the authorities. Returned to Taurinos for trial in the murder of Abbé Alvar, Boudes was convicted and sentenced to life in prison.

Branch Davidians

Ronald Reagan was still enjoying his first term of office, in 1983, when 23-year-old Vernon Wayne Howell turned up at the Mt. Carmel religious commune, outside Waco, Texas. The illegitimate, dyslexic son of a Dallas native, born when his mother was barely 14, Howell combined a love of heavy metal music with a fascination for the Bible, reportedly memorizing most of the New Testament before he was 13 years old. He was raised in the Seventh Day Adventist church, but was ejected at age 21, for disrupting services by "ranting and raving." Howell preferred to think of it as religious persecution, but he had other problems on his mind when he reached Mt. Carmel, confessing worry over his penchant for excessive masturbation. Cult leader Lois Roden, then 67 years young, decided that what Vernon needed was a woman's touch, and so she took him to her bed.

Mt. Carmel was the headquarters of a fundamentalist sect called the Branch Davidians, which traced its roots to the 1930s. In those days, Bulgarian immigrant Victor Houteff had led a minor walkout from the Adventist church, creating his own Davidian SDA cult with a base outside Waco. At Houteff's death, in 1955, his widow moved the cult to nearby Mt. Carmel, where she began predicting Christ's return at Easter 1959. It was another disappointment, leading to a rift within the congregation, 50 die-hard followers — rechristened Branch Davidians — remaining at Mt. Carmel under the leadership of "prophet" Ben Roden. In 1978, Ben went the way of all flesh, and widow Lois took over the commune, but son George soon defected to lead his own splinter group, loudly contesting her rule of the cult.

Vernon Howell, meanwhile, was starting to experience some "revelations" of his own, proclaiming that he was the final angel sent by God to supervise the Last Days of the planet. After Lois Roden died, he left Mt. Carmel with a group of 25 disciples, leading them on an aimless trek through the Southwest before they settled near Palestine, Texas. The move left George Roden in charge of Mt. Carmel, where he spent much of his time denouncing Howell as a bastard, an adulterer, a "rock and roll musician, and a Satan worshiper." Word got around that Vernon planned on taking Mt. Carmel away from George, by force if necessary, and Roden responded by challenging Howell to a ghoulish test of faith. In October 1987, Roden exhumed the corpse of an 85-year-old woman buried at the ranch, declaring that whichever "prophet" raised her from the dead should rule the cult. Instead of joining in the fun, Howell tried to have his rival jailed for corpse abuse, but Waco's sheriff shrugged the whole thing off as a sick joke.

The stage was set for violence, and Howell got the ball rolling on November 3, 1987, when he led a team of seven men in camouflage fatigues, all armed, to infiltrate Mt. Carmel and secure a photo of the corpse, to make the sheriff take him seriously. Roden saw them coming and cut loose with a machine gun, touching off a twenty-minute battle in which George was slightly wounded. Vernon and his crew were jailed, but quickly posted bond, while Roden was locked up for contempt of court in an unrelated case, after filing what his prosecutor called "some of the most obscene and profane motions that probably have ever been filed in a federal courthouse." In Roden's absence, Vernon and his loyalists quickly occupied the commune. At their trial in 1988, on charges of attempted murder, Howell and company proclaimed that they had only meant to frighten Roden, and charges were dismissed when jurors failed to reach a verdict in the case.

Back at Mt. Carmel, Vernon was feeling his oats. George Roden was out of his hair, committed to a mental institution after killing a man, and Howell moved to solidify his hold over the cult. He married 14-year-old Rachel Johnson, and she bore him two children before he decided that one wife was less than his due. Before long, he was building up a harem which he called the "House of David," with his peripheral "wives" ranging in age from their teens to early fifties, some reportedly as young as ten or 12 years old. Howell claimed he chose his mates on spiritual merit; it was mere coincidence that he selected only the attractive girls and women from his flock. At one point, Vernon made a trip to Israel, hoping to "convert the Jews," but when that effort failed, he wound up back in Waco, telling his disciples that the ultimate apocalypse would strike in Texas, rather than the Holy Land, as he had once declared.

In terms of doctrine, Vernon grew increasingly extreme and dictatorial. He formed a private goon squad, dubbed the "Mighty Men," and in August 1989 he declared himself the only Branch Davidian allowed to have a wife — in fact, he was entitled to as many as his heart desired. All other marriages within the cult were instantly annulled, a move which drove some loving couples to defect from Mt. Carmel. Those who remained did their best to rationalize the new rule, one telling reporters, "We as Davidians aren't interested in sex. Sex is so assaultive, so aggressive. [Vernon] has shouldered that burden for us." On his way to godhood, in 1990, Howell legally changed his name to "David Koresh," a merger of the Old Testament's King David and the Hebrew name for Cyrus, the Persian Conqueror of Babylon, who permitted Jews to return to Israel. On the side, he began to bill himself as the reincarnation of Jesus, telling his disciples that "if they remained faithful, God would one day return and take them to heaven in his spaceship." As befit a god, Koresh occupied the only room at Mt. Carmel with air-conditioning or television, often sleeping until 2:00 P.M., while his flock did grunt work on the farm and sweltered in the Texas heat. At worship services, convened three times a day, Koresh would rant for hours on end about the evil world outside the commune and his own exalted role in Bible prophecy. As God's last earthly representative, he was entitled to absolute power. "It means that the prophet owns everything," he said, "your house, your money, even your underwear. That means when the prophet comes to your house at night and asks you to strip naked, you are obligated by God to hand over your underpants."

Increasingly, he warned his followers about the danger posed by "Babylon," investing them with paranoid delusions that the state or federal government was working overtime to crucify the second Christ. "We will put a weapon in everyone's hand," Koresh proclaimed. "If you want to die for God, you must be willing to kill for God." He changed the name of Mt. Carmel to Ranch Apocalypse and started building up an arsenal of weapons, said by cult defectors to include a .50-caliber machine gun and at least 300 other firearms, some 11 tons of firepower in all. A bus was buried at the compound, serving as a bunker for the army of the Lord. In 1992, a UPS deliveryman reported to the feds that he had dropped a heavy carton at the ranch and it had ruptured, spilling hand grenades. By that November, agents of the Treasury Department's Bureau of Alcohol, Tobacco, and Firearms had sufficient testimony in their files to justify warrants for a search of the ranch and Koresh's arrest.

What happened next remains a subject of enduring controversy. Critics say that federal agents could have taken David any time they wanted to, when he went shopping for supplies, guitars, or guns. Instead, they stalled for three months, planning a commando raid against the ranch itself on February 28. The day before their scheduled strike, the Waco *Herald-Tribune* began a series which denounced the Branch Davidian cult as a "menace in our community," increasing paranoia at the ranch as David's sheep prepared themselves for war. Next morning, when the black-clad raiders made their move, an hour-long battle left ten persons dead — six cultists and four members of the strike force — with another 24 ATF agents wounded. At least one of the Davidians was reportedly wounded by federal gunfire, then executed by his brethren to "put him out of his misery." Koresh himself was shot, and told his mother he was dying, but he managed to hang on for another 51 days, while FBI agents laid siege to the ranch.

In David's mind, the standoff was a vindication of his own apocalyptic prophecies. He had predicted the government would come to wipe his people out, and there its agents were, camped on the highway with their guns and armored vehicles. It was a golden opportunity to spread his word before a global audience. On April 10, he penned a letter to the outside world that read: "The law is mine, the Truth is Mine. I AM your God and You will bow under my feet. I AM your life & your death. I AM the Spirit of the prophets and the Author of their testimonies." In case anyone missed the point, Koresh wrote another letter the following day, declaring that "My hand made heaven and earth. My hand shall also bring it to an end. Your sins are more than you can bear."

Eight days later, on April 19, 1993, the FBI got tired of waiting, moving in with tanks and tear gas. Futile gunfire sputtered from the barricaded house, before a fire broke out — perhaps ignited by a tear-gas canister, or set deliberately on orders from Koresh; no one will ever know. When the smoke cleared, Koresh and 75 of his followers were dead in the ruins, including 25 children, 12 of them reportedly the prophet's own. Autopsy results showed that Koresh had been shot in the forehead, an apparent suicide, while his second in command, Steve Schneider, was shot in the mouth. Seventeen others, including five children, had been shot before they burned, including one woman shot in the back, and a two-year-old boy was apparently stabbed to death. Eight members of the cult escaped the blaze, some with their clothes in flames, and 11 of David's disciples — including some not present at the ranch on February 28 — were ultimately tried for murder of the four dead ATF men. At their trial, in 1994, all 11 were acquitted of murder and conspiracy, although five were convicted of manslaughter, seven others on miscellaneous firearms violations.

Brown, John

By the late 1840s, controversy over slavery had deeply divided America, with opponents denouncing the "peculiar institution" as immoral, while slave owners cited Bible verses to prove it a "positive good." Above the Mason-Dixon Line, some Christian abolitionists were not content to sermonize or passively await the Second Coming as a means to solve their problem. Harriet Beecher Stowe became the movement's chief propagandist, with publication of her novel *Uncle Tom's Cabin*, but her brother, Henry Ward Beecher, adopted a more militant role. More than 3,000 New England ministers had signed petitions opposing passage of the Kansas-Nebraska Act, which permitted settlers in those territories to decide for themselves if slavery would be allowed, and when petitions failed, Rev. Beecher called for open combat. "Let it be settled now," he thundered from his pulpit. "Bring the champions. Let them put their lances in rest for the charge. Sound the trumpet, and God save the right." Champions needed weapons, though, and Beecher was happy to supply them, shipping rifles — known as "Beecher's Bibles," after their deceptive packaging — to anti-slavery zealots in the territory that would soon be known as "Bleeding Kansas."

No warrior for the cause did more to fire up abolitionist resistance or increase slaveowners' paranoia than a religious fanatic named John Brown. A New York native, born at the turn of the century, Brown read his Bible faithfully without absorbing any of the scriptures that supported slavery. He was among the Northern "champions" who answered Rev. Beecher's call to stand and fight in Kansas, and by May of 1856, Brown's patience had approached the breaking point.

He was outraged, on May 21, when proslavery forces led by a racist U.S. marshal, raided the free-soil community of Lawrence. They burned the town's only hotel, along with several homes, and demolished the newspaper office, killing two men in the process. Four days later, Brown and a half-dozen gunmen, including four of his sons, retaliated at Potawatomie, Kansas, slaughtering five Southern men and boys, several of whom were mutilated with Brown's favorite saber. The bloody one-two punch touched off a full-scale shooting war in "Bleeding Kansas," with at least 200 persons killed in sundry skirmishes by January 1861.

Brown's favorite tactic was to sweep down on a farm owned by slaveholders, murder any white men he could find, and liberate as many of his "colored brothers" as agreed to join the ranks of his expanding private army. If Brown also helped himself to horses and assorted other stolen property along the way, such items were the rightful spoils of war — a holy war, at that — and it would still be months before Brown's small guerrilla band began receiving cash from abolitionists in the United States and Canada. By that time, he was leaning toward the notion of a more dramatic gesture, something that would leave a mark on race relations in America, perhaps provoking a general slave revolt across the South.

In July of 1859, Brown moved to Harper's Ferry, Virginia, home of the unguarded Federal Arsenal. He used a pseudonym and introduced himself to neighbors as a cattle buyer, but procuring livestock was the last thing on his mind. He had $4,000 in his pocket, donated by northern abolitionists, and a fantastic scheme was already unfolding in his mind. Brown meant to seize the arsenal, arm local slaves, and lead his liberated army southward through the Appalachians, spreading freedom as he went. It was a pipe dream, and supporters like the savvy Frederick Douglass tried to talk Brown out of it, but he would not be swayed. By mid-October, 21 of his guerrillas had arrived in town, and they were spoiling for a fight. The raid went forward on a Sunday night, the sixteenth of October, and while Brown indeed secured the arsenal, his plans collapsed beyond that point. There was no general uprising of slaves in answer to his call, and local whites besieged his unit in the arsenal before U.S. Marines arrived to call for Brown's surrender. Brown held out through that night, but his small force was overrun the next day, by professional soldiers. The butcher's bill was 18 dead on both sides, including two of Brown's sons, with several more wounded. As for the prophet of armed liberation, John Brown was transported to Charlestown for trial, where he was swiftly convicted and hanged.

Bruneau, Abbé

Abbé Bruneau, of Laval, was another French priest who used murder to cover his lesser crimes in the 19th century. Like **Abbé Boudes** before him, Bruneau was more concerned with money than immortal souls, a weakness that led him to embezzle 1,500 francs from the church in December 1893. When his supervisor, Abbé Fricot, sat down to check the books on January 2, 1894, Bruneau panicked, with deadly results.

Abbé Fricot was missing at 7:00 o'clock that evening, when the dinner bell rang, and Bruneau told the servants he was "out," his whereabouts unknown. A search began at once and lasted through the night. Next morning, Fricot's battered corpse was found at the bottom of an old well, pinned under two feet of water by a crude pile of logs. Examination of the body indicated that the priest had been savagely beaten, perhaps for as long as two hours, before a crushing blow to the skull ended his life.

As police began their investigation, Abbé Bruneau abruptly changed his story. In the new version, he had seen Fricot loitering near the old well, and later returned to find his colleague dead, an apparent victim of suicide. Hoping to spare Fricot's reputation and save the church from scandal, Bruneau claimed, he had thrown logs atop the corpse to simulate a homicide. By that time, however, Bruneau was suspected in a series of other crimes, including arson for profit and the murder of a florist in Laval, whose throat was cut during a robbery. Convicted of killing Abbé Fricot, Bruneau was sentenced to death. A crowd of 16,000 turned out to watch him keep his date with Madame Guillotine.

Capital Punishment

American advocates of the death penalty often quote scriptures in support of their cause, but modern capital crimes, at least outside of the Islamic world, are no longer defined as holy writ. There was a time in the United States, however, when adherence to Old Testament standards was a literal matter of life and death — a grim state of affairs which certain zealots wistfully regard as the Good Old Days.

For all the textbook talk about religious liberty in early America, tolerance was hard to come by in the colonies. Maryland's famous Toleration Act of 1649 was written only after years of bloody civil war between Protestants and Catholics in Lord Baltimore's colony, and its final terms were as harsh as the Puritan blasphemy laws. Under terms of the act, flogging, fines and prison were prescribed for any "persons reproaching any other within the province by the name or denomination of Heretic, Schismatic, Idolater, Puritan, Independent, Presbyterian, Popish priest, Lutheran, Calvinist, Anabaptist, Brownist, Antinomian, Round-Head, Separatist, or by any other name or term, in a reproachful manner relating to the subject of religion." At that, only *Christians* were protected, Marylanders being still at liberty to persecute any Jews or atheists they might discover in the neighborhood. And textbooks likewise fail to mention that the Toleration Act was swept away in later years, when Protestants rose up to seize the government of Maryland and pass new laws excluding Catholics from the colony.

Massachusetts legislators took a page from *Deuteronomy* (21:18-21), quoting some of the scripture verbatim when they crafted America's first law on juvenile delinquency:

> If any man have a stubborn or rebellious son, of sufficient understanding and years, *viz fifteen years* of age, which will not obey the voice of his Father, or the voice of his Mother, and that when they have chastened him, will not harken unto them; then shall his Father or Mother, being his natural Parents, lay hold of him, and bring him to the Magistrates assembled in Court, and testifie unto them, that their Son is Stubborn and Rebellious, and will not obey their voice and chastisement, but lives in sundry notorious Crimes, such a son shall be put to death.

Nowhere were religious statutes more intrusive or abusive than in dealing with the sex lives of the early colonists. Such "crimes" as simple fornication and adultery were most often punished by humiliation, as in Hawthorne's *Scarlet Letter*, but other sexual transgressions — such as homosexuality and bestiality — were capital offenses under Old Testament guidelines, and the ultimate penalty *was* invoked from time to time. Governor John Winthrop, of Massachusetts, described the case of 18-year-old William Hackett, caught buggering a cow one Sunday, in 1641, by a woman who had stayed home sick from church:

> When the day of execution came, after he had been at the lecture, he went to the place of execution sadly and silently, and being up the ladder, he said nothing; but the cow (with which he had committed that abomination), being brought forth and slain before him, he broke out into a loud and doleful complaint against himself, bewailed his sinful course of life, his disobedience to his parents, his slighting and despising their institutions and the instructions of his dame, and other means of grace God had offered him, etc.
>
> Then Mr. Wilson, the pastor of Boston (the rest of the elders and the people there present joining with him), prayed earnestly to the Lord for him a good space. He attended duly thereto, and prayed also himself, crying oft and earnestly for mercy; yet with a trembling body, and amazed with the apprehension of death so near at hand, to which he quietly yielded himself, when he was required.
>
> There is no doubt to be made but the Lord received his soul to his mercy.

The following year, at Plymouth, Governor William Bradford recorded a similar case:

> There was a youth whose name was Thomas Granger. He was servant to an honest man of Duxbury, being about sixteen or seventeen years of age. (His father and mother lived at the time at Sityate.) He was this year [1642] detected of buggery, and indicted for the same, with a mare, a cow, two goats, five sheep, two calves, and a turkey. Horrible as it is to mention

> but the truth of the history requires it. He was first discovered by one that accidentally saw his lewd practice towards the mare. (I forebear particulars.) Being upon it, examined and committed, in the end he not only confessed the fact with that beast at that time, but sundry times before and at several times with all the rest of the forenamed in his indictment. And that his free confession was not only in private to the magistrates (though at first he strived to deny it) but to sundry, both ministers and others; and afterwards upon his indictment, to the whole court and jury, and confirmed it at his execution.
>
> And whereas some of the sheep could not so well be known by his description of them, others with them were brought before him and he declared which they were and which were not.
>
> And accordingly he was cast by the jury and condemned, and after executed about the 8th of September, 1642. A very sad spectacle it was; for first the mare and then the cow and the rest of the lesser cattle were killed before his face, according to the law, *Leviticus* 20:15, and then he himself was executed. The cattle were all cast into a great and large pit that was digged of purpose for them and no use made of any part of them.

When no eyewitness to a sex crime was available, investigation of the charge was sometimes more bizarre than the alleged offense. Governor Theophilus Eaton, of New Haven colony (later Connecticut), was called upon to witness the trial-by-masturbation of one Thomas Hogg, accused in 1646 of fathering a piglet that resembled him, it being also wall-eyed on one side:

> The governor and deputy, intending to examine him, caused him to be [led] down to Mrs. [Lamberton's] yard, where the swine were, then bid him scratt [i.e., scratch] the sow that had the monsters and immediately there appeared a working of lust in the sow, insomuch as she poured out seed before them and then they asked what he thought of it, he said he saw a hand of God in it. Afterwards, he was bid to scratt another sow as he did the former but it was not moved at all, which Thomas Hogg acknowledged to be true but said he never had to do with the other sow.

Despite the "evidence" provided by his porcine paramour, Hogg was convicted only on the lesser charges of filthiness, lying, and pilfering. He was sentenced to a severe whipping, followed by prison time "with a mean diet and hard labor that his lusts may not be fed." The sow and piglet's fate was not recorded.

When it came to religious dissent, no sect was so harshly persecuted in the colonies as the Society of Friends, best known as Quakers. They were Christians, to be sure, but they were also pacifists who balked at taking oaths and scorned the formal hierarchy of religion, clinging stubbornly to their beliefs in spite of any threats. When banished, they would frequently return, and Quaker women sometimes demonstrated in the nude against their persecutors, in a show of self-abasement which the ruling clergy labeled sexual degeneracy.

Quakers had been persecuted in England from the day they went public, in 1646, and founder George Fox was frequently imprisoned for his opposition to the Church of England. Ten years passed before the first two Quakers — women from Barbados — stepped ashore in Massachusetts to a rather hostile welcome from the Puritans. They were immediately jailed, stripped naked, and examined for "witch marks." When that search failed, the women were deported, and their books were burned in public, to expunge their lurking evil from the midst of righteous Christendom.

On balance, banishment was the best Quakers could expect from their reluctant hosts in America. A Quaker woman transported from England to Massachusetts in 1657 was sentenced to twenty lashes for her membership in "the accursed sect," before she was expelled. The Friends who followed her were subject to flogging, ear-cropping, branding, or tongue-boring with a hot iron. In 1658, Plymouth Pilgrims enacted a new law to protect their colony from "manifest opposers of the true worship of God," declaring that "No Quaker Rantor or any other such corrupt person shall be admitted to be a freeman of this Corporation." That same year, the Massachusetts general court raised the ante, imposing an automatic death sentence on any Quaker who returned to the colony after being expelled.

Nor were the Chosen People bluffing. One contemporary tabulation of violence against Massachusetts Quakers over the next three years included:

> 1. Two honest and innocent women stripped stark naked and searched after such an inhuman manner, as modesty will not permit particularly to mention.
>
> 2. Twelve strangers in that country, but free-born of this nation, received twenty-three whippings, the most of them being with a whip of three cords with knots at the ends, and laid on with as much strength as could be by the arm of the executioner, the stripes amounting to three hundred and seventy.
>
> 3. Eighteen inhabitants of the country, being free-born English, received twenty-three whippings, the stripes amounting to two hundred and fifty....

> 5. Two beaten with pitched ropes, the blows amounting to an hundred and thirty nine, by which one of them was brought near unto death, much of his body being beaten unto a jelly, and one of their doctors, a member of their church, who saw him, said, *it would be a miracle if ever he recovered, he expecting the flesh should rot off his bones,* who afterwards was banished upon pain of death....
>
> 10. One laid neck and heels in irons for sixteen hours.
>
> 11. One very deeply burnt on the right hand with the letter **H** after he had been whipt with above thirty stripes.
>
> 12. One chained to a log of wood the most part of twenty days, in an open prison, in the wintertime....
>
> 14. Three had their right ears cut by the hangman of the prison, the door being barred, and not a Friend suffered to be present while it was doing, though some such desired .... [Emphasis in the original]

And those survivors were the *lucky* ones. Quakers Marmaduke Stephenson and William Robinson were hanged on Boston Common, in October 1659, for refusing to vacate the colony. A third defendant, Mary Dyer, was forcibly evicted, but she later returned to Massachusetts and was hanged. A fourth Quaker was hanged in 1661, with 28 more on the waiting list when King Charles II ordered a halt to the executions.

Witches, of course, were the ultimate dissidents, and in retrospect, it is surprising that the Puritans took so long to discover witches in their midst. The **Inquisition** had been executing “heretics” and “sorcerers” in Europe since the 13th century, with witches added to the list by Pope Innocent VIII in 1484. Detailed instruction in the identification and torture of suspects was provided two years later, with the publication of *Malleus Maleficarum*, and perhaps a quarter-million victims or more were condemned before the madness ran its course. European Protestants were eager to display their piety by finding witches of their own, and failed attorney Matthew Hopkins gained notoriety as Britain's "witchfinder general" in the 1640s, boasting that he "sent to the gallows more witches than all the other witch hunters in England."

With that background, and God's demand for execution of witches in *Exodus* 22:18, it was predictable that Puritans should be concerned about the threat of those who frolicked with "familiar spirits." Plymouth was the first colony to enact a death penalty for witchcraft, in 1636, followed closely by Connecticut (in 1642) and "tolerant" Rhode Island (in 1648). New Netherlands' skeptical Dutchmen were generally immune to the hysteria, though trials convened soon after England seized the colony in 1646, renaming it New York. Pennsylvania lagged behind the pack, its two witch prosecutions brought by Swedish settlers, up from Delaware, and William Penn prevented either case from reaching trial. Virginia's witch hunts backfired on the faithful, with slander suits pressed against several accusers, but general skepticism did not prevent Grace Sherwood from being imprisoned for witchcraft in 1706. Six years later, in South Carolina, several suspects were mobbed and tortured by superstitious Anglicans; their case was later dismissed, but local authorities refused to prosecute the would-be lynchers who had injured them.

Overall, suspected witches had the most to fear in New England, where Cotton Mather and his ilk seized any opportunity to sit in judgment of their peers. America's first witch, Alse Young, was executed at Windsor, Connecticut, in

May 1647, spared the continental tradition of burning by an English fondness for the gallows. Mary Johnson was the next convicted, sentenced to public flogging at Hartford in August 1648, but whipping apparently failed to cleanse her soul, and she was hanged at Wethersfield, Connecticut, four months later. John and Joan Carrington followed her to the Wethersfield gallows in March 1651, with Goody Bassett hanged at Stratford two months later. Goodwife Knapp was executed for witchcraft at Fairfield, Connecticut, in December 1653, and Lydia Gilbert suffered the same fate 11 months later, at Windsor. Hartford Puritans hanged Nathaniel and Rebecca Greensmith in January 1662, closely followed by the execution of Mary Barnes, at Farmington. Connecticut's last witch, one Mary Sanford, went to the gallows at Hartford, in June 1662.

By that time, the good people of Massachusetts were tired of watching while their neighbors had all the fun. Cotton Mather jumped into the witch-hunting business with both feet in 1688, investigating the alleged possession of the Goodwin family, said to be cursed by an elderly Irish servant. The evidence was ambiguous in that case, but not so at Salem, four years later. Finally, after years of gnashing his teeth on the sidelines of America's mini-Inquisition, Mather was about to get the break he had been praying for.

The Salem "outbreak" began, fittingly enough, at the home of a local minister, Rev. Samuel Parris. Several children were reportedly afflicted with convulsions at the Parris home, interpreted as symptoms of possession by the Devil. Under questioning, the children fingered Rev. Samuel's live-in servant, a slave named Tituba, as the source of their affliction. She, in turn, was smart enough to save herself with a confession, naming two elderly white women as the witches responsible for her own fall from grace. Those suspects, in turn, saw the writing on the wall and fingered others, basking in the spotlight of their roles as heretics-turned-heroes. Dozens were arrested in the next few months, with the harshest treatment reserved for those who refused to confess. Between May and September of 1692, 14 women and five men were hanged as witches in Salem; another man died under torture, while refusing to confess imaginary sins, and yet another woman died in prison, while awaiting disposition of her case. As an aside, the frantic Puritans also executed several domestic animals, identified as "familiars" who stubbornly declined to assume human form and admit their dealings with Satan.

The Salem witch craze finally collapsed when clever suspects started naming various prominent individuals as fellow heretics, but Cotton Mather went to his grave believing he had done a public service by exposing the cancer of witchcraft, while also admitting that some innocent people had suffered. He also got a book out of the deal, published in 1693 as *Wonders of the Invisible World*, which supplied "an account of the sufferings brought upon the country by witchcraft." Back home, meanwhile, things had changed with the ascension of King Charles II to the throne, in 1660. A skeptic who regarded claims of witchcraft and black magic as superstitious nonsense, Charles led a movement that returned by slow degrees to common sense. Witchcraft remained a capital offense in England until 1736, but the last conviction was recorded 24 years earlier, in Leicester.

Such laws and punishments appear bizarre today, but growing numbers of American Christians advocate an immediate return to the colonial system of Bible-based executions. These so-called "Christian Reconstructionists" are devoted to the concept of "dominion theology," which calls for a reversion to the bad old days of rigid theocracy, with a hand-picked elite interpreting and imposing Biblical law, complete with a list of capital crimes drawn from the Old Testament. The political arm of Christian Reconstructionism in America is the U.S. Taxpayers Party, which proclaims that "all civic law should emerge from biblical law." Furthermore, "The U.S. Constitution establishes a republic under God; not a democracy." If anyone missed the point, movement spokesmen have declared that "supernatural Christianity and democracy are inevitable enemies." In 1995, the USTP's national committee included the following stalwart Christians:

- ✞ Rev. Matthew Trewhella, convicted arsonist and friend of the paramilitary "militia" movement.
- ✞ David Shedlock, communications director for Operation Rescue in Iowa, who led demonstrations at a Des Moines synagogue in November 1992, chanting at the assembled worshipers, "Leave your religion! Go to the true religion!"
- ✞ Rev. Michael Bray, convicted women's health-care clinic bomber and a signatory of Paul Hill's "justifiable homicide" declaration.
- ✞ Jeffrey Baker, of Florida, a spokesman for the so-called "10th Amendment Militia, Church Status," who likewise advocates killing abortionists. When not promoting murder, he preaches that supermarket bar codes are Satan's "mark of the beast," and that the Jewish star of David is a symbol of the "New World Order's" plot to dominate mankind.
- ✞ Randall Terry, convicted felon and founder of Operation Rescue, who accused the GOP and Ralph Reed's Christian Coalition of having "sold out the Law of Heaven." "The horrifying truth," Terry told one avid audience, "is that much of the Christian right, led by the

Christian Coalition, has become the mistress of the Republican Party. The party has seduced us, used us, lied to us and made empty promises to us... Now that the religious right mistress has made herself available for the political bedchamber, certain Christian leaders are pimping for us, declaring our willingness to betray our King and lie with the whoremongers of child killing, homosexuality, etc., as long as we get to be near the throne." **[See also: "Pro-Life" Movement]**

Carrawan, George Washington

Reverend George Carrawan grew up in the toughest Southern Baptist tradition. A native of North Carolina, whose father died when George was still a toddler, he was raised by a Bible-quoting mother who had more faith in hellfire than in salvation. Even so, Carrawan was 27 years old before he was baptized and heard "the calling" to become a minister himself. His style drew parishioners to the Goose Creek Baptist Church, but there were some disturbing quirks in the preacher's personality, as well. His fiery temper coupled with obsessive jealousy, to the point that he accused another minister of seducing his wife. Then, when Elizabeth Carrawan died abruptly after 18 years of marriage, the pastor provoked further scandal by marrying his young housekeeper, Mary Bell, three weeks after the funeral. (Between the two wives, Carrawan would father 20 children, three of whom survived.)

Rev. Carrawan was 53 years old when another pastor in the region, Rev. Alvin Swindell, began hinting to friends that Elizabeth Carrawan may have been poisoned. Carrawan, meanwhile, was up to his old tricks, accusing Mary of adultery with any man in the vicinity, but his strict view of fidelity did not stop Carrawan from impregnating a 16-year-old member of his congregation. It was the last straw, prompting elders of the Goose Creek church to fire him, but Carrawan blamed Rev. Swindell, once confronting him with a shotgun, backing down in the presence of inconvenient witnesses.

By November 1852, Carrawan's paranoia had found a new target, in schoolmaster Clinton Lassiter. From all appearances, Lassiter was friendly with the Carrawans, several times spending the night at the minister's house, at Rev. George's suggestion, but the friendship was too good to last. The men quarreled, and Carrawan was heard to complain that Lassiter had "made advances" toward Mary, also slashing at George with a knife in the heat of an argument. Carrawan went so far as to have his wife swear out a complaint of attempted rape against Lassiter, but Mary soon recanted the lie, and Lassiter sued Carrawan for slander, winning a judgment for $2,000 in damages.

That should have been the end, but Lassiter had reckoned without Carrawan's vicious temper. Bright and early one Monday morning, the teacher vanished on his way to school, and he was still missing six days later, when searchers found his body in a shallow woodland grave, killed by a shotgun blast in the back. George Carrawan had been the only local resident of substance who refused to join the search for Lassiter, and suspicion deepened when he fled town that Saturday night, soon after the body was found. In his absence, witnesses came forward to describe the ambush shooting, and authorities were waiting with a warrant when Carrawan returned to Goose Creek in January 1853.

The one-time minister spent ten months in jail before his trial convened, with 30 prosecution witnesses lined up to testify against only six for the defense. Jurors deliberated overnight, and they had barely finished announcing their guilty verdict the next morning, when Carrawan drew a single-shot pistol and fired point-blank at Prosecutor Edward Warren. A locket worn beneath his clothes saved Warren from a fatal chest wound, whereupon the defendant pulled another gun, before deputies could restrain him, and shot himself in the head. This time, his aim was true, and Carrawan was dead before he hit the floor.

Carson, Michael and Susan

The bright, pampered daughter of a wealthy newspaper executive, born September 14, 1941, Susan Barnes appeared to have every advantage in life. In fact, severe dyslexia left her functionally illiterate when she dropped out of high school at age 16. It hardly mattered, with her family's money, and she soon married well, to Arizona businessman Leland Hamilton, bearing the first of two children at age 17. With motherhood behind her at an early age, Susan settled into a comfy routine of tennis, jogging, and country-club parties... but something dark and deadly simmered just below the surface, waiting to erupt.

Leland and Susan separated in 1970, the children remaining with Susan in Scottsdale for a time, until they wearied of their new lifestyle and went to live with their father. At home, Susan had begun to act "crazy," spelling her first name with a "z" and dabbling in the occult, smoking pot and dropping acid, indulging in "artistic" vandalism, sampling an estimated 150 lovers — by her own count — between the breakup of her marriage and November 1977. By that time, she had settled on Islam as her religion of choice, but "Suzan" was unable to read the Koran or anything else, absorbing prescribed doctrine from lectures, making up bits and pieces to suit herself as she went along.

On Thanksgiving Day 1977, Susan met James Clifford Carson, nine years her junior and recently divorced from his wife in Phoenix. They were on a double date, Susan paired with one of Carson's former classmates from the University of Iowa, but weed and acid blurred the guidelines of propriety, and they wound up in bed together. Next morning, Carson moved into Susan's unfurnished Scottsdale townhouse. It was love at first sight, Susan quickly informing Carson that his "true name" was Michael, "the name of an angel in the Bible."

It might have been an odd choice for a Moslem, but Carson didn't mind. They were "Michael and Suzan" from that moment on, blending their mutual love of drugs and loony-tune politics into new and dangerous configurations. Carson's father was a ranking oil-company executive, tapped as an energy advisor to President Nixon in the early 1970s, but "Michael" was the family's black sheep. Weakened by a childhood illness that turned his bones brittle, Carson had become a bookworm, leaning toward Marxist tracts and founding a tiny SDS chapter in his Tulsa, Oklahoma, high school. Later, he drifted into the Twilight Zone of San Francisco's Haight-Ashbury district, somehow winding up at the University of Iowa, where he immersed himself in left-wing campus politics.

Now, he had "Suzan." Carson was absolutely smitten by her intelligence and sexual know-how, her gift of gab and wide experience in the occult. Susan was also obsessed with nudity, and they spent most of their days at the townhouse stark naked, dressing reluctantly when they were forced to go out for fresh supplies of food or drugs. In the summer of 1978, they sold their meager belongings and flew to Europe, stopping in London long enough to be "married" — sans license, in a free-form hippie ceremony — on June 21.

Back in Scottsdale as summer waned, Susan ran afoul of the law with her penchant for exhibitionism. Neighbors reported a nude woman cavorting on the lawn, and a flying squad of police rolled out to catch the show. Invading the townhouse without a warrant, officers found marijuana on the premises and slapped the cuffs on Susan. They refused to let her dress before the trip downtown, requiring her naked body as "evidence" of indecent exposure. In court, after months of legal wrangling, the felony drug counts were dismissed and Susan pled guilty to the exposure charge, receiving a sentence of six months probation. She emerged from the experience profoundly changed, embittered toward the government and laws in general, devoted to the prospect of a Moslem "holy war." As far as Carson was concerned, whatever Susan said was tantamount to gospel; if she said a revolution was required to cleanse the land with blood, so be it. He would tag along.

Early 1981 found the couple in the Haight-Ashbury, soaking up chemicals, sponging room and board from various acquaintances. Their last known benefactor in the Haight was Karen Barnes (no relation to Susan), a 23-year-old doper, failed actress, and topless dancer who made room for "Suzan and Michael" in her basement flat on Shrader Street. None of them had been seen for several days when Karen's landlord stopped by on March 7 and found her dead, her skull crushed with a blunt instrument, stabbed 13 times in the face and throat. As an afterthought, the killer had draped Karen's body with a quilt, slipping a pillow under her head. The name "Suzan" was scrawled across Karen's refrigerator in crayon, and neighbors recalled her live-in guests, but self-styled Moslems "Suzan and Michael" were nowhere to be found in San Francisco.

By mid-March the Carsons were well into Oregon, hiking the Cascades and staking out an abandoned shack on a peak Susan dubbed "Allah's Mountain." In early May, she "felt the call of Los Angeles" and sent James off on an aimless two-week pilgrimage, thumbing rides around the Golden State while Susan kept the home fires burning in Oregon. Carson returned on May 24 to find her half-starved and hysterical, raving about the harassment she had suffered in his absence, from "witches" living nearby. James nursed her back to a semblance of health, plotting revenge on the neighbors, but he never got the chance to act. In August, before his plans were finalized, a ranger from the Bureau of Land Management arrived to evict them from their shack.

They hit the road with a vengeance, drifting through New Mexico, Arizona, Colorado, Montana, circling back to California. At Garberville, in Humboldt County, they found work on a marijuana farm, harvesting and curing the black-market crop. It was a fairly profitable occupation, and they earned enough to winter in Portland, Oregon, shunning regular work while Carson cranked out a rambling manuscript titled *Cry for War*. In essence, it was a mock-Islamic blueprint for revolution, complete with a hit list including such diverse targets as President Ronald Reagan, California Governor Jerry Brown, British Prime Minister Margaret Thatcher, the Ayatollah Khomeini, and cult killer Charles Manson. With spring's arrival, the self-ordained Islamic assassins drifted south once more, in search of prey.

March 1982 found them at Big Sur, California, where they rented a tree house from a local construction worker. Everything was cool at first, until they quarreled with their landlord and he sent a pistol-packing thug to kick them out. "Michael" took a beating in the process, but Susan was unwilling to let the matter drop. At her insistence, Carson brewed himself a batch of Molotov cocktails and went looking for revenge, torching the tree house, his landlord's cabin, and a tent occupied by his recent assailant. Holed up at an abandoned cabin in the wake of their blitz, Carson found a rusty .38 revolver and a box of ammo. Susan took it as "a sign."

Back in Humboldt County by April, they helped plant and irrigate the new marijuana crop, Carson standing guard with a rifle to keep narcs and poachers at bay. Trouble arrived in the form of Clark Stephens, a hard-core San Diego junkie who went out of his way to irritate the Carsons. Tension reached its peak on Clark's third day at the ranch, following an altercation in which he hurled sexual insults at Susan. Three rounds from the rusty .38 shut him up for good, and Susan helped drag his corpse into the woods, where it was burned with kerosene and buried in a shallow grave.

The Carsons kept on drifting. On Tuesday, May 11, they were trudging through the Trinity National Forest, when they met a sheriff's posse on a search-and-rescue mission. Fearing arrest, they struck off through the trees at top speed, leaving the bewildered deputies to search their cast-off packs. Inside, they found a stolen driver's license, "Michael's" box of ammunition, and a manuscript of *Cry for War*.

The hunt began.

Eight days later and far to the south, James was arrested in Monterey Park on suspicion of rape, booked with an alias from the stolen driver's license lost in Trinity County. Police were looking for a long-haired, bearded rapist, but the latest victim took one look at Carson and pronounced him innocent. He was long gone, reunited with Susan, when careless officers found his loaded .38, stashed in the back seat of their patrol car, and new warrants were issued. A pattern was forming, but police still didn't know who they were looking for, or where the fugitives might be found.

Another piece of the puzzle was added on May 17, when the skeletal remains of Clark Stephens were found in

Humboldt County. "Michael and Suzan" were down on the list as prime suspects, but where had they gone? Police in northern California were desperate for leads, coordinating efforts with their brothers to the south, finally catching a break through Carson's sheer stupidity. Asked for a reference in Monterey Park, he had given his jailers the name of Susan's ex-husband, in Scottsdale. Phone calls and a visit brought the game full circle, Leland Hamilton more than happy to fill in the blanks for his visitors in uniform.

The lawmen knew their suspects now, but finding them would still take time.

Thumbing rides near Bakersfield on January 11, 1983, the Carsons were picked up by motorist John Hellyer and driven to Santa Rosa, 75 miles north of San Francisco. Along the way, Hellyer offended Susan by patting her knee and rubbing his leg against hers, dropping comments which she interpreted as satanic witch-speak. She had decided to kill Hellyer by the time they reached Santa Rosa, spending the night with a friend of Hellyer's before continuing the drive north. "Michael," she told Carson in bed, "either you kill that demon or I will."

Next morning, as Hellyer prepared to drop the couple at their chosen off-ramp, James drew a pistol and demanded money. They fought for the gun, tumbling from the pickup, and Susan lent a hand, stabbing Hellyer with her trusty boot knife. James finished their victim off with two shots in the head, but a passing motorist had seen it all, racing to alert police. The Carsons fled in Hellyer's pickup, finally ditching the truck in a vineyard and lighting out on foot. They were captured separately, trying to ford the Napa River at different points.

James told the Napa County booking officer his name was "Michael Bear," but he was running out of time and luck.

Arraigned for Hellyer's murder on January 28, the Carsons were held over for trial without bond. Six weeks later, the news hit San Francisco after "Michael" wrote a peevish letter to the *Chronicle*, demanding publicity for himself "in the important press." One of the subscribers was a San Francisco homicide detective working on the case of Karen Barnes, still searching for "Suzan and Michael." Interviews were arranged on May 4 ... and the Carsons confessed everything.

Karen Barnes, according to the transient killers, had been marked for execution as a "witch" who dabbled in black magic and tried to steal Susan's "Moslem warrior" for some extramarital sex. In defense of their action, the Carsons cited matching texts from the Koran and Holy Bible, proclaiming: "Thou shalt not suffer a witch to live." John Hellyer was another witch, in Susan's estimation, and both male victims had sealed their own fates by "sexually abusing" Susan — Stephens through his insults, Hellyer by patting and "rubbing against" her leg.

Defense attorneys for the Carsons requested a psychiatric evaluation on October 23, 1983, but both defendants were judged sane and competent for trial. Eight months later, in June 1984, both were convicted of killing Karen Barnes, drawing terms of 25 years to life on July 2, 1984. Identical sentences were later pronounced in the cases of Stephens and Hellyer, providing a virtual guarantee that neither witch-hunter will ever make parole.

Castria, James

On January 17, 1995, a resident of Arizona telephoned police in Staten Island to request assistance. The caller was concerned about her sister, Susan Engel, and her elderly brother-in-law Lowell. Neither had responded to messages left on their answering machine over the weekend; East Coast relatives had no idea where they had gone, and they had not checked into any local hospital. Patrolmen checked their tidy flat, at the Cassidy-Lafayette senior citizens' complex, and found nothing out of place. Indeed, the couple had been last seen on January 9, as they left the complex for their regular morning walk. Police traced them as far as the Chinese restaurant where they ate lunch, and there the trail went cold.

Detectives played their last card at the bank where Lowell and Susan Engel kept their savings. Susan had received an $85,000 inheritance in July 1993, and $45,000 of that money had remained in November 1994, when it was suddenly withdrawn and placed into a new account, held jointly with someone named James Castria. A series of withdrawals swiftly drained the new account, until its January balance stood at a pitiful $1.62.

Police went looking for their one and only suspect, tracing him to the Faith of Gospel Church in Clifton, New Jersey. Their man was *Reverend* James Castria, age 45, a clergyman well liked by his parishioners. Rev. Castria knew the missing couple well: in fact, he had introduced them in 1988, after Lowell's first wife died, and Castria had performed their wedding ceremony that July. They kept in touch after the Engels moved to Staten Island, and he had reluctantly agreed to share a bank account at Susan's request, since the aging couple had problems managing money. Castria further admitted to making several withdrawals from the joint account — all perfectly legal — but insisted that the money had been taken out with the permission of the Engels, based on Castria's promise to pay it back.

So far, so good... but then detectives learned that Castria had moved his family to a new $250,000 home in January, just about the time the Engels disappeared. Two months later, the Engels were found in Pennsylvania, beaten to death with a blunt instrument, Rev. Castria denied any knowledge of their death, obliging investigators with blood and hair samples for forensic comparison. He was scheduled for another interview, at the state police barracks in Swiftwater, Pennsylvania, on March 25, but Castria never made it. Instead, he packed his bags and fled, next seen in the crumpled wreckage of his car, after it struck a bridge abutment in the Catskill Mountains, traveling at 80 miles per hour.

Rev. Castria died in hospital, without regaining consciousness, and his passing left police with an unsolved mystery. Was the fatal car crash an accident, or suicide, as suspected by police? Their only clue was Castria's Bible, left behind in a trash bag at his church. Thumbing through it, detectives found two passages underlined in adjacent chapters of *Exodus*. The first: "Thou shalt not kill." The second: "Eye for eye, tooth for tooth, hand for hand, foot for foot."

Chivington, John M.

America's Civil War had dragged on for three bloody years when Colorado Governor John Evans decided the time was ripe to drive Cheyenne and Arapaho Indians from their mineral-rich hunting grounds. To execute his order, Evans called upon Colonel John Chivington, a one-time presiding elder of the Nebraska Methodist Conference, now military commander for the Colorado territory. Known as the "fighting parson," Chivington made no secret of his rabid hatred for Native Americans. His policy, proclaimed in a speech at Denver, was simplicity itself: "Kill and scalp all Indians, big or little. Nits make lice!" The members of his Third Colorado Regiment, mostly hundred-day volunteers from rugged mining camps who sought to avoid military service in the larger war, were aptly described by Governor

Evans: "They have been raised to kill Indians, and they must kill Indians."

That is precisely what they did at Sand Creek, under Col. Chivington's supervision, on November 29, 1864. Surrounding the camp of Chief Black Kettle, Chivington's men ignored a white flag of surrender and an American flag raised by the Cheyenne, charging the camp from all sides. As per Chivington's credo, the Cheyenne were killed without regard to age or gender, many of the women raped, their bodies grossly mutilated after death. Seven cavalry troopers died in the battle, mostly by "friendly fire" from their comrades, while the Cheyenne body count remains in dispute: various sources cite an Indian death toll between 163 and 400, but all agree that a majority, perhaps as many as two-thirds, were unarmed women and children. When three of his officers protested the slaughter, Chivington raged, "Damn any man who sympathizes with Indians. I have come to kill Indians, and believe it is right and honorable to use any means under God's heaven to kill Indians."

"Christian Identity" Movement

The strange cult known as Anglo-Israelism — in the United States, as "Christian Identity" — dates from 1840, give or take, although it did not reach America until the mid-1880s, when disciple Edward Hine arrived from England, for a "visit" that would ultimately span four years. The gospel he carried with him, part of the "British Israelite" movement, taught that Britons and their descendants constitute the "ten lost tribes of Israel." It was a peculiar doctrine, with no solid basis in scripture, but Hine found many in the United States and Canada who were eager to believe. By the time he went home, in February 1888, the Brooklyn-based Anglo-Israel Association was ready to spread the good news nationwide.

A leading advocate of Anglo-Israelism in the 1920s was Rev. Reuben Sawyer, an Oregon clergyman and paid recruiter for the **Ku Klux Klan**. The Klan connection made it easier for Sawyer to promote his cult's belief in two distinct and separate groups of humankind: "Adamic" individuals were whites created in God's own image, while "pre-Adamic" peoples included the nonwhite races, acknowledged as "created beings" but *not* God's offspring, vaguely associated with Lucifer and his failed rebellion in heaven. As literal spawn of the Devil, nonwhites were less than human, morally unclean.

New Englander Howard Rand was the dominant voice of Anglo-Israelism in America, from the late 1920s through the end of World War II, emerging as the movement's most determined and energetic evangelist. Converted to the sect in 1927, Rand met with a group of Detroit businessmen soon after, to create the Anglo-Saxon Federation of America (ASFA). Word spread rapidly after the group's first convention, in May 1930; within a year, active chapters were reported in California, Oregon, Illinois, and Florida. One of the early Detroit recruits was William J. Cameron, editor of Henry Ford's notorious *Dearborn Independent*, which ran a long series of anti-Semitic features in the 1920s. Through Cameron, the ASFA began forging links to the far-right fringe of American politics, building from a September 1931 alliance with Fred Marvin's American Coalition of Patriotic Societies. Cameron was also well known for his ties to Kurt Ludecke, a Nazi propagandist from Germany who plied his trade in America after the Munich beer hall *pütsch* sent Adolf Hitler and some of his cronies to prison.

Despite such connections, and his own confirmed alcoholism, Cameron became the public face of the ASFA for nearly a decade, manning the helm while Rand pulled strings behind the scenes. By the time Cameron was eased out of office, in the late 1930s, Anglo-Israelism had undergone a series of changes that produced the modern "Christian Identity" movement in North America, discarding even the Anglo-Israel label, with its implication of foreign entanglements. One area of rapid growth was Los Angeles, where the membership in Identity cults grew by 381% between 1920 and 1930. Charles Fox Parham, hailed by some as the father of modern Pentecostalism, preached the Identity line in L.A. from 1924 onward, and the ASFA was heavily involved in founding Kingdom Bible College, in 1930. Another Identity evangelist who set up shop in L.A., around 1935, was Rev. Joe Jeffers of Kingdom Temple, who was also a member of the Silver Shirt Legion. Yet another Identity spokesman in Los Angeles was Rev. Clem Davies, a Canadian transplant with ties to both the Silver Shirts and KKK. William Pelley, meanwhile, spread the Identity creed through his lectures and writing, while publicly denying any personal belief in Anglo-Israelism.

Rev. Gerald L.K. Smith, constantly seeking a vehicle for personal advancement, attached himself to every significant Identity spokesman in America, during the 1930s and '40s. One such was Ellsworth Perkins, formerly associated with Aimee Semple McPherson in Los Angeles, who now told congregations, "I shall not deny that I believe that the White nations of Western Europe are the lost ten tribes of Israel, and an integral part of Israel." Another Smith associate was Rev. Wesley Swift, the son of a Methodist preacher who deserted his father's church in revulsion against its propagation of a "social gospel." Resettled in California by the mid-1930s, Swift preached in a succession of desert communities around Southern California, attending Kingdom Bible College and rubbing shoulders with the pro-Identity Covenant Evangelistic Society, whereby he was apparently converted to the racist cult. (Swift's widow told a different story, crediting her husband's conversion to his association with Rev. Gerald Winrod and the Ku Klux Klan.) In years to come, Smith and Swift were the closest of friends, collaborating on a range of racist projects that would carry them from L.A. to Capitol Hill.

Silver Shirt *führer* William Pelley, meanwhile, for all his disavowals of Anglo-Israelism, continued to promote ASFA teachings through both his paramilitary "storm troop" and his short-lived Christian Party. Pelley added his own twist to the formula, spouting various crackpot "prophecies" derived, he said, from the study of tunnels in the Great Pyramid of Egypt. Among those revelations was Pelley's prediction that the Depression would end on the night of September 16, 1969, "and not one moment sooner!" It would be another thirty-two years before the Millennium began, on September 17, 2001, with the nations of Earth united under "the Christ form of government." Election results for 1936 ruled Pelley out as a part of that exalted regime: his Christian Party polled fewer than 1,600 votes in Washington State; even the Communists did better, with only the sad Prohibition Party tasting Pelley's dust.

Every religion needs its own theology, and Identity authors were working overtime through the Depression, struggling to shore up their fuzzy beliefs. Frederick Haberman published *Tracing Our Ancestors* in 1934, asserting that Cain and "the later sons of Adam" married pre-Adamite women "of the Turanian or Mongolian race," producing offspring with superior physical strength but diminished spiritual capacity. In

Haberman's history, the Adamites lived in "the forty Cities of Takla Makan," somewhere in the Turkestan desert, until they drifted into sin and were annihilated by a localized deluge. Cain's descendants, meanwhile, "migrated into the valley of the Euphrates as early as 3800 B.C.," where Haberman describes them turning to the worship of Satan.

It was all heady stuff, fabricating history out of thin air, and anyone could jump in for the hell of it. Beginning in 1936, Identity author P.E.J. Monson argued the case for dual seedlines of mankind — the "God line" descended from Abel, and the "Satan line" descended from Cain. In Monson's scenario, enough members of the "Satan line" survived Noah's flood — apparently overlooked by all-seeing Jehovah — to continue as a threat, their religion embodied in the Catholic Church, with the Pope reigning as "Prime Minister of the Devil." Lest the Jews be forgotten, a series of anonymous pamphlets were published in Canada during World War II, including a "Chart of Racial Origins from Biblical Sources." The bashful author accepted the *Protocols of Zion* as an accurate blueprint for Jewish domination of the world, attacking Zionists as "Ashkenazim of Turko-Mongol blood." "The cry of 'anti-Semitism' raised by the Zionists," he or she went on, "is purely propaganda, and has no basis in fact, as the Ashkenazim are neither Jews nor Semitic by blood or race." The pamphlets further distinguished between "Semitic" and "Asiatic" Jews, branding Cain as the same "Sargon" who founded "the synagogue of Satan."

Christian Identity believers have become increasingly paranoid and militant since the late 1960s, moving toward a point where many (if not most) believe themselves to be at war with the so-called "Zionist Occupational Government" (ZOG) in Washington, D.C. It should not be presumed that every group wearing the "Identity" label is armed and dangerous per se, but *The Directory of Christian Identity*, published annually by the Virginia Christian Israelites, includes the following among its list of congregations which provide "a proper and correct explanation of the scriptures":

- ✞ Church of Jesus Christ, led by pastor Thom Robb in Harrison, Arkansas. Robb is David Duke's successor as national director of the Knights of the Ku Klux Klan, from which position he has declared, "There is war in America, and there are two camps. One camp is in Washington, D.C., the federal government controlled by the Antichrist Jews. Make no mistake about it — their goal is the destruction of our race, our faith, and our people. And our goal is the destruction of them. There is no middle ground. We're not going to take any survivors, any prisoners. It's us or them."
- ✞ Crusade for Christ, based in Little Rock and led by retired U.S. Army colonel Gordon ("Jack") Mohr. A paid orator for the John Birch Society between 1969 and 1980, Mohr graduated to Identity religion and spent the 1980s hosting "freedom festivals" which featured paramilitary training for members of the KKK and other far-right groups.
- ✞ Church of Jesus Christ Christian, led by Wesley Swift's aging widow in Escondido, California.
- ✞ National Christian Church, led by longtime neo-Nazi Oren Potito, of Ocala, Florida.
- ✞ Crusade Against Corruption, a Georgia-based gay-hating group led by lifelong Klansman and convicted church bomber Jesse Stoner.
- ✞ Church of Jesus Christ Christian (a.k.a. Aryan Nations), formerly led by Richard Butler at Hayden Lake, Idaho.

- ✞ Christian Defense League, a Louisiana racist group led by Rev. James K. Warner, whose "credits" include thirty-odd years of association with George Lincoln Rockwell, David Duke, and other neo-Nazi leaders from coast to coast.
- ✞ New Christian Crusade Church, founded by Warner and now led by like-minded pastor Craig Demott.
- ✞ Sons of Liberty, another organization founded by James Warner, operating from the same Louisiana town as his New Christian Crusade Church.
- ✞ *The Seditionist*, a newsletter published by ex-Klansman and self-styled "Aryan warrior" Louis Beam, an associate of the Aryan Nations and other crypto-fascist groups. Beam draws the title for his newsletter from the federal sedition indictment which drove him into hiding and briefly placed him on the FBI's Ten Most Wanted list in 1987.

Another listing in the national Identity directory is that of the so-called "Christian Posse," a.k.a. Posse Comitatus, based in Tigerton, Wisconsin. Despite its public title, though, the "posse" should not be mistaken for a group of smiling door-to-door evangelists. The Posse Comitatus — literally "posse of the county" — was organized in Portland, Oregon, by William Potter Gale and Henry Beach, spreading quickly through a dozen states in the early 1970s. "Identity" trappings aside, the group opposes paying taxes and insists that there is no legitimate authority above the county sheriff's office. That philosophy led to Gale's conviction for tax evasion, in October 1987, and he died six months later, while his sentence was under appeal. By that time, though, the aging colonel had become superfluous, eclipsed in the early 1980s by Posse spokesman James Wickstrom, Identity minister of the Life Science Church in Wisconsin, who rails against "niggers" and Jews, exhorting his followers to "[h]ave no pity on those in office who have taken and destroyed your rights and have been responsible for the aborting of our children and the death of our sons with chemicals and the death of our sons in war and the stealing of our rights."

That message was taken to heart by the Posse's first "martyr," in February 1983. Gordon Kahl was both a Posse member and a loyal disciple of the Texas-based Gospel Doctrine Church of Jesus Christ, when he was convicted of income tax evasion in 1977. Released on five years probation, Kahl returned to his native North Dakota, thereby violating terms of his release. It took a team of U.S. marshals six years to attempt retrieving him, outside Medina, and the net result was a bloody fiasco. When the smoke cleared, two federal agents were dead, with three more lawmen and Kahl's son wounded, and Kahl was on the lam, hiding out with friends from the Identity movement. In hiding, he wrote a letter to Wickstrom, describing America as "a conquered and occupied nation — conquered and occupied by the Jews." Kahl made his way to Arkansas before an informant betrayed him, and he was killed in a second shoot-out with authorities on June 3, 1983.

James Wickstrom mourned for Kahl, but he had problems of his own. Jailed in 1984 on charges of creating an illegal "township" and proclaiming himself the new "judge," he served 13 months for impersonating a public official. Wickstrom's sentence was commuted on the condition that he stay away from right-wing paramilitary groups, but the lure proved irresistible. In August 1990, resettled in Pennsylvania, he was convicted a second time and sentenced to 38 months in prison for conspiracy to distribute $100,000 in counterfeit bills.

Another militant branch of the Identity movement, in this period, was James Ellison's Covenant, Sword, and Arm of the Lord (CSA), established in Arkansas during 1971 on 224 acres purchased from the Fellowship of Christian Athletes. The fortified compound — dubbed "Zarephath-Horeb" after a Biblical purging place — quickly became a haven for ex-convicts, junkies, and assorted misfits, ruled by Ellison and a counsel of "elders," subsisting on income from gun sales and a sawmill on the property. CSA gunsmiths provided automatic weapons to "freedom fighters" from various militant groups, and fugitives such as Gordon Kahl were always welcome in the bosom of Ellison's community. Following Kahl's death at the home of a CSA member in June 1983, the group became more militant, its home base officially designated as "an arms depot and training ground for Aryan Warriors." That August, Ellison and "elder" Bill Thomas set fire to the Metropolitan Community Church in Springfield, Missouri, to protest the church's support for gay rights. A week later, Thomas and other CSA members burned a Jewish community center in Bloomington, Indiana. In November 1983, Thomas and Richard Snell bombed a natural gas pipeline near Fulton, Arkansas, dawdling in the neighborhood long enough for Snell, with Stephen Scott's help, to rob and kill a Jewish pawnbroker. A month later, James Ellison became the first Identity leader to formally declare war against "ZOG," marking the occasion with abortive assassination attempts on a federal judge and an FBI agent the CSA blamed for Gordon Kahl's death. Ellison and five of his disciples pled guilty to federal weapons charges in August 1985, with Ellison sentenced to five years in prison. Other CSA members were subsequently convicted of bombing and arson charges in Arkansas, Missouri, and Indiana. Richard Snell was executed for the pawnbroker's murder in 1995, thus providing the movement with another "holy martyr."

For all its violence, the CSA could never hold a candle to another Christian Identity faction, organized in 1983 by hard-core members of the CSA, Ku Klux Klan, and the Aryan Nations. Dubbed the Order, or the Silent Brotherhood, this new faction had its roots in a racist novel, *The Turner Diaries*, published five years earlier by "Andrew McDonald" — real name William Pierce, a former member of the American Nazi Party, now *führer* of his own National Alliance. *The Turner Diaries* became an instant best-seller among far-right fanatics who dote on its melodramatic tale of white warriors rebelling against an American police state run by communistic Jews. Self-styled tax protester and Identity lecturer Robert Jay Matthews was obsessed with the novel's "message" and dreamed of putting its plan into action in modern America. In 1983, he met some like-minded "patriots" at Richard Butler's Aryan Congress in Idaho, and the Order was launched that October, claiming over 30 members at its peak.

The group's first effort was the October 1983 robbery of an adult video store in Spokane, Washington, which netted the spectacular sum of $369.10. Next, the silent brothers turned to counterfeiting, using Rev. Butler's printing press at Hayden Lake, but their product was so shabby that one member was quickly arrested. By year's end, they had turned to bank robbery, looting two Seattle establishments for a total of almost $29,600. The April 1984 bombing of a Seattle porno theater was followed the next day by an armored car heist, netting the Order about $235,000. According to federal authorities, money from that and later robberies was freely distributed to racist leaders across the United States, allegedly including Richard Butler, Robert Miles, and other front men for the Identity movement. Order members also bombed a Boise synagogue (inflicting little damage) in April 1984, and scored their first fatality in May with the execution of loose-lipped "brother" Walter West, suspected of talking out of turn. In June 1984, controversial Jewish talk show host Alan Berg was gunned down by an Order hit team in Denver. The following month, Matthews and company stopped a Brinks truck near Ukiah, California, and relieved the guards of some $3.6 million. It was all downhill from there, however, with a series of near-misses and shoot-outs with the FBI dogging the Aryan warriors through 1984. Matthews himself was cornered and killed on Whidbey Island, in Puget Sound, that December. When the smoke cleared, 28 of his disciples stood convicted on various charges, facing prison terms that ranged from three to 250 years.

Federal prosecutors were so optimistic in the wake of those trials, that they tried to break the neo-Nazi movement's back with charges of sedition, filed against 14 leaders of the fringe, including Butler, Miles, and rabid Klansman Louis Beam. The case looked solid, with James Ellison, fugitive Klansman Glenn Miller, and Bob Matthews' common-law wife standing by as prosecution witnesses, but it was clearly a mistake to hold the trial in Fort Smith, Arkansas, where all 14 defendants were acquitted by a snow-white jury in the spring of 1988.

By that time, there were rumbles of an "Order II," organized at Hayden Lake in 1985, by past and present members of the Aryan Nations. If the original Order had been menacing, however, its new incarnation bore a greater resemblance to the gang that couldn't shoot straight. Member Elden Cutler was jailed in August 1985, for his role in an abortive contract-murder plot, and the new Order's counterfeiting efforts, launched six months later, fared no better than the bungled attempts of Matthews and friends. The new team started planting bombs in March, but their first attempt — at a Jewish-owned trucking company — turned out to be a dud. They did manage to set off a blast at a Kootenai County car dealership, owned by a critic of the Aryan Nations, but that triumph was spoiled two weeks later, when member Kenneth Shray was executed as a suspected informer. In September 1986, the home of a Catholic priest who criticized Butler's fanatics was firebombed. Two weeks later, the new Order set off four bombs in Coeur d'Alene, as diversions for a planned series of robberies, but the holdups fell through and five members were arrested. Highly limited in both imagination and mobility, the Order was effectively crushed by 1988, with six members in prison and several nervous turncoats hiding in protective custody.

By that time, though, a new force was emerging in the heartland of America, embodied in the form of "citizen militias," many of them linked to far-right racist groups, enamored of the anti-Semitism preached by ministers of the Identity movement. A forerunner of that trend, the so-called Arizona Patriots, was launched in 1982 by former Western movie star Ty Hardin. Having fled a Hollywood he loathed for its pervasive Jewish influence and later run afoul of IRS accountants for evading income taxes, Hardin settled in the Arizona desert and organized his own local tax-protest movement, heavily flavored with Christian Identity dogma, closely linked to "Jack" Mohr's Christian Patriot's Defense League. By June 1984, the Arizona Patriots were operating from a 320-acre compound near Kingman, soliciting funds through Mohr's CPDL newsletter, and issuing nonsensical "indictments" on every elected official in the state. Plans for the group's first armored car robbery were hatched in January 1986, with elderly member Jack Oliphant serving as the "brains" of the scheme, but the befuddled plot dragged on so long that FBI agents ran out of patience and indicted nine Patriots for conspiracy that December. Oliphant and three others pled guilty in the summer of 1987, drawing federal prison terms. By that time, two other Arizona Patriots were jailed on weapons and explosives charges. Testimony at their trials — wherein both were convicted — alleged that members of the Patriots had planned attacks on federal buildings. It is doubtless a "coincidence" that suspected Oklahoma City bomber and mass murderer Timothy McVeigh moved to Kingman in 1993, living with an army pal who was associated with the Arizona Patriots, and that McVeigh allegedly set off a "practice" bomb near Kingman, during February 1995.

From coast to coast, the latest crop of paramilitary racist groups, described by friend and foe alike as "citizen militias," are heavily influenced by the doctrines and spokesmen of Christian Identity. Some examples include:

- ✝ James "Bo" Gritz, vice presidential candidate of the far-right Populist Party in 1988 (with ex-Klan wizard David Duke, whom he repeatedly repudiated), who found a new audience in Identity circles after his defeat. Gritz is a close associate of Identity minister Pete Peters. By the time Gritz ran for president on the Populist ticket, in 1992, associate Jack McLamb — a former cop from Arizona — was openly recruiting law enforcement officers for the militia movement nationwide. Gritz himself, in the '92 campaign, recommended that supporters of his cause should organize militias for themselves.
- ✝ Eva Lamb, a neighbor and reputed associate of Aryan Nations leader Richard Butler, founded the Idaho Organized Militia in 1992.

- ✞ John Trochmann, founder (with his brother and nephew) of the Militia of Montana, is a reported member of the Aryan Nations and a frequent guest at the neo-Nazi group's compound at Hayden Lake, Idaho. By 1992, two years before he launched the paramilitary faction known as MOM, Trochmann was already well known in Identity circles, having filed legal papers asserting his personal "sovereignty" as a "free white Christian man."
- ✞ M.J. ("Red") Beckman, another influential voice in the Montana militia movement, is an Identity propagandist and author of *The Church Deceived* (1984), which described Jews as followers of Satan who control "our government, our major media, our banks and legal profession." From his home in Billings, Beckman writes, "They talk about the terrible holocaust of Hitler's Germany. Was that not a judgment upon a people who believe Satan is their God?"
- ✞ Association de Libertas, a Texas-based "Christian Patriot" group with close ties to Trochmann's Militia of Montana, which pursues a goal of stripping political power from minority "14th Amendment citizens" in the United States.
- ✞ "Elohim City," a Christian Identity outpost straddling the Arkansas-Oklahoma border. Residents include identified veterans of Jim Ellison's Covenant, Sword, and Arm of the Lord. Two weeks before the deadly Oklahoma City bombing of April 1995, blast suspect Timothy McVeigh was welcomed as a guest in the community, presumably because he had friends there and shared in their beliefs.
- ✞ Mark Reynolds, an Identity disciple and leader of an Oregon militia group, who proclaims that "[l]aws to execute sodomites would surely put a quick end to people dying from AIDS they got in a restaurant or the dentist's

> chair! So-called tolerance is anti-Christian and lukewarm." In March 1995, Reynolds warned that if the federal government kept "pushing people the way they are doing, people like [U.S. Attorney General Janet] Reno will end up hanging from telephone poles or trees."

A less public, but equally sinister faction of the Identity fringe is the so-called Phineas Priesthood, named for a Biblical character in the twenty-fifth chapter of *Numbers*. Phineas, it is said, averted God's plague on Israel by ramming a spear through the bodies of an Israelite man and a Midianite woman. Their crime: race-mixing. Self-appointed spokesman for the group, Identity believer Richard Kelly Hoskins of Lynchburg, Virginia, has sketched a bizarre history of the Phineas Priesthood in his book *Vigilantes of Christendom* (1990). According to Hoskins, secret members of the "priesthood" have included such diverse historical figures as Robin Hood, Jesse James, and John Wilkes Booth. In more recent times, the group reportedly attracted Byron De La Beckwith, a former Klansman and convicted assassin of civil rights leader Medgar Evers. Beckwith himself was ordained as an Identity minister in 1977, and often preached the tale of Phineas to racist congregations in the South. Hoskins described the zealous dedication of the Phineas Priests to their racial holy war:

> As the Kamikaze is to the Japanese, as the Shi'ite is to Islam, as the Zionist is to the Jews, so the Phineas Priesthood is to Christendom. Regardless how the world sees them, they see themselves as the latest in a long line of God's servants stretching back into antiquity.

But does the group *exist?* Hoskins has taken to denying it in recent interviews — but, then again, he also denies knowing Beckwith, a lie exposed by Beckwith's wife, who says of Hoskins, "We just love him. We go way back." Before the heat came down, Hoskins was pleased to write, "It makes little difference whether you agree or disagree with the Phineas Priesthood. It is important that you know that it exists, is active, and in the near future may become a central fact of your life." Rev. Jarah Crawford, an Identity spokesman who ordained Beckwith in the cult, has also discussed the Phineas Priesthood in his book *Last Battle Cry* (1986), and *The New York Times* recognized the group's existence in October 1991, describing its members as "God's executioners." **[See also: Ku Klux Klan; "Pro-Life" Movement]**

"Christian Reconstructionists": See Capital Punishment

Church of the Creator

A right-wing cult espousing racist views that make those of **"Christian Identity"** seem moderate by comparison, the Church of the Creator was chartered as a nonprofit religious organization in August 1973. Its founder and "pontifex maximus" was Ben Klassen, a one-time Florida state legislator who made a fortune in real estate before he became a professional hater in the early 1970s. His first neo-Nazi venture, the short-lived Nationalist White Party, was founded in 1970 and served as the foundation of his later, more successful enterprise.

Initially chartered in Florida, Klassen's Church of the Creator moved its headquarters to North Carolina in 1982 and remained there for the next decade, while planting chapters worldwide and forging friendly ties with fascist groups from Canada to Europe, Australia, and South Africa. The church's motto is "RAHOWA!" — short for *"Racial Holy War"* — and Klassen makes no bones about his wish to rid the world of Jews and nonwhite "mud people," using tactics that include "murder, treachery, lying, deceit, mass killing, whatever it takes." Klassen alienated some traditional bigots with his denunciations of "Jewish Christianity," but his troops are frequently in evidence when Klansmen and skinheads rally to strut their stuff. Racism aside, Klassen's church offers a potential tax break for opponents of the hated "Jewish Occupational Government," by proclaiming all members clergymen under the advertised slogan of "every Creator a reverend."

One "minister" who took the call for "RaHoWa!" seriously was George David Loeb, of Arlington, Florida. Outspoken in his hatred of minorities, Loeb twice faced potential eviction from his condominium complex on charges of harassing black neighbors. His tactic was simple, as outlined in a letter written to a member of the **Ku Klux Klan**:

> The frequent use of the word nigger should lead to a widespread and violent black uprising that should give whites (and possibly police) the opportunity to kill large numbers of them with impunity. It is our feeling as Creators that shrinking the numbers of blacks worldwide is one of the highest priorities.

On May 17, 1991, Loeb shot and killed a black US Navy veteran of Desert Storm, following a near-miss collision in a Neptune Beach parking lot. Fleeing the state with his wife, "Reverend" Loeb was captured in Poughkeepsie, New York, a month later, while trying to shoplift some groceries. Back in Florida, the 35-year-old "Creator" claimed self-defense, alleging that his victim had threatened him with a brick, but witnesses disagreed, and he was convicted of murder on July 29, 1992. A jailhouse suicide attempt was foiled the next day, and Loeb's sentencing date was advanced to August 12 when he declared a hunger strike. The trial judge sentenced Loeb to life imprisonment, with no parole for the first 25 years.

Klassen's church, in the meantime, was undergoing some cosmetic changes. Its pontifex maximus was 72 years old in 1990, when he named as his successor "Reverend" Rudy Stanko, a church member from Nebraska. Unfortunately, Stanko was then serving six years in federal prison, on a conviction for selling tainted beef to the government school-lunch program, and his installation as head of the church was postponed until his release. By the time Stanko was freed in December 1991, however, things had changed. In May 1992, "after much deliberation," Klassen announced "Reverend" Charles Altvater, of Baltimore, as his new heir apparent. Klassen declined to discuss "the Rudy Stanko fiasco," although Stanko remained a Creator in good standing and fired off a letter of congratulation to Altvater. Rev. Charles was out of luck, however, replaced as church leader that autumn, by Brandon O'Rourke. Klassen finally stepped down, while remaining as the cult's most revered figure, and church headquarters was moved to O'Rourke's home city of Milwaukee.

"Church of the Lamb of God": See LeBaron, Ervil

Constanzo, Adolfo de Jesus

Miami-born on November 1, 1962, Adolfo Constanzo was the son of a teenaged Cuban immigrant. He was still an infant when his widowed mother moved to Puerto Rico and acquired a second husband. There, Adolfo was baptized a

Catholic and served the church as an altar boy, appearing to accept the standard tenets of the Roman faith. He was ten years old when the family moved back to Miami, and his stepfather died a year later, leaving Adolfo and his mother financially well-off.

By that time, neighbors in Little Havana had begun to notice something odd about Aurora Constanzo and her son. Some said the woman was a witch, and those who angered her were likely to discover headless goats or chickens on their doorsteps in the morning. Adolfo's mother had introduced him to the santeria cult around age nine, with side trips to Puerto Rico and Haiti for instruction in voodoo, but there were still more secrets to be learned, and in 1976 he was apprenticed to a practitioner of palo mayombe. His occult "godfather" was already rich from working with local drug dealers, and he imparted a philosophy that would follow Adolfo to his grave: "Let the nonbelievers kill themselves with drugs. We will profit from their foolishness."

Around the same time, Constanzo's mother recalls that her son began displaying psychic powers, scanning the future to predict such events as the 1981 shooting of President Ronald Reagan. Be that as it may, Adolfo had problems foretelling his own future, including two arrests for shoplifting — one involving the theft of a chainsaw. On the side, he had also begun to display bisexual inclinations, with a strong preference for male lovers.

A modeling assignment took the handsome young sorcerer to Mexico City in 1983, and he spent his free time telling fortunes with tarot cards in the city's infamous "Zona Rosa." Before returning to Miami, Adolfo collected his first Mexican disciples, including Martin Quintana, homosexual "psychic" Jorge Montes, and Omar Orea, obsessed with the occult from age 15. In short order, Constanzo seduced both Rodriguez and Orea, claiming one as his "man" and the other as his "woman," depending on Adolfo's romantic whim.

In mid-1984, Constanzo moved to Mexico City full-time, seeking what his mother called "new horizons." He shared quarters with Quintana and Orea, in a strange *ménage à trois,* collecting other followers as his "magic" reputation spread throughout the city. It was said that Constanzo could read the future, and he also offered *limpias* — ritual "cleansings" — for those who felt they had been cursed by enemies. Of course, it all cost money, and Constanzo's journals — recovered after his death — document 31 regular customers, some paying up to $4,500 for a single ceremony. Adolfo established a menu for sacrificial beasts, with roosters going for $6 a head, goats for $30, boa constrictors at $450, adult zebras for $1,100, and African lion cubs listed at $3,100 each.

True to the teachings of his Florida mentor, Constanzo went out of his way to charm wealthy drug dealers, helping them schedule shipments and meetings on the basis of his predictions. For a price, he offered magic that would make dealers and their hit men invisible to police, bulletproof against their enemies. It was all nonsense, of course, but smugglers drawn from Mexican peasant stock, with a background in *brujeria,* were strongly inclined to believe. According to Constanzo's ledgers, one dealer in Mexico City paid him $40,000 for magical services rendered over three years' time.

At those rates, the customers demanded a show, and Constanzo recognized the folly of disappointing men who carried Uzi submachine guns in their armor-plated limousines. Strong medicine required first-rate ingredients, and Adolfo was rolling by mid-1985, when he and three of his disciples raided a Mexico City graveyard for human bones to start his own *nganga* — the traditional cauldron of blood employed by practitioners of palo mayombe. The rituals and air of mystery surrounding Constanzo were powerful enough to lure a cross section of Mexican society, with his clique of disciples including a physician, a real estate speculator, fashion models, and several transvestite nightclub performers.

At first glance, the most peculiar aspect of Constanzo's new career was the appeal he seemed to have for ranking law enforcement officers. At least four members of the Federal Judicial Police joined Constanzo's cult in Mexico City: one of them, Salvador Garcia, was a commander in charge of narcotics investigations; another, Florentino Ventura, retired from the *federales* to lead the Mexican branch of Interpol. In a country where bribery — *mordida* — permeates all levels of law enforcement and federal officers sometimes serve as triggermen for drug smugglers, corruption is not unusual, but the devotion of Constanzo's followers ran deeper than cash on the line. In or out of uniform, they worshipped Adolfo as a minor god in his own right, their living conduit to the spirit world.

In 1986, Ventura introduced Constanzo to the drug-dealing Calzada family, then one of Mexico's dominant narcotics cartels. Constanzo won the hard-nosed dealers over with his charm and mumbo-jumbo, profiting immensely from his contacts with the gang. By early 1987, he was able to pay $60,000 cash for a condominium in Mexico City, buying himself a fleet of luxury cars that included an $80,000 Mercedes-Benz. When not working magic for the Calzadas, or other clients, Adolfo staged scams of his own, once posing as a DEA agent to rip off a coke dealer in Guadalajara, selling the stash through his police contacts for a cool $100,000.

At some point in his odyssey from juvenile psychic to high-society witch, Constanzo began to feed his *nganga* with the offerings of **human sacrifice**. No final tally for his victims is available, but 23 ritual murders are well documented, and Mexican authorities point to a rash of unsolved mutilation-slayings around Mexico City and elsewhere, suggesting that Constanzo's known victims may only represent the tip of a malignant iceberg. In any case, his willingness to torture and kill total strangers — along with close friends — duly impressed the ruthless drug dealers who remained his foremost clients.

In the course of a year's association, Constanzo came to believe that his magical powers alone were responsible for the Calzada family's continued success and survival. In April 1987, he demanded a full partnership in the syndicate and was curtly refused. On the surface, Constanzo seemed to take the rejection in stride, but his devious mind was working overtime, plotting revenge.

On April 30, Guillermo Calzada and six members of his household vanished under mysterious circumstances. They were reported missing on May 1, police noting melted candles and other evidence of a strange religious ceremony at Calzada's office. Six more days elapsed before officers began fishing mutilated remains from the Zumpango River. Seven corpses were recovered in the course of a week, all bearing signs of sadistic torture — fingers, toes, and ears removed, hearts and sex organs excised, part of the spine ripped from one body, two others missing their brains.

The vanished parts, as it turned out, had gone to feed Constanzo's cauldron of blood, building up his strength for greater conquests yet to come.

In July 1987, Salvador Garcia introduced Constanzo to another drug-running family, this one led by brothers Elio and Ovidio Hernandez. At the end of that month, in Matamoros, Constanzo also met 22-year-old Sara Aldrete, a Mexican national with resident alien status in the United States, where she attended college in Brownsville, Texas. Adolfo charmed Sara with his line of patter, noting with arch significance that her birthday — September 6 — was the same as his mother's. Sara was dating Brownsville drug smuggler Gilberto Sosa at the time, but she soon wound up in Constanzo's bed, Adolfo scuttling the old relationship with an anonymous call to Sosa, revealing Sara's infidelity. With nowhere else to turn, Sara plunged full-tilt into Constanzo's world, emerging as the *madrina* — godmother or "head witch" — of his cult, adding her own twists to the torture of sacrificial victims.

Constanzo's rituals became more elaborate and sadistic after he moved his headquarters to a plot of desert called Rancho Santa Elena, 20 miles from Matamoros. There, on May 28, 1988, drug dealer Hector de la Fuente and farmer Moises Castillo were executed by gunfire, but the sacrifice was a disappointment to Constanzo. Back in Mexico City, he directed his drones to dismember a transvestite, Ramon Esquivel, and dumped the grisly remains on a public street corner. His luck was holding, and Constanzo narrowly escaped when Houston police raided a drug house in June 1988, seizing numerous items of occult paraphernalia and the city's largest-ever shipment of cocaine.

On August 12, Ovidio Hernandez and his two-year-old son were kidnapped by rival narcotics dealers, the family turning to Constanzo for help. That night, another human sacrifice was staged at Rancho Santa Elena, and the hostages were released unharmed on August 13, Adolfo claiming full credit for their safe return. His star was rising, and Constanzo barely noticed when Florentino Ventura committed suicide in Mexico City on September 17, taking his wife and a friend with him in the same burst of gunfire.

In November 1988, Constanzo sacrificed disciple Jorge Gomez, accused of snorting cocaine in direct violation of *el padrino's* ban on drug use. A month later, Adolfo's ties to the Hernandez family were cemented with the initiation of Ovidio Hernandez as a full-fledged cultist, complete with ritual bloodletting and prayers to the *nganga.*

Human sacrifice can also have its practical side, as when competing smuggler Ezequiel Luna was tortured to death at Rancho Santa Elena on February 14, 1989; two other dealers, Ruben Garza and Ernesto Diaz, wandered into the ceremony uninvited, and promptly wound up on the menu. Conversely, Adolfo sometimes demanded a sacrifice on the spur of the moment, without rhyme or reason. When he called for fresh meat on February 25, Ovidio Hernandez gladly joined the hunting party, picking off his own 14-year-old cousin, Jose Garcia, in the heat of the moment.

On March 13, 1989, Constanzo sacrificed yet another victim at the ranch, gravely disappointed when his prey did not scream and plead for mercy in the approved style. Disgruntled, he ordered an Anglo for the next ritual, and his minions fanned out with their noses to the ground, abducting 21-year-old Mark Kilroy outside a Matamoros saloon. The sacrifice went well enough, followed two weeks later by the butchery of Sara Aldrete's old boyfriend, Gilberto Sosa, but Kilroy's disappearance marked the beginning of the end for Constanzo's homicidal family.

A popular premed student from Texas, Mark Kilroy was not some peasant, transvestite, or small-time pusher who could disappear without a trace or an investigation into his fate. With family members and Texas politicians turning up the heat, the search for Kilroy rapidly assumed the trappings of an international incident... but it would be Constanzo's own disciples who destroyed him in the end.

By March 1989, Mexican authorities were busy with one of their periodic antidrug campaigns, erecting roadblocks on a whim and sweeping the border districts for unwary smugglers. On April 1, Victor Sauceda, an ex-cop turned gangster, was sacrificed at the ranch, and the "spirit message" Constanzo received was optimistic enough for his troops to move a half-ton of marijuana across the border seven nights later.

And then, the magic started to unravel.

On April 9, returning from a Brownsville, Texas meeting with Constanzo, cultist Serafin Hernandez drove past a police road-block without stopping, ignoring the cars that set off in hot pursuit. Hernandez believed *el padrino's* line about invisibility, and he seemed surprised when officers trailed him to his destination in Matamoros. Even so, the smuggler was arrogant, inviting police to shoot him, since the bullets would merely bounce off.

They arrested him instead, along with cult member David Martinez, and drove the pair back to Rancho Santa Elena, where a preliminary search turned up marijuana and firearms. Disciples Elio Hernandez and Sergio Martinez stumbled into the net while police were on hand, and all four were interrogated through the evening, revealing their tales of black magic, torture, and human sacrifices with a perverse kind of pride.

Next morning, police returned to the ranch in force, discovering the malodorous shed where Constanzo kept his *nganga,* brimming with blood, spiders, scorpions, a dead black cat, a turtle shell, bones, deer antlers — and a human brain. Captive cult members directed searchers to Constanzo's private cemetery, and excavation began, revealing 15 mutilated corpses by April 16. In addition to Mark Kilroy and other victims already named, the body count included two renegade federal narcotics officers — Joaquin Manzo and Miguel Garcia — along with three men who were never identified.

The hunt for Constanzo was on, and police raided his luxury home in Atizapan, outside Mexico City, on April 17, discovering stockpiles of gay pornography and a hidden ritual chamber. The discoveries at Rancho Santa Elena made international headlines, and sightings of Constanzo were reported as far away as Chicago, but in fact, he had already returned to Mexico City, hiding out in a small apartment with Sara Aldrete and three other disciples. On May 2, thinking to save herself, Sara tossed a note out the window. It read:

> Please call the judicial police and tell them that in this building are those that they are seeking. Give them the address, fourth floor. Tell them that a woman is being held hostage. I beg for this, because what I want most is to talk — or they're going to kill the girl.

A passerby found the note, read it, and kept it to himself, believing it was someone's lame attempt at humor. On May 6, neighbors called police to complain of a loud, vulgar argument in Constanzo's apartment — some say, accompanied by gunshots. As patrolmen arrived at the scene, Constanzo spotted them and opened fire with an Uzi, touching off a 45-minute battle in which, miraculously, only one policeman was wounded.

When Constanzo realized that escape was impossible, he handed his weapon to cultist Alvaro de Leon Valdez — a professional hit man nicknamed "El Duby" — with bizarre new orders. As El Duby recalls the scene: "He told me to kill him and Martin [Quintana]. I told him I couldn't do it, but he hit me in the face and threatened me that everything would go bad for me in hell. Then he hugged Martin, and I just stood in front of them and shot them with a machine gun."

Constanzo and Quintana were dead when police stormed the apartment, arresting El Duby and Sara Aldrete. In the aftermath of the raid, 14 cultists were indicted on various charges, including multiple murder, weapons and narcotics violations, conspiracy, and obstruction of justice. In August 1990, El Duby was convicted of killing Constanzo and Quintana, drawing a 30-year prison term. Cultists Juan Fragosa and Jorge Montes were both convicted in the Esquivel murder and sentenced to 35 years each; Omar Orea, convicted in the same case, died of AIDS before he could be sentenced. Sara Aldrete was acquitted of Constanzo's murder in 1990, but was sentenced to a six-year term on conviction for criminal association. Constanzo's *madrina* insisted that she never practiced any religion but "Christian santeria"; televised reports of the murders at Rancho Santa Elena, she said, took her by complete surprise. Jurors disagreed in May 1994, when Sara and four male accomplices were convicted of multiple murders at the ranch; Aldrete was sentenced to 62 years, while her cohorts — including Elio and Serafin Hernandez — drew prison terms of 67 years.

The cult of blood and pain, meanwhile, endures. Police in Mexico City investigated the ritual murders of 74 victims between 1987 and 1989, with similar crimes recorded from Veracruz. A relative of Martin Quintana told authorities, in June 1989, that Constanzo's first *madrina* was still at large, practicing her homicidal magic around Guadalajara. And from jail, before his death, Omar Orea declared, "I don't think that the religion will end with us, because it has a lot of people in it. They have found a temple in Monterrey that isn't even related to us. It will continue." **[See also: Human Sacrifice]**

Covenant, Sword and Arm of the Lord: See "Christian Identity" Movement

Crusades

A series of **religious wars** that spanned the best part of two centuries, the Crusades derived from the Roman Catholic Church's effort to eclipse competing imperial powers. Targets of the various campaigns included European Jews (blamed for various "crimes" including the crucifixion of Jesus and the advent of bubonic plague), Islamic "infidels," and disciples of Eastern Orthodox Christians (who formally split from the Roman Church in AD 1054). As in our surveys of religious wars and **terrorism**, no conclusive body count is possible for the Crusades, but victims on all sides certainly numbered in the hundreds of thousands, perhaps in the millions.

Pope Urban II launched the First Crusade in 1095, when he rallied European knights to march on Jerusalem and "save" the Holy Land from Seljuk Turks who threatened Byzantine Emperor Alexius I. The Crusaders finally reached Jerusalem in 1099, slaughtering resident Jews and Muslims with such abandon that one observer reported their horses "wading bridle-deep" in blood.

The Second Crusade was declared by Pope Eugenius III, in 1147, after Turks recaptured the fiefdom of Edessa from Christian occupation troops. Crusaders were repulsed in defeat after an abortive assault on Damascus in 1148.

Pope Gregory VIII inaugurated the Third Crusade, in 1187, after Muslim warlord Saladin recaptured Jerusalem. Sparing no melodrama, the Pontiff declared, "Cursed be the man who holds back his sword from shedding blood." It was a rousing sentiment, but quarrels between Christian commanders prevented them from reaching Jerusalem, and the drive petered out after five years of futile combat.

In the Fourth Crusade (1201-04), Pope Innocent III conceived a new angle of attack, proposing that Christian troops should attack Muslim forces in Egypt, but the Crusade was diverted to completely different purposes and the attack on Egypt was never attempted.

Eight years later, inspired by the rantings of a French "child prophet," thousands of young people left their homes to join a bizarre Children's Crusade. The untrained "warriors," many of them under twelve years old, set sail for the Holy Land in 1212, but few returned, the majority dying in shipwrecks or winding up sold into slavery by unscrupulous skippers. Another group of several thousand children traveled overland to Italy, but they were turned back by church officials, many succumbing to hunger, disease, or exposure in transit.

Stung by the humiliation of the ludicrous Children's Crusade, Pope Honorius III launched a new campaign to seize Egypt in 1217, but flooding in the Nile River Valley blocked the Crusaders' advance on Cairo, and they retreated, more disillusioned than ever, in 1219.

Holy Roman Emperor Frederick II took a stab at diplomacy nine years later, his Sixth Crusade more of a talking war, and while he secured a ten-year treaty with Sultan Kamil in 1229, ceding Jerusalem and other holy places to the Christian West, Kamil's concessions provoked violent dissent among Muslims, with renewed fighting when the treaty expired in 1239. Five years later, Turkish forces recaptured Jerusalem.

The Seventh Crusade, beginning in 1248, was a joint effort of Pope Innocent IV and King Louis IX of France. Once again, the goal was Jerusalem; and once again, Crusaders failed to reach their destination. This time, Louis himself was captured, forced to pay a literal king's ransom before the crusade ran out of steam in 1254.

Flush with their long string of victories, Muslim forces under Sultan Baybars overran Antioch in 1268, and French King Louis IX launched the Eighth Crusade two years later, to recoup Christian losses. It was a fatal mistake: Louis died of illness in Tunisia, and his tattered army turned for home before year's end.

The Ninth (and last) Crusade was an English project, launched by Prince Edward to relieve King Louis, but the French monarch was already dead when Edward's troops reached North Africa in 1271. He managed to complete a truce at Acre the following year, and returned home to claim the English throne, but Muslim forces were merely biding their time. In 1289, they captured Tripoli, while Acre — the last Christian outpost in the Holy Land — fell two years later, effectively closing out the Crusades. **[See also: Biblical Bloodshed; Inquisition; Religious Wars; Terrorism]**

David, Rachal

Charles Longo was the son of a New York physician, raised without religious training, who somehow emerged from a four-year stint in the Marine Corps as a devoted Mormon. Baptized in 1958, he left for Uruguay as an LDS missionary in March 1960. Over the next 11 months, church officials in Uruguay remarked on Longo's curious behavior, and he was back in the States by February 1961, dodging recommendations that he seek psychiatric treatment. Enrolled at BYU that fall, Charles was known around campus as "an extremely devout man," but doubts were raised, in the words of Longo's faculty advisor, "when he blessed his first son to be a prophet."

It would take some time for that son to appear, but Longo and his Swedish-born wife, Margit Ericsson, were well on their way by 1963, with the birth of daughter Eva. Another girl, Elizabeth, was born in 1964, followed by Frank in 1965, Deborah in 1966, Joseph in 1969, Bruce in 1970, and Rebecca in 1972. Long before then, however, Charles Longo had run afoul of the church that seemed to dominate his life.

By 1965, Longo regarded himself as God's prophet on earth, destined to lead the LDS church in a worldwide revival. Ranking elders disagreed, and when Charles persisted in his heresy, he was formally excommunicated in June 1969. By that time, though, he had collected a cult of disciples, some 12 adults and 31 children, who joined their messiah in a one-bedroom house in Manti, Utah. When not preaching The Word, Charles practiced knife-throwing and worked on his karate skills. He wore a three-foot sword and threatened those who angered him, including a local judge. His sermons to the faithful included a promise to "lop off thousands of heads," if necessary, to promote the word of God.

In 1970, that Word decreed that Charles should change his name to one that sounded more religious. Henceforth, he would be "Immanuel David," while Margit became "Rachal David." Some of the children were also renamed, while others, apparently, were considered pious enough as they were. In 1971, the Davids moved to Duchesne, Utah, sharing a two-bedroom house with three other families, promoting Immanuel's curious take on the scripture. Neighbors were told that he expected a shipment of gold which would leave his commune "in clover," while he finalized plans to "take over the universe." Despite high hopes, the cult scraped by on food stamps and unrepayable loans, with bad debts piling up by the day. At last, when the heat grew too intense, David fled with his family to Salt Lake City, living in a series of hotels.

And, overnight, their luck appeared to change. They suddenly had cash to burn, dining at expensive restaurants and settling the tab with $100 bills, shelling out an estimated $75,000 in rent alone over two years' time. In July 1978, Immanuel ordered two $47,000 pianos, seemingly confident of his ability to pay on delivery. Meanwhile, the David children shied away from school, and rarely left their hotel suite. In public, they were forbidden to speak without their father's permission. Immanuel himself ballooned to some 300 pounds, billing himself to the faithful as a one-man merger of Jehovah, Jesus, and the Holy Ghost.

Police, however, suspected that the prophet's business dealings were far from holy. By late 1976, several of his associates were in jail or facing indictment on various charges, and the FBI was tracking Immanuel on suspicion of wire fraud. That December, shots were fired into the family's hotel suite by persons unknown, and their car was set afire in the parking lot. On August 1, 1978, Immanuel borrowed a van and drove into the desert outside town, where he connected a hose to the exhaust pipe and gassed himself to death. His body was found the next day, and Rachal, informed of his fate, voiced concern that her family would soon be ousted from the Dunes Hotel for lack of funds.

Early on the morning of August 3, Rachal led her seven children onto the balcony of their 11th-story suite, 250 feet above the street. A crowd of 50 horrified pedestrians stood watching as she tossed her children over, one by one, then leaped behind them. "There was no emotion in the thing," one witness told the press. "They didn't scream and they didn't seem to fight." Incredibly, one victim — 15-year-old Eva — managed to survive the plunge, spending a year in hospital before she was released to a foster home. At this writing, no status report is available on the remainder of Immanuel David's cult.

Danites: See Mormons

"Death Angels": See Nation of Islam and **"Temple of Love"**

Desnoyers, Guy

Father Guy Desnoyers was the village priest of Uruffe, in eastern France. He was also a tireless Don Juan, servicing many of his female parishioners in ways that had nothing to do with religion. When one of his paramours, 19-year-old Regina Faye, got pregnant in 1956, Father Desnoyers first suggested that she have an abortion, but the girl refused. She also balked at leaving town, to save the church from scandal, and Desnoyers grew desperate. Borrowing a car from another of his girlfriends, Desnoyers took Regina for a drive in the country, where he shot her in the head, then mutilated her body, killing the eight-month-old infant in her womb. Arrested for the murder, he freely confessed, explaining that he had taken pains to kill the unborn child because it was "the fruit of sin." Officials in the Catholic Church pulled strings to spare Desnoyers from the guillotine, and he received a prison term of life. Even that was too much for the padre, however, Desnoyers pleading from his cell that, if released, he would gladly spend the rest of his life in a Trappist monastery. President Georges Pompidou was impressed enough to commute Desnoyers' sentence, but the priest forgot his promise, instead retiring from the church to marry a divorcée with two children who had comforted him in prison.

Dongsaenkaew, Tip

A professional exorcist in Thailand, 57-year-old Tip Dongsaenkaew had practiced her art in the village of Rai Patana, 315 miles northeast of Bangkok, for ten years before she ran afoul of the law. Her troubles began when relatives of Sommai Chaipanya, a 38-year-old mother of two, approached her for help in April 1996. Chaipanya was subject to sporadic outbursts of hysteria, blamed by exorcist Tip on a demon called "Pob," who devours human intestines. The treatment called for Chaipanya to stand naked, while Tip flogged her head and genitals with a dried sting ray's tail. The patient escaped after two days of flogging, whereupon Tip approached the family and demanded payment in the sum of 4,000 baht (about $160). When Chaipanya's relatives refused to pay, Tip kidnapped the woman and proceeded with her brutal "cure," resulting in her death and the filing of a murder charge against Tip Dongsaenkaew.

Durrant, William Henry Theodore

At first glance, Theodore Durrant appeared to be what well-placed women and their single daughters would call a "good catch." Still in his twenties, courteous, well-groomed, a doctor in training at San Francisco's Cooper Medical College, he was also devoutly religious, serving as assistant superintendent for the regular Sunday School at Emmanuel Baptist Church. Unknown to those around him, though, the young man had a darker side. His dual obsessions were religion and sex, although in the latter field, he would confide to a fellow med student, "I have no knowledge of women."

That didn't stop young ladies from being drawn to Durrant like moths to a flame, however, and one of his strongest admirers was 18-year-old Blanche Lamont, a parishioner at Emmanuel Baptist. On April 3, 1895, they were seen together by numerous witnesses, making their way toward the church, where Blanche was last seen alive on the sidewalk outside. She had been missing several days, curiously unreported by her family, when Durrant began dropping broad hints that she might have "gone astray." On the side, he was pawning her jewelry and pocketing the cash.

Police were clueless as to Blanche's disappearance, but another young woman at Emmanuel Baptist, 21-year-old Minnie Williams, was talking her head off, telling friends that she "knew too much" about the case, hinting darkly that Blanche had met with foul play. On April 12, she was seen arguing with Theo Durrant on the street outside the church, but they seemed to patch things up, and she was holding his arm, cuddling close, as they went back inside.

Next morning, a Saturday, members of the church Ladies' Society were stunned to find Minnie's lifeless, blood-smeared body wedged inside a church cupboard. Half naked, she had been stabbed in both breasts, her wrists slashed, and her own underwear had been jammed in her mouth. Police waited a day before searching the rest of the church, thereby disrupting Easter Sunday services, but it was worth the effort. Once they forced the boarded-over door to Emmanuel Baptist's 120-foot belfry, they found Blanche Lamont's body: she was naked, strangled, raped after death, her clothing jammed into the belfry rafters. Her corpse had been arranged so neatly, head propped up on wooden blocks, that police immediately cast about for "someone who knows something about medicine."

Theo Durrant was the natural suspect, all things considered, and he was swiftly indicted for Blanche Lamont's murder. Conviction was even more rapid, jurors setting a new record with deliberations lasting barely five minutes. Appeals delayed Durrant's date with the gallows for nearly two years, but he was finally hanged on April 3, 1897 — the very anniversary of Blanch Lamont's brutal slaying.

"Ear Murders": See "Temple of Love"

Eto, Sachiko

Police in Sukagawa, Japan, had multiple reasons to search Sachiko Eto's home on Wednesday morning, July 5, 1995. They were investigating an assault and missing-persons case, to start with, and a neighbor had complained of rancid odors emanating from the house. In fact, he said, it smelled like rotting flesh.

The initial victim, still alive and talking in a local hospital, complained that she had been beaten with clubs by Eto, a 47-year-old self-styled "faith healer," and other members of the cult that shared her home. The clubbing was an exorcism, she explained, one of many carried out by Eto in an effort to rid her disciples of their "animal souls." Sachiko also bragged that she could resurrect disciples, if the beatings went too far and they should wind up dead.

From what police found in the guru's home, however, it appeared that she could use some practice when it came to resurrection. Six corpses littered the house, in various stages of decomposition, the freshest of them bearing marks from beatings that had claimed their lives. Eto was jailed on charges of inflicting bodily harm; arrested with her were her daughter, 23-year-old Yoko Otomo; 21-year-old Hiroshi Nemoto; and 45-year-old Michio Sekine.

Eto's co-defendants were all live-in members of the faith healer's cult, and they were intimately linked to the victims. Otomo's husband, missing since the preceding summer, was among the dead; so, too, was Michio Sekine's 47-year-old wife. The other dead included 50-year-old Mamoru Miki, his wife Kazuko, and their teenage daughter Satoe — an entire family beaten to death after they made the mistake of moving in with Eto and her followers.

In custody, Sachiko Eto admitted beating her six disciples to death with drumsticks, but denied intent to kill. Michio Sekine confessed to beating his wife, as part of an exorcism ritual, and described their three young children joining in the fun. In fact, they said, it was a practice for cult members to beat their own relatives during exorcisms, as an act of "love." Police missed the point, and with confessions in hand, the charges were upgraded to murder in the slaying of Kimiko Sekine, apparently the first to die.

Frazier, Patricia Ann

It was 4:00 A.M. on February 22, 1980, when police in Wichita Falls, Texas, were summoned to the home of Patricia Ann Frazier. A babysitter had called to report that Frazier's daughter, four-year-old Khonji Wilson, had been killed. At the apartment complex, patrolmen found the child stretched out on the front seat of her mother's car. She had been stabbed repeatedly, her heart cut out and placed on the floorboard, carefully wrapped in a washcloth. In Frazier's apartment, a blood-soaked mattress told them they had found the murder scene.

Patricia Frazier had a history of drug abuse and mental problems; four years earlier, she had been hospitalized in California, following a nervous breakdown. Now, she said that demons had appeared to her, demanding that she cut her daughter's heart out as a kind of sacrifice. Psychiatrists described her as delusional, and an April hearing found her incompetent for trial, consigning her to a hospital for the criminally insane.

Frazier had improved enough to stand trial in October 1980, but the defense produced a battery of analysts who diagnosed her as a paranoid schizophrenic. Prosecutors disagreed, contending that Frazier had murdered her child because the girl was inconvenient to a new romance, and ten jurors agreed, but two others held out for acquittal, and a mistrial was declared on November 4.

The state was prepared to try again, in May 1981, but Frazier's attorney had a new wrinkle. This time, he claimed that Patricia's delusions were caused by "cinematic trauma," a result of watching *The Exorcist* on television two days before she killed her child. Psychologist Leon Morris signed off on the theory, testifying that the movie "crystallized her delusions she was suffering from and made her feel that her daughter was possessed and was trying to destroy her." Found incompetent for trial a second time, Frazier was returned to the asylum and subsequently released without further charges. At last report, she was in California, living with her mother and pursuing a daily regimen of medication to control her delusions.

"Gay Bashing"

Homosexuals are second only to abortionists in the raw fury they evoke from fundamentalist Christians. In this case, at least, there is some Biblical basis for the animosity, with the Old Testament prescribing death for gays in the books of *Leviticus* and *Judges*. And, from the recorded statements of our nation's leading fundamentalists, it is apparent that a fair percentage of God's people wish those ancient laws were in effect today.

Jerry Falwell's Moral Majority lifted the fallen banner of homophobia after Anita Bryant's brief fling at gay-bashing in the late 1970s. Branding AIDS a "gay plague," Falwell went on to describe homosexuals as "brute beasts... part of a vile and satanic system [that] will one day be utterly annihilated, and there will be a celebration in heaven." In 1981, California's Moral Majority leader, Dean Wycoff, told the press, "I agree with **capital punishment**, and I believe homosexuality is one of those sins that could be coupled with murder." (Even Falwell balked at that, calling Wycoff's plan to execute gays "ridiculous and unthinkable.") Televangelist Pat Robertson, meanwhile, declares that: "Homosexuality is an abomination. Many of those people involved with Adolf Hitler were Satanists, many were homosexuals. The two things seem to go together."

With so much heat involved, it comes as no surprise that incidents of harassment and violence directed at real or imagined gays have increased dramatically in recent years. One watchdog group, the National Gay and Lesbian Task Force, recorded 20 murders from 1985 alone in which "homosexual orientation appeared to be a relevant factor." A more recent canvas of five major American cities disclosed 8,303 "gay-bashing" incidents between 1988 and 1993.

Most prominent ministers stop short of calling for direct attacks on gays, and Pat Robertson took the unusual step of threatening lawsuits against several television stations in November 1995, after they aired public service spots produced by the Parents, Families and Friends of Lesbians and Gays (PFLAG), presenting quotes from Robertson, Falwell, and Helms as examples of rampant homophobia in the United States. Far-right spokesmen for the **"Christian Identity"** movement, however, are typically less cautious in their words and deeds. Ted Weiland, a Nebraska Identity minister, reminds us that "God said they are to be put to death, and it wasn't necessarily to be done in a 'merciful' manner. Homosexuals were to be put to death by stoning." From North Carolina, **Ku Klux Klan** spokesman Greg Beckett advises that "The only way this deadly disease [AIDS] can be stopped is by purging the guilty and infested parties that subscribe to these lifestyles among us." In Georgia, meanwhile, the "Crusade Against Corruption" — led by former Klansman and convicted church bomber J.B. Stoner — doesn't want to do away with AIDS at all. Rather, its members appear in public brandishing placards that declare: "Praise God for AIDS." And, according to Arkansas Klansman Thom Robb, another Identity minister, "The good news is that every ten minutes a queer gets AIDS."

The results of such tough talk are seen on police blotters across the country. Randall Evans, a member of the homicidal Order, was jailed in 1983 for assaulting a gay man in Oregon. Two years later, Identity spokesman James Ellison — then leader of the Covenant, the Sword and the Arm of the Lord

— was convicted of setting fire to a church that welcomed gay parishioners in Springfield, Missouri. In November 1987, three members of the Klan-connected White Patriot Party were indicted for shooting five men in a bookstore they believed to be a gay hangout: three of the victims were killed. In December 1990, a San Diego teenager was accosted by Nazi skinheads who called him a "faggot," then stabbed him to death. Two gay men were shot to death, with a third wounded, in Minneapolis during August 1991.

And so it goes. Ironically, one of the Identity movement's leading spokesmen, Rev. Richard Butler of the Aryan Nations, has found it necessary to defend himself on charges of sexual impropriety. In the early 1970s, before he moved his group to Idaho, Butler was arrested in California on charges of "lewd conduct near a school playground." No details were forthcoming, but a decade later, in 1982, Butler addressed the issue in a letter to his followers, admitting the arrest while insisting that he was "not a homosexual child molester." Instead, Butler claimed, he had been "set up" for the bust by a man he described as a police informant and a "practicing homosexual." **[See also: Terrorism]**

Griffin, Michael: See "Pro-Life" Movement

Heaven's Gate

At first, the story played like something from *The X Files*. It began with a package in the mail, containing a letter and two videocassette tapes. The letter was a farewell message — in effect, a suicide note. On the tapes, 39 individuals appeared, most of them in pairs, bidding good-bye to their loved ones, explaining that they were on their way to another, better life among the stars. A UFO was coming for them. It would carry them away, once they "shed" their bodily "containers" via suicide.

"Our 22 years of classroom here on planet Earth are finally coming to conclusion — 'graduation' from the Human Evolutionary Level," read the letter. "We are happily prepared to leave this world and go with Ti's crew."

The recipient of the package recognized most of those on the tape. He was, in fact, a former member of the cult to which they all belonged, a group that lately called itself Heaven's Gate. Alarmed by the possibility of a mass suicide, the man notified his employer, Nick Matzorkis, and directed him to the cult's headquarters, a $1.6 million mansion complete with swimming pool and tennis courts, located in the exclusive celebrity enclave of Rancho Santa Fe, 30 miles north of San Diego, California. Matzorkis drove to the site, went inside, and emerged moments later, shaken and stunned, to summon the authorities.

Inside the house, all 39 members of the local cult lay dead. Its leader, 65-year-old Marshal Applewhite, was alone in the master bedroom, while his followers were distributed five to a bedroom. All 39 were dressed identically in black shirt, matching pants, and new black Nike sneakers. All had short-cropped hair, initially confusing deputies who thought that most of them were men. Each body occupied a bunk bed, all but two draped with triangular purple shrouds covering the face and upper body. Each had some form of identification in his or her shirt pocket, along with a $5 bill and some quarters. Packed suitcases stood near the bodies, as if the dead had been planning to go on a trip.

Which, as it turned out, they had.

County medical examiner Brian Blackbourne reported that the dead included 21 women, aged 28 to 72, and 18 men, ages 29 to 65. All but one were Americans, the lone exception packing a Canadian driver's license. Two were black, the rest Caucasian, including a handful of presumed Hispanics. Ten of the dead hailed from New Mexico, nine from Texas, four each from California and Colorado, three each from Arizona and Utah, one each from the states of Florida, Minnesota, Ohio, and Washington; of the two remaining, one carried an international driver's license, while the last had none. Some of the victims had died from a drug overdose, others from asphyxiation, with written instructions found on their bodies describing the technique in detail.

According to the evidence and written notes, each member of the cult had consumed a dose of phenobarbitol, mixed in a pudding or applesauce and chased with shots of vodka. After swallowing the lethal mixture, each lay down with a plastic bag over his or her head and waited calmly for death. The suicides were carried out in shifts — 15 on each of two successive days, with nine more on the third and final day. Survivors had cleaned up after each death shift, arranging the bodies, removing plastic bags and throwing them away before draping the corpses in their purple shrouds. The last two cleanup men had no one to assist them: they alone were found with plastic bags still wrapped around their heads.

As the authorities began, too late, to check the death cult's history, they learned that it had been around for over 20 years. At one time or another, it was advertised by different names, but the core ideology never changed: a spaceship was coming to swoop up true believers and carry them to paradise in outer space. When it arrived, the faithful would discard their bodies and move on. Nothing on earth could hold them back.

The father of the cult was a peculiar messiah indeed. Marshall Herff Applewhite was born at Spur, Texas — 240 miles west of Dallas — in May 1931, the son of a Presbyterian minister. He graduated from high school in Corpus Christi, in 1948, and briefly studied for the ministry, soon shifting his interest to music. In 1952, he graduated from Austin College, in Texas, but his further education was interrupted by a stint in the U.S. Army Signal Corps, from 1954 to '56. In 1959, he earned his master's degree in music from the University of Colorado at Boulder. Two years later, he was hired as choral director for the University of Alabama, moving on to teach music at Houston's University of St. Thomas from 1966 to 1970. In his spare time, between 1964 and '68, Applewhite performed with the Houston Grand Opera, frequently singing lead parts.

His "normal" life began unraveling sometime in the late 1960s, climaxed with his dismissal from St. Thomas in 1970, over "health problems of an emotional nature." He took a shot at psychotherapy, but nothing seemed to put his mind back on an even keel. Divorced by 1972, Applewhite met Bonnie Lu Nettles, a divorcée with four children who had abandoned a nursing career in favor of astrology. Applewhite shared her interest in the stars, and they soon joined forces as partners in life, living briefly in Las Vegas, moving on to Oregon, where they reportedly experienced a "spiritual awakening." For Applewhite, the process included castration, but neither conversion nor gelding affected morality. In August 1974, he was jailed in Texas on charges of auto theft and stealing credit cards.

Meanwhile, the cult rolled on. Applewhite and Nettles liked to call themselves "The Two," posing as extraterrestrials on a mission of salvation. In the mid-1970s, they began to call themselves "Bo" and "Peep," later "Do" and "Ti" (pronounced "doe" and "tee," like the musical notes), to demonstrate that their "earth names" meant nothing. Not only were they aliens walking around in "host bodies," said Bo and Peep, they were also the two "witnesses" described in the *Book of Revelations*, who ascend to heaven in a cloud — interpreted to mean UFO. Recruits were cautioned to avoid drugs, alcohol, and sex — the latter prohibition so complete that female acolytes wore baggy shirts to hide their breasts, while at least seven males in the final suicidal clique had followed Applewhite's example by submitting to castration.

At a glance, the cult's theology was eclectic to a fault, blending tenets of Eastern and Western religions with New Age philosophies and flying saucer "facts." Bonnie Nettles "shed her container" in 1985, a victim of cancer, but Applewhite and company hailed her as a pioneer, gone on ahead to pave their way to the heavens. "Do" labored on with "Ti," recruiting disciples first through public meetings, then by word of mouth, and finally with the assistance of the media. In May 1993, billing itself as "Total Overcomers Anonymous," the cult paid $30,000 for a three-quarter-page ad in *USA Today*, leading off with the tongue-in-cheek headline UFO CULT RESURFACES WITH FINAL OFFER. That ad read, in part:

> The Earth's present "civilization" is about to be recycled — "spaded under." Its inhabitants are refusing to evolve. The weeds have taken over the garden and disturbed its usefulness beyond repair.

On January 17, 1994, when an earthquake rocked Los Angeles, the cult thought its moment had come. Within hours of the shakeup, Applewhite's people were on the street, passing out leaflets that trumpeted WE TOLD YOU SO! Still, the elusive aliens did not arrive. Something was missing. More work was required.

In January 1994, Applewhite launched a nine-month, cross-country series of free public meetings, spreading the word from coast to coast. By September 1995, the cult was on-line as "Undercover Jesus" and/or " ET Presently Incarnate," Off-line, members preferred to call their outfit "Heaven's Gate," supporting themselves in fine style with a commercial business — "Higher Source" — that designed custom Internet web sites for any and all comers.

Indeed, Heaven's Gate had its own home page on the World Wide Web, and browsers could have told from reading it that something strange was up among Do's disciples. Appearance of the Hale-Bopp comet was their tip-off, believers convinced that the great "mother ship" was concealed in its tail. As the web page told its readers:

> The joy is that our Older Member in the Evolutionary Level above human (the Kingdom of Heaven) has made it clear that Hale-Bopp's approach is the "marker" we've been waiting for — the time for the arrival to take us home to "Their World" in the literal heavens... We fully desire, expect and look forward to boarding a spacecraft from the Next Level very soon. There is no doubt in our mind that our being "picked up" is inevitable in the very near future...
>
> If you study the material on this website you will hopefully understand our joy and what our purpose here on Earth has been. You may even find your "boarding pass" to leave with us during this brief "window"...
>
> We will, between now and our departure, do everything we can for those who want to go with us. But

we cannot allow them to interfere with or delay our return to Him.

It was suggested, after the fact, that Applewhite may have duped his followers into mass suicide by telling them his body was "disintegrating" with cancer, but autopsy results showed no trace of the disease. Survivors of the cult remain convinced that the Mother Ship is drawing closer day by day, if not in the shadow of Hale-Bopp, then somewhere near at hand — at least in cosmic terms. Their friends and loved ones did not commit suicide, they say: they have simply moved on.

Hernandez, Cayetano and Santos

Unscrupulous scam artists from Yerba Buena, in the Mexican state of Tamaulipas, the Hernandez brothers organized a local cult in early 1963, persuading gullible farmers that the "mountain gods" would shower them with riches if they demonstrated proper piety and made unselfish sacrifices. Sex was the preferred form of devotion, with women submitting themselves to Santos, while Cayetano serviced the men. Dissension spread over time, when the promised blessings failed to materialize, and the brothers went shopping for a solution in Monterrey. There, they met Magdalena Solis, a blonde lesbian prostitute, persuading her and her brother Eleazor to impersonate the mountain gods for a share of the take.

Villagers in Yerba Buena were briefly appeased by the ruse, but even steamy sex with deities paled in comparison to hard cash. When their disciples grew restless again, the Hernandez brothers called for a human sacrifice, with two of their most vocal critics beaten to death, their blood consumed by the faithful from ceremonial bowls. Over the next few weeks, six more doubters were dispatched in similar style.

Old-fashioned jealousy finally doomed the cult, Magdalena Solis flying into a rage when one of her female devotees began sharing sexual favors with Santos Hernandez. The "goddess" demanded an immediate sacrifice, with the teenage girl bound to a cross and beaten to death. While her body was being burned, Magdalena fingered another member of the cult as a heretic, watching her disciples hack the man to pieces with machetes on the spot.

Unknown to participants in the ghoulish rite, they were also observed by a teenage witness not affiliated with the sect. Police were skeptical, but they dispatched a patrolman to check out the cult's mountain lair, just in case. When the officer disappeared, along with his guide, a flying squad was sent to Yerba Buena from the capital at Ciudad Victoria. They found two mutilated corpses, the policeman's heart ripped from his chest, and rifle fire erupted when the squad approached the cave the cult had fortified. Three officers were wounded in the shootout, but the odds were on their side. When the smoke cleared, police found Santos Hernandez dead from bullet wounds. His brother was missing, later identified as a victim of assassination by a rival candidate for priesthood in the cult. The resident "gods" and twelve disciples were convicted of murder, drawing long terms in prison.

Hill, Paul: See "Pro-Life" Movement

Homosexuality: See "Gay Bashing"

Howell, Vernon: See Branch Davidians

Human Sacrifice

If history begins, as Philip Groisser says, in the Near East, so too begins the chronicle of human sacrifice — and it begins with children. Many Jews and Christians are emphatic in denying (or persistent in ignoring) this part of their history, but they cannot escape the fact that our Judaeo-Christian heritage has roots in bloody soil.

The Holy Bible is ambiguous in treatment of the subject. In *Genesis*, Chapter 4, we are told how God's preference for Abel's blood sacrifice over Cain's vegetarian offering prompted mankind's first murder, and later, in Chapter 22, Jehovah orders Abraham to sacrifice his only son. That exercise, apparently, was just a test of character and faith, canceled at the penultimate moment, but later (*Exodus* 22:29), God calls upon the Israelites to sacrifice "the firstborn of thy sons." The order seemed straightforward, unequivocal, and yet we are informed (*Ezekiel* 20:26) that Israel's sacrifice of children was in fact a *punishment* inflicted by this selfsame God, "that I might make them desolate, to the end that they might know that I am the Lord."

Elsewhere in scripture, we read that sacrifice of children is abominable when the victims are offered "to Molech" (*Leviticus* 18:21; *Jeremiah* 32:35). Specific prohibitions of child sacrifice are issued to the Levites (*Deuteronomy* 18:10) and Israelites (2 *Kings* 17:17; *Ezekiel* 20:31), with a death sentence reserved even for "strangers" who sacrificed their offspring in territory occupied by God's chosen people (*Leviticus* 20:2-4). A seeming contradiction rises in the divine prohibition against sacrificial offerings of the blind, lame or sick (*Malachi* 1:8), but we may console ourselves with the hope that those instructions applied only to lower animals.

It was not always so, however. King Solomon reportedly conducted sacrifices to Molech and Chemosh in the 10th century BC (1 *Kings* 11:7-8), and the rituals were continued in Judah three centuries later, by King Ahaz (2 *Kings* 16:3) and his grandson Manasseh (2 *Kings* 21:6; 2 *Chronicles* 33:6). Both sacrificed to Molech, we are told, and while it was assumed for many years Molech was a pagan god, more recent scholarship suggests that the "name" may, in fact, be a technical term for the act of child sacrifice itself, without reference to a specific deity. Indeed, 2 *Samuel* 21:1-9 describes King David's participation in the sacrifice of seven men at the beginning of a barley harvest, with an eye toward ending famine in the land.

The myths of ancient Greece abound with sacrificial homicides, but modern scholars are inclined to question whether they reflect real-world events, or something more akin to rumblings from the group subconscious. Indeed, while some feminist historians prefer to believe that ancient Greeks never practiced human sacrifice at all, on balance, their conclusions sound a good deal more like wishful thinking. Greek historian Pausanius was well aware of bloody rituals conducted on the summit of Mount Lykaion, in Arcadia, but he chose not to examine them in detail. "I could see no pleasure in delving into this sacrifice," he wrote. "Let it be as it is and was from the beginning." Others maintain that the cult of Zeus Lycaeus — variously described by scholars as a sect of "werewolves" or bear-worshipers — "definitely" practiced human sacrifice. Evidence of ritual murders exists from at least a dozen locations in ancient Greece, including Athens itself, with the "recipients" including Zeus, Kronos, Artemis, Ares, Dionysus, Hermes, and various mythical heroes.

If the evidence of Greek human sacrifice remains controversial in some circles, there is no doubt whatsoever about ancient Rome. The Romans were eclectic people, borrowing their gods and rituals from races as diverse as the Egyptians,

Greeks, and the Etruscans who preceded them in northern Italy, by way of Asia Minor — who, themselves, divined the future from the entrails of slaughtered prisoners, in a ritual dubbed *hostiae consultatoriae*. Emperor Commodus (AD 180-192) continued that grisly method of fortune telling and passed it on to his successor Caracalla (AD 211-217), despite the fact that human sacrifices were outlawed in the Roman Empire after AD 196. Constantine V (AD 741-75) was among the most notorious of imperial bloodletters, one observer noting that he "was not particular about whose corpse should find its way to his altar," as long as it was fresh. Predictions aside, ancient Romans also practiced the rites of *expiatio*, designed to restore a disrupted balance between man and various higher powers through the offer of animal or human sacrifice. In 216 BC, after Hannibal crushed the Roman army at Cannae, the entire Senate pitched in for a cleansing ceremony that included the live burial of two couples — one Greek and one Gaulish — at the cattle market in Rome.

The wide-ranging Phoenicians were both excellent seamen and zealous practitioners of child sacrifice, who carried their beliefs and rituals to the ends of the known world. Their most successful colony, at Carthage in North Africa, was a hotbed of ritual murder, with child sacrifice routinely practiced from the eighth century BC until Rome destroyed the city in 146 BC. Archaeologists have unearthed thousands of urns at old Carthage, holding the calcined remains of young children, along with small birds and animals — the latter probably intended as substitutional sacrifices. Greek author Kleitarchos, writing in the third century BC, described Carthaginians offering their children to Kronos, and while there is also an occasional mention of blood rites devoted to Saturn, most of the tiny victims were apparently sacrificed to Tanit or Ba'al

Hammon. The facial rictus produced by cremation is responsible for Kleitarchos coining the term "sardonic laughter."

When Roman legions expanded the empire, they took their religion along, as witnessed by the ancient fortress at Reculver, in Kent, where infant skeletons were excavated from the walls in 1966. Human sacrifice, of both children and adults, was not a Roman import to the conquered lands, however. Julius Caesar's campaigns in Gaul and Britain (58-51 BC) produced copious evidence of Celtic human sacrifice, with the Druid priesthood officiating in most cases. Caesar himself described the Celtic ritual of building giant wicker effigies, inside which human victims were confined and ritually burned alive. Other victims were drowned in special cauldrons or decapitated, sometimes shot with arrows or impaled. Dio Cassius reports that Boudicca's Iceni hanged Roman noblewomen in the grove of Andastre, afterward slicing off their breasts and stitching the severed flesh to their lips, but most Celtic ritual murders were more prosaic, with decapitated and dismembered victims buried in foundations, or within the rings of "Druid circles" such as those at Stonehenge. Some of the more ghastly reports are dismissed by modern historians as flagrant wartime propaganda, but the occurrence of human sacrifice in ancient Gaul and Britain cannot be doubted. Only in the first century AD, long after Caesar's invasion, would Pomponius Mela report that ritual slaughter in Gaul had ceased.

It would appear that Mela's confident obituary for ritual murder in Britain was premature, to say the least. We know, for instance, that the practice of "blessing" new construction projects with human remains continued well after Mela's report. The fortress at Reculver, built with children in its walls, was of third-century construction, and other public buildings — such as the church at Darrington, in Yorkshire, with a skull removed from its foundation in 1895 — were erected on human remains. In Britain's fenlands, likewise, those who neglected to maintain the critical sea walls, thus producing floods, became a part of the foundation when a new wall was constructed.

In Scandinavia, the Norsemen sacrificed both animals and human beings to their deities, including Odin, who preferred his offerings suspended from the limbs of trees. Historian Adam of Bremen, writing in the 11th century AD, quotes a 70-year-old Swede who recalled a childhood scene of dangling corpses in the sacred grove at Old Upsalla. "Tollund Man," in Denmark, was likewise hanged or strangled, buried with the rope around his neck, as an offering to the goddess Nerthus, guardian of agricultural fertility. Further south, the Elbe or Western Slavs paid homage to the war god Svarozhich, whose temple stood at Radegast, near Leipzig. Various Slavonic tribes trooped through the temple, offering human sacrifices in an effort to secure the gift of prophecy, or to reward Svarozhich for the blessings they had already received. In AD 1066, following a Slavic victory in battle, the winners beheaded John, Bishop of Mecklenburg, and presented his skull to their god as a token of gratitude.

By that time, the Christian church was well on its way to a full-scale **Inquisition**, beginning with the suppression of Gnostic "heretics" after AD 392. Gnostic dualism — regarded by many scholars as the theological root of modern Satanism — was inherently repugnant to the early church, as was the sect's die-hard opposition to childbirth in an "evil" world. Historian Epiphianus described, in rather florid terms, the alleged Gnostic method for disposing of unwanted offspring:

> If one of them happens to allow the sperm to penetrate the woman and make her pregnant, listen to the outrage that they dare to perform. At the right moment they extract the embryo with their fingers and take this aborted infant and crush it with pestle and mortar; when they have mixed in honey, pepper and other spices and perfumed oils to lessen their nausea, every member of this troop of swine and dogs, each taking a piece of the aborted child in their fingers. And so, when they have finished their cannibal feast, they end with this prayer to God: "We have not been deceived by the Archon of lust, but we have retrieved our brother's transgression." And this they consider the perfect Passover.

As European explorers "discovered" new parts of the globe, from the 14th through the 16th centuries, they found the aboriginal inhabitants of almost every land pursuing diverse forms of human sacrifice. In Africa, the very "heart of darkness," victims were dispatched for the same reasons others had been slaughtered in the Middle East and Europe: to insure good harvests and avert disasters; to predict the future; to provide a blessing of specific temples, palaces, and such; to serve their executioners as duty-bound ambassadors into the spirit realm. In parts of Africa, convicted criminals were utilized in sacrificial rites, while other tribes preferred the blood of kings. As late as 1881, the monarch of Ashanti (now a part of Ghana) mixed the blood of 200 virgins with the mortar used to build his new palace. Inevitably, when African slaves were carried away to the New World, their tribal religions went with them, mutating over time into the modern-day cults of voodoo, santeria, palo mayombe, macumba, and others — all of which maintain traditions of animal sacrifice, with the occasional "long pig" or "goat without horns" thrown in for special occasions.

Throughout vast Asia it was much the same. In Mandalay, once the royal capital city of Upper Burma (now Myanmar), men were buried alive as offerings to the earth deity, in an effort to make buildings secure, while next-door in Siam (now Thailand) victims were crushed in pits for identical reasons. The Khonds, a tribe of Orissa, offered human sacrifices to assist their harvests, well into the mid-19th century. The chosen victims, called *Meriah*, were frequently descendants of prior offerings, blessed — or cursed — by their blood line to fill a predetermined role in Khondish ritual. At killing time, the chosen one was led into a virgin forest, there anointed with oil and turmeric, after which he was drugged before being killed by one of a variety of methods, his body cut into pieces, and burned in a ritualistic way.

The Assassin cult, a Muslim splinter group in Persia (now Iran), organized in the 11th century, took its name from the descriptive adjective *hashashin* ("users of hashish"). Members viewed murder as a sacred duty to their god and earthly ruler, but their frequent use as mercenary hit men during the Crusades has blurred the line between which slayings were considered holy work and which were simply business. Inasmuch as killers were dispatched with an elaborate ritual, including use of sex and psychedelic drugs to generate "visions" of the paradise that awaited faithful servants of the cult, there may have been no real distinction on the part of those who did the killing. The sect was theoretically destroyed by Mongol invaders under Hulaku, grandson of Genghis Khan, in 1256, with some 12,000 cult members slain, but French observers noted remnants of the group surviving into the early 19th century.

It may be sheer coincidence that the "demise" of the Assassins coincided with the birth of yet another homicidal cult, this time in India. Dating from the early 13th century, the sect called *thag* — Hindi for "deceiver" — saw its members labeled "thugs" in a corruption of the label they appointed for themselves. Cultists were also known as *Phansigars*, after the Hindi word for "noose," since they preferred to strangle victims with the *rumal* (scarf) each member wore around his waist. Thugs worshipped Kali, the Hindu goddess of destruction, and aside from random homicide, their rituals also incorporated masochistic elements, in which devotees were flogged and mutilated by their priests, hoisted aloft with hooks in their flesh, while the ecstatic audience chanted, "Victory to Mother Kali." It is impossible to say how many victims were annihilated by the thugs in the 600 years before they were suppressed by British military force. Colonial records indicate that some 4,500 thugs were convicted of various crimes between 1830 and 1848, with at least 110 sentenced to death for murder. One of those, Thugee Buhram, single-handedly disposed of 931 victims before his arrest in 1840, and British authorities estimate that cultists accounted for some 40,000 homicides in the year 1812 alone. Assuming this to be a record year, even ten times the normal body count, it is apparent that the thugs must still have slaughtered millions of victims during their 600 years of active hunting.

It was the New World, though, which broke all standing records for ritual homicide. Spanish *conquistadors* in Central and South America found native cultures in place which had equaled the architectural feats of Egypt, while surpassing the ritual blood-baths of Carthage and darkest Africa. Here, whole societies existed *for the purpose* of conducting human sacrifice en masse, relying on a steady stream of slaves and prisoners of war to keep their crimson altars occupied. One lapse, they feared, would blight their harvests, cause all manner of catastrophes, perhaps even prevent the sun from rising.

Anyone who has concerned himself with human sacrifice for any length of time is perfectly familiar with its practice by the Inca and the Aztecs. It requires a more exacting study, though, to learn and understand that those bloodthirsty cultures were the end result of ages during which specific homicidal rituals were refined to what practitioners of the 15th and 16th centuries regarded as perfection.

Several thousand years before the Aztecs sold themselves as mercenary warriors to the Tepanec kingdom of Atzcapotzalco, children were sacrificed by decapitation and other methods in the Tehuacán Valley, 120 miles southeast of modern Mexico City. El Tajin, in northern Veracruz, gave rise to a people obsessed with human sacrifice in the Late Classic period (AD 600-900), who combined their blood rites with a native ball game, offering the captain of the losing team to their Death God, recording the events in detailed bas reliefs. Toltec shamans, in the Post-Classic period, invented the *tzomplanti* skull racks that would later decorate proud Aztec temples, incorporating cannibalism as part of their morbid ritual. Another Post-Classic culture, the Zapotecs — based at Mitla, some 25 miles southwest of modern Oaxaca City — were still going strong in the 17th century, when Father Burgoa reported the continuing slaughter of "numberless" victims. When Mixtecs invaded the Zapotec territory, their warlord 8 Deer "Jaguar Claw" (AD 1063-1115) sacrificed members of competing royal families, thus merging religion with power politics. The Tarascan kingdom, never conquered by its avaricious Aztec neighbors, practiced both human sacrifice and auto-sacrifice (spilling one's own blood) in honor of the mighty war god *Wakúsecha*, whose earthly form was on loan to King Kasonsí.

Amid such carnage, the Maya, Aztecs, and Inca stand out for a combination of style and sheer ferocity. Human offerings were frequent and continuous in all three cultures, although scholars still debate the final Aztec body count. Some early sources speak of as many as 80,000 victims slaughtered over four days, an epic killing that was undoubtedly a challenge to priests restricted to the use of obsidian daggers. Conversely, there is no denying that the sacrifices were both frequent and prolific, including communal cannibalism and grisly rites in which priests were called upon to wear the fresh skins of their victims. Ironically, such practices would ultimately work against the natives, as they gave their Christian conquerors a fair excuse to raze their temples, confiscate their gold, and slaughter those who would not be converted — albeit at swordpoint — to the worship of a brand-new god.

In North America, white settlers found no native cult of sacrifice to rival those below the Rio Grande. Only the Natchez people of the lower Mississippi practiced wholesale sacrifice at their important funerals, dispatching wives, relatives, and friends of the deceased to join him in the afterlife. On such occasions, total strangers sometimes volunteered to join the parade of death, and parents unrelated to the dear departed had been known to sacrifice their children, basking in the adulation that resulted from their generosity. A few miles farther north, Pawnee practitioners worshipped the sun and morning star, the latter deity requiring an annual human sacrifice. Because the Pawnee were too civilized to kill their own, they would abduct an adolescent girl from some adjacent tribe and treat her royally for six months, before she was eventually killed with arrows, by the removal of her heart, or by slow roasting. The coddling time was thought to put their captive in a more cooperative mood, thereby insuring that her spirit would be properly respectful in negotiating with the morning star for future blessings on the tribe.

White prejudice dictates that if there is a place on earth where human sacrifice still lingers, it must be in darkest Africa — and sadly, in this instance, the assumption is correct. On both sides of the equator, practitioners of native witchcraft (often lumped together with the catch-all tags of "medicine" or *ju-ju*) have been active in performing human sacrifices to the present day.

Beginning in Nigeria, we find a long series of "murders for magic," including the removal of particular organs for ritual use, reported among the Tiv people, from 1938 through 1949. The Tiv use certain body parts for different rituals — the knee cap, genitals, a tibia, the brain — and feel that every mother owes one child to the *mbatsav* ("league of witches") as a living sacrifice. Ritual headhunting sent three Tiv practitioners to the gallows in the 1940s, but belief is not restricted to ignorant bushmen. Isaiah Oke, in his book *Blood Secrets*, presents first-hand evidence of a ritual called *iko-awo*, performed at the request of a modern Nigerian army officer, in which the victim was flayed alive, his gutted corpse preserved as a point of contact with the spirit realm.

In July 1987, the *Nigerian Tribune* reported the case of a man who hired a *ju-ju* priest to sacrifice his own 13-year-old nephew. The boy was decapitated, his body dumped in a canal, while his head reposed in a box at the uncle's home. The relic was later introduced as evidence in court, with the uncle and his parents — the victim's grandparents — convicted of murder. In May 1988, the *African Guardian*, published in Lagos, Nigeria, declared that native shamans were using human blood, plus the breasts and pubic hair of murdered women, to produce magic charms. A short time later, Nigerian essayist Wilson Asekombe wrote that "human sacrifice will soon become the number two cause of accidental [sic] death in West Africa, second only to traffic accidents."

Zimbabwe (formerly Rhodesia) has been another site of continuing ritual murders. Back in 1922, elders of the Mtwara tribe sacrificed their own chief's son to the rain goddess, believing that he had seduced a virgin scheduled to portray the goddess in a yearly celebration, thereby bringing on a brutal drought. Six tribesmen were convicted of murder and sentenced to death in that case, but their sentences were later commuted. Half a century later, Dr. John Thompson, heading Rhodesia's forensic service from 1963-77, described the case of a herdsman who butchered sacrificial victims and sold their "magic" organs to witch doctors. His downfall, leading to another death sentence, occurred when he supplied his foreman with a package of spare "beef," which happened to include two fingers and a human ear.

Basutoland (now Lesotho) witnessed a series of 130 ritual murders between 1940 and 1958, related to procurement of human tissue — used in making a charm called *diretlo* — for magical purposes. Prior to imposition of British colonial rule in 1868, the samples had been lifted from rivals killed in war; without that ready source of victims, tribal shamans turned upon their own, removing flesh and organs from live victims who either died in the process or were murdered afterward to guarantee their silence.

Two hundred miles to the northeast, in tiny Swaziland, eight persons were hanged in July 1981, as authorities sought to curb a new outbreak of "medicine" murders, condemned by the nation's prime minister as a "totally disgraceful and barbaric practice." Even militant South Africa has its problems with human sacrifice, where makers of *muti* (a synonym for *diretlo*) remain sporadically active to the present day. A series of nineteen ritual murders, committed in the "independent homeland" of Venda between 1982 and 1984, sent twelve practitioners to death row, including a deputy cabinet minister and his son.

In the western hemisphere, African *ju-ju* traditions survive in such variant forms as voodoo, santeria, abaqua, macumba, and others, while the Bantu religion of palo mayombe has also taken root with rituals including human sacrifice. Reports of ritual murder emanate periodically from Haiti, where voodoo is the dominant religion, and a young Cuban girl was sacrificed as far back as 1903, by practitioners of palo mayombe. More recently, around Havana in 1978, devotees of abaqua murdered the entire 20-member cast of a stage play that publicized their cult's secret rituals.

In strife-torn Peru, human sacrifice remains a daily fact of life, dating back to the time of the Incas. For some practitioners, the ritual offering of human lives is believed to insure bountiful crops, control the weather, and prevent such natural catastrophes as floods and earthquakes. These rituals, called "paying the earth," are also employed by wealthy businessmen, including mine owners and beer distributors, to insure continued prosperity. Various local festivals and holidays demand a human sacrifice, and regional narcotics smugglers (as in Mexico, Bolivia, and elsewhere) rarely make a move without spilling blood to appease the gods in advance. In parts of Peru, a sect of cultists called *liquichiri* specialize in the extraction of fat from human victims. The end product, called *cebo*, is believed to be especially useful in rituals aimed at acquiring new vehicles, ranging from automobiles to jet aircraft.

While isolated human sacrifices have been documented throughout Peru from the 1940s to the present day, some *yatiri* — shamans for hire — have traditional killing grounds of their own. One such, near Puno, is Mt. Santa Barbara, the site of several sacrifices in the early 1980s. A female victim, killed there in 1982, was found with her breasts cut off, her vagina slashed, and her face painted black. Around Yunguyo, ritual murders are so common that Mayor Horacio Benavides circulated a petition in May 1988, calling on the provincial prosecutor's office to investigate "abnormal elements of people who are practicing paganism or perhaps the narcotrafficker *pistacos* [vampires]." Today, despite several well-publicized cases resulting in prosecution and convictions, the ceremonial murders continue.

In neighboring Chile, human sacrifice is such an established tradition that the courts recognize "compulsion by irresistible psychic forces" as grounds for acquittal in cases of ritual murder. Where police have tried to discourage the practice, Mapuche Indians complain of more frequent droughts and earthquakes, now that fewer children are offered to the gods. In 1960, following a period of earthquakes near Puerto Dominguez, Clara Huenchillan decapitated two of her own children as a sacrifice; prosecutors declined to press charges when Clara blamed the murders on a dream, inspired by "many witches" in the neighborhood. In 1985, at Lago Bundi, Juana Namuncura was suspected (but never charged) of sacrificing her own great-grandchild to appease the elements. A year later, cultists in Vista Hermosa blamed Osvaldo Salamanca's chronic illness on a "vampire demon" which they exorcised by driving a wooden stake through the heart of his nine-year-old nephew.

Mexico, home of the Aztecs, has also experienced its share of human sacrifices in modern times, from the ritual bloodletting of the **Hernandez** brothers in the 1960s to the grisly deeds of Adolfo **Constanzo** and company, linked to at least 23 sacrificial murders between 1987 and 1989. Police in Mexico City investigated ritual slayings of 60 adults and 14 infants during the same period, with more deaths reported around Veracruz. With the exposure of Constanzo's cult in 1989, it was tempting to blame him for all such crimes, but in fact, the ceremonies have continued since Constanzo's death in a shootout with police. As prosecutor Guillermo Ibarra explained, "We would like to say, yes, Constanzo did them all, and poof, all those cases are solved. And the fact is, we believe he was responsible for some of them, though we'll never prove it now. But he didn't commit all of those murders, which means someone else did. Someone who is still out there." **[See also: Biblical Bloodshed]**

Inquisition

The *Crusades* were still in progress when leaders of the Roman Catholic Church picked up disturbing vibes of dissidence within their sprawling European empire. Everywhere they turned, it seemed that Jews or pagan peasants flaunted Rome's authority to chart the "one true faith," and even certain Christian sects displayed a subversive tendency to think for themselves on matters of doctrine. Such heretics were dangerous, as demonstrated when Eastern Orthodox Christians bailed out in AD 1054, to establish their own headquarters at Constantinople.

Clearly, something had to be done, and while the Roman Catholic Church had started killing heretics around Orléans, in 1022, it took some time for the new housecleaning to gather momentum. Pope Adrian IV declared a crusade against the dualist Cathar sect in 1159, but his death that same year prevented the purge from taking effect. The Cathari and their spiritual offspring were still giving Rome fits in 1204, when Pope Innocent III graced his legates with authority "to destroy, throw down, or pluck up whatever is to be destroyed, thrown down, or plucked up and to plant and build whatever is to be built or planted." All the papal manhunters lacked, henceforth, was a compelling motive, and that was provided in 1208, when Rome offered the land and property of any heretics to those who cut them down.

The Albigensian Crusade against Cathari worshipers in southern France began that same year and dragged on until 1229, claiming as many as 1,000,000 lives by some estimates. Twelve thousand were said to have been slaughtered at the Cathedral of St. Nazaire alone, while Bishop Foulques of Toulouse executed another 10,000. When the crusaders surrounded Béziers, and a field officer reportedly asked the commanding legate how to distinguish between loyal Catholics and Cathars, that worthy is quoted as having replied, "Kill them all, for God knows his own." When the slaughter was finished, papal observers claimed 20,000 dead, but other sources place the body count between 60,000 and 100,000, one noting that "even the dead were not safe from dishonor, and the worst humiliations were heaped upon women."

Two years after the close of the Albigensian Crusade, in 1231, Pope Gregory IX established the Holy Inquisition as a separate tribunal, with fire selected as the sole appropriate mode of execution for heretics. In 1244, the Council of Narbonne ruled that all sentences must include flogging, without mitigation for family, old age, or illness. Torture was formally approved as a means of extracting confessions in 1252, by Pope Innocent IV (remaining on the church's books until 1917). Four years later, inquisitors were granted papal authority to absolve their assistants for any acts of violence. In 1262, inquisitors were further empowered to absolve each other for crimes of bloodshed, thus removing the last, slim vestige of restraint.

Historians typically divide the Inquisition into three phases — Medieval, Spanish, and Roman — but the distinction is an exercise in glib semantics. The Spanish Inquisition, with its special attention to Jews, was supervised by Dominican Tomás de Torquemada, appointed as Inquisitor General by Pope Sixtus IV. The Roman Inquisition, meanwhile, was distinguished from its Medieval predecessor only by a name change, in 1542, when Pope Paul III reassigned the effort to a new Congregation of the Inquisition. In short, the Inquisition was a Roman Catholic show from start to finish, and attempts to shift the blame amount to nothing more than a belated exercise in public relations.

(In all fairness, we must add that Protestants sometimes killed "heretics" too. So did Jews and Muslims. From the 11th century on into the Middle Ages, the persecution of Karaites (a heretical Jewish sect) by flogging them to death, if unrepentant, was a common practice in Castile. Of course, this practice took place with the permission of the Christian Kings of Castile.)

No one, it seemed, was secure as the dragnet for heretics went on. No group was apparently "more Catholic" than the crusading Knights Templar, organized in 1118 as bodyguards for pilgrims trekking to the Holy Land, but times change. By the early 14th century, the Templars had prospered to such an extent that they were considered the bankers of Europe, holding substantial IOUs from mighty kings and queens. A declaration of heresy would erase those debts, while putting the vast wealth of the Templars up for grabs, and so it was as early as 1307, when the Templars were accused of crimes including homosexuality, black magic, and the worship of a demon known as Baphomet. Leader Jacques de Molay and his ranking lieutenant were burned in Paris in 1314. The Templars' wealth was never found.

Accusations of sorcery and black magic were hardly new in Medieval Europe, but their application to the Templars signaled a dramatic change of direction for the Holy Inquisition. Belief in witchcraft had been declared heretical in AD 906, but its influence remained strong among European peasants, and the first official prosecution did not occur until 1275, when a woman was burned at Toulouse. In 1320, as the major heretical sects began to thin out, Pope John XXII gave his inquisitors new work by authorizing the full-scale investigation of sorcery. Pope Innocent VIII took matters a step further in 1484, ordering Dominican inquisitors Henry Kramer and Jacob Sprenger to prepare a formal handbook for witch-hunters. Their *Malleus Maleficarum* ("Hammer of Witches") was published two years later, with 30 editions printed by 1669.

For the next three centuries, Europe was ravaged by witch hunts that dwarfed the earlier persecution of heretics. Historian R.H. Robbins has described it as "the shocking nightmare, the foulest crime and deepest shame of western civilization," with estimated body counts ranging from 30,000 to a high of nine million. (At least 90 domestic animals were also tried and executed for witchcraft, after Pope Innocent VII warned inquisitors to keep an eye out for "familiar spirits.") From the 16th century onward, Protestant "reformers" rivaled Catholics in their brutal handling of suspected witches, with one Lutheran prelate — Benedict Carpzov — boasting that he had personally ordered 20,000 executions.

Where greed had often fueled the Inquisition's fires in the 14th and 15th centuries, witch-hunting added a new and disturbing sexual component. Female "witches" outnumbered males by approximately five to one, and sexual mutilation was a staple form of interrogation. Rape of female prisoners was encouraged, at least under Roman Catholic inquisitors, through their policy of allowing men identified as "zealous Catholics" to visit witches in private, while female visitors were banned. Indeed, the people of Toulouse were so convinced that inquisitor Foulques de Saint-George arraigned women for the sole purpose of molesting them, that they took the unusual (and potentially fatal) step of gathering evidence against him.

Before the smoke cleared, German witch-hunters had burned at least 30,000 suspects, while some 5,000 were executed in France, and another 7,500 or so in Scotland. Europe's witchcraft hysteria finally faded in the 17th century, with a corresponding decrease in trials. Holland executed its last "witch" in 1610, England in 1684, America in 1692, Scotland in 1722, and France in 1745; even the zealous Germans had called it quits by 1775. **[See also: Capital Punishment]**

International Society for Krishna Consciousness

Swami A.C. Bhaktivedanta Prabhupada came to the United States from India, in September 1965. Landing in Boston, he soon moved on to New York, hawking copies of the Hindu *Bhagavad-Gita* ("The Song of the Lord") and preaching about Krishna, the avatar of Vishnu — a boyish, mischievous god who played the flute and frolicked in bright fields of flowers all day. The vision was a hippie's dream, and Swami Prabhupada soon had a small clique of followers in Manhattan, donning saffron robes and shaving their heads, chanting "Hare Krishna" in the back room of his curio shop when they weren't out working the streets.

One of Prabhupada's early recruits was Keith Ham, the 28-year-old son of a fundamentalist preacher, with a doctorate in religious studies, who met the swami on a street corner in Manhattan's East Village. Ham moved in with the krishnas that night, and when he broke the news by telephone, his father denounced his decision as "the work of the devil." Satisfied to take his chances, Ham became "Kirtanananda Bhaktipada," swiftly rising through the ranks to serve as Swami Prabhupada's right-hand man.

From all appearances, the swami was a man of strong convictions, who practiced what he preached — including pacifism, chastity, and vegetarianism. Unfortunately for his movement in America, he was also an extremely busy man, traveling incessantly on business for the International Society of Krishna Consciousness (ISKCON). In Prabhupada's absence, Keith Ham ran the show, and soon his ego ran amok. As one ex-member of the cult explains, "Kirtanananda decided that Swami Prabhupada was an old fart who didn't know as much as he did about marketing a new idea."

In 1968, Ham purchased 130 acres of land outside Moundsville, West Virginia, to build a settlement he called New Vrindaban, after the Indian village where Krishna supposedly lived. The first winter was brutal, driving the unprepared krishnas away from their "city," but they returned in the spring, and this time they came to stay, expanding their beachhead to some 2,800 acres by 1983. There was trouble with the locals from day one, complaints of rock-throwing incidents and the occasional sniping, but Ham persevered, running New Vrindaban as his personal fiefdom, ordering marriages and divorces on a whim, directing every facet of his loyal disciples' lives. In June 1973, two local men invaded the settlement, brandishing guns, to "rescue" a 15-year-old girl from the cult. Shots were fired, and while no one was wounded, the incident served to heighten krishna paranoia.

Ham reported the attack to Swami Prahbupada, and a surprising answer came back from the holy man in India:

> When New Vrindaban has been attacked twice, thrice, why are you not keeping guns? Where violence is, there must be violence. We are not followers of Gandhi's philosophy. Ours began on the fields of war. If somebody attacks you, you must protect yourselves to your best capacity.

In other words, the gloves were off. Ham made the most of his instructions from the swami, stockpiling weapons at New Vrindaban, encouraging his followers to do likewise in temples across the country. He also began recruiting a new class of disciples, emphasizing strength and criminal cunning over knowledge of Hindu philosophy. One such was New Vrindaban's medic, Nick Tsacrios, a disgraced Florida physician and sometime drug addict who had served prison time for selling cocaine. When West Virginia lawmen started checking local krishnas out through FBI computer files, they were amazed to see how many boasted rap sheets worthy of career criminals.

Celebrity endorsements aside, by the late 1970s, ISKCON was all about money and power. Aside from New Vrindaban, plus various temples and shops nationwide, the cult owned Fischer Mansion in Detroit (once occupied by the founder of Cadillac Motors), and a twelve-story, multimillion-dollar building on Manhattan's West 55th Street. Swami Prahbupada died in 1977, at age 81, leaving his global empire theoretically divided into 11 districts, each with its own guru, the batch of them collectively responsible for running ISKCON. As one former krishna explains, "He thought he was leaving the movement to eleven bishops. What he really did was create eleven competing popes." In the circumstances, a power struggle was inevitable, and Keith Ham was determined to win. The swami's corpse was barely cold when Ham declared that his fellow gurus were "in *maya*" — that is, living in sin — and called upon them to accept his leadership. When they refused, the stage was set for a religious civil war.

The shooting started out in California, with disciple Alexander Kulik. Kulik lived at the exclusive Rancho La Costa resort, near San Diego, and paid his tab by smuggling hash oil into California, laundering the money through Prasadam Distributing International, spending millions to build ISKCON temples in San Diego and L.A. In October 1977, one of PDI's employees, Steve Bovan, was murdered gangland style — nine shots, no witnesses — in Newport Beach. Six hours later, Kulik was arrested with a million dollars worth of heroin in his car; another half-million in skag was retrieved from his condo at La Costa. More arrests followed, effectively dismantling Kulik's wing of ISKCON. At his trial, the drug lord said he did it all for Krishna and Swami Prahbupada, but he would be forced to serve the time alone.

Another hotbed of krishna crime was northern California, around Berkeley, where guru Hans Kary — a.k.a. "Hansadutta" — billed himself as "a secretary for God." His second in command was James Patrick Underwood, alias "Jiva," a San Quentin alumnus who ran the temple's all-female *sankirtan* team, alternately bedding and beating the women, supplying them with "uppers" so that they could spend long hours selling incense on the streets, each earning an average $400 per day. Guru Kary eventually got jealous of Underwood and took command of the ladies away from him, at gunpoint, using his own special talents to keep them inspired. On the side, Kary dreamed of being a rock star, but his self-produced albums — including a cheery number titled *Nice But Dead* — fell short of burning up the charts.

Kary's luck ran out in February 1980, when police raided the 480-acre ISKCON ranch at Mount Kailasa, north of San Francisco. They missed the stolen goods they were expecting, but turned up an arsenal including a grenade launcher, three rifles, four shotguns, two pistols, and some 2,000 rounds of ammunition. A short time later, krishna Dennis Lee Richardson was arrested at the Berkeley temple, leading police to a storage locker where they found four more rifles, four shotguns, and another 400 rounds of ammo. The guru's own Mercedes-Benz gave up two rifles, two pistols, and a submachine gun fitted with a silencer, insuring Kary of a free ride up the river on illegal weapons charges.

It was gratifying to see his rivals picked off one by one, but Keith Ham still had business of his own to conduct, at New Vrindaban. As in other temples, one of his chief moneymakers was the female *sankirtan* team, led by polygamous wifebeater Dennis Gorrick, a.k.a. "Dharmatma." Gorrick's contribution to the cult, aside from having sex with every woman on his team, consisted of teaching them to lie and steal. Dharmatma's ladies posed as military widows, "concerned parents" soliciting funds for a special school, even members of the National Organization for the Reform of Marijuana Laws — anything, in short, that would lead total strangers to open their hearts and their wallets. Hanging out at professional sports events, they sold counterfeit posters and bumper stickers, printed on a special press the cult had purchased for $110,000. And, if all else failed, they stole whatever they could get their hands on. One of Gorrick's "wives," Sharon Wilson, had a rap sheet that included arrests for shoplifting in Toronto, Canada; theft by deception in Indianapolis (two counts); soliciting without a permit in Norfolk, Virginia (three counts); plus various other charges in Orlando, Florida, and Austin, Texas.

The Krishna cult was big business by 1980, and Keith Ham was in the driver's seat, but his days were numbered. Before he knew it, the unholy violence would be striking close to home.

Swami Kirtanananda dedicated a lavish Palace of Gold at New Vrindaban in 1980, its domed roof plated with 22-karat gold, while the walls were sheathed in 200 tons of marble and onyx. New Vrindaban itself was expanding, up from its original 130 acres to some 2,884 by 1983. With the temple completed, it became a major tourist attraction, welcoming 200,000 paying visitors per year. On the side, federal investigators estimate that ISKCON banked another $10.5 million between 1983 and '85, from sales of bootleg T-shirts, caps and bumper stickers bearing likenesses of famous (copyrighted) cartoon characters.

That kind of cash becomes addictive in a hurry, and the leaders of the cult would not permit their income or their image to be jeopardized by misfits in the ranks. One such was Charles St. Denis, a.k.a. "Chakradara," a 250-pound alcoholic and junkie who ran a nursery at New Vrindaban. Personality aside, St. Denis had incurred the enmity of krishna enforcer Thomas Drescher (alias "Tirtha") by allegedly encroaching on some property that Drescher claimed. St. Denis was also accused of raping another cultist's wife, but he denied the charge and cheerfully accepted when the husband, Daniel Reid, invited him to "party" in June 1983. Arriving at the designated site, St. Denis was met by Reid and Drescher, who shot him 12 times and buried him in a shallow grave. For good measure, Chakradara's house was also burned, netting a $40,000 insurance payoff for New Vrindaban.

Cultist Steve Bryant was another potential embarrassment, a gun nut and fanatical John Bircher who left New Vrindaban in 1984, when his wife began withholding sex. He blamed Kirtanananda for stealing his family, denouncing the cult to anyone who would listen, finding a welcome audience among rival Krishna groups as he wandered across the country. Over time, as the authorities ignored his charges, Bryant's rage evolved into a plot to kill Kirtanananda and a list of other "bogus gurus." When Kirtanananda was assaulted by a deranged krishna at New Vrindaban in October 1985, hospitalized for five weeks, he blamed Bryant for the attack. There was no evidence of a connection, but it hardly mattered. Swami Kirtanananda had decided to make an example of Bryant, using him as "a monkey on a stick" — a reference to the Indian practice of impaling one monkey to keep others from raiding commercial banana groves. On May 22, 1986, Bryant was sitting in his van, parked on a street in Los Angeles, when a krishna assassin shot him twice in the head with a .45-caliber pistol.

Further north, in Berkeley, California, ISKCON guru Hansadutta — née Hans Kary — suffered an apparent mental breakdown in August 1984, firing thirty shots into a Cadillac dealership for no apparent reason, and shooting up a liquor store moments later. Captured with three pistols, a shotgun, and $8,627 in cash, Kary fumed as the incident scuttled his plan to steal an army payroll from Fort Ord. By December 1985, he had moved to New Vrindaban with a handful of hard-core disciples, scheming with Kirtanananda to seize control of the "renegade" Berkeley temple. A month later, 15 raiders looted the cult's Mt. Kailasa farm of three cars, 23,000 books, and $15,000 in cash. Guru Atreya Risha filed a civil suit against New Vrindaban and won his case in early

1987, with Kirtanananda and company ordered to pay the Berkeley temple $40,000 in damages.

By that time, state and federal investigators were closing in on ISKCON, pursuing charges that ranged from fraud and gunrunning to multiple murder. Thirty residents of New Vrindaban were interrogated over Steve Bryant's slaying, with Tom Drescher convicted and sentenced to life without parole in December 1986. Drescher was also convicted of killing Charles St. Denis, and three other cultists joined him in prison on arson charges, related to the burning of St. Denis's home. New Vrindaban was raided in January 1987, with computer records seized that documented a yearly income of five to six million dollars from various *sankirtan* scams. Kirtanananda himself was indicted in May 1990, with two disciples, on three counts of racketeering, one count of conspiracy to murder, and six counts of mail fraud. He dismissed the charges as "absurd," but a jury disagreed, convicting him of racketeering and fraud in 1991. The guru's luck was holding, though: a federal appeals court subsequently overturned that verdict, ruling that the jury had been prejudiced by "irrelevant" testimony regarding abuse of women and molestation of children at New Vrindaban. Tried again in 1996, Kirtanananda was once more convicted of racketeering and sentenced to federal prison.

Jewish Defense League: See Terrorism

Johns, Jerald Curtis

The other members of his small church in Los Angeles referred to him as "Mr. Bible Johns," for his devotion to the Lord. Jerald Johns carried his Bible everywhere, it seemed, and he always had a quote from scripture ready for every occasion. His devotion to charity work was legendary... but the man they all respected for his piety also possessed a darker side.

In 1973, before he came to Jesus, Jerald Johns had served six months in jail for raping an exotic dancer, whom he followed home from work one night. Two years later, following a second rape, he was diagnosed as a mentally disordered sex offender and packed off for two years at Patton State Hospital. Johns was barely out of the hospital a month, when he was nabbed again for two attempted rapes. This time, he wrote the judge: "After having failed in my third attempt to live a wholesome and constructive life, I wanted nothing but to die. But I discovered Christ after being paroled and adopted a daily lifestyle that included daily readings from the Bible."

Clearly, it wasn't working.

The praying rapist's last rampage began in January 1982 and continued for over two years, police suspecting that he may have victimized as many as 100 women. Bible Johns worked an area of ten square blocks in Hollywood, invading homes at night, cowing his victims with death threats to make them perform on demand. His targets ranged in age from 24 to 71, and unlike Johns himself, all but one of them was white.

The sole exception was Sandra Trine, cornered with her roommate when Johns invaded their Hollywood apartment on the night of December 10, 1982. Threatening the women with a screwdriver, Johns raped both of them repeatedly and forced them to perform oral sex, the latter act turning lethal when Sandra choked to death on her own vomit.

Now, it was a murder case, but police still had no leads on their suspect beyond descriptions of a stocky black man, five-foot-ten, perhaps 200 pounds, with a mustache. It was June 4, 1984, when patrolmen spotted 32-year-old "Bible" Johns acting suspiciously in Hollywood and matched his demeanor to the description. Members of his parish were incredulous, finally concluding that Johns must be possessed by the devil, since Satan "only attacks the strong ones."

Johns initially pled innocent to murder and 89 other felony counts involving 11 victims, but he changed his tune when prosecutors agreed to waive the death penalty. The court rejected a defense attempt to place Johns back in Patton State Hospital, preferring a sentence of 142 years in prison that ruled out parole for the first 71 years.

Jones, Jim: See "People's Temple"

Jouret, Luc: See Order of the Solar Temple

Kahane, Rabbi Meir: See Terrorism

Kahl, Gordon: See "Christian Identity" Movement

Koresh, David: See Branch Davidians

Klinger, David: **See Nuske, Matthew**

"Know-Nothings": **See "Nativist" Movement**

Ku Klux Klan

Organized as a social club for Confederate war veterans in 1866, the original Ku Klux Klan — drawing its name from the Greek *kuklos*, for "circle" — was reorganized as a political terrorist movement the following year. Its primary targets were "uppity" blacks and Republican "carpetbaggers" who sought to improve the lot of former slaves in Dixie. Despite frenzied violence in 12 states — including some 2,000 murders, plus innumerable floggings, rapes, castrations, brandings, shootings, and lesser assaults — the first Klan was rarely involved in religious conflict. Anti-Semitism surfaced only twice: at Greensboro, Alabama, in 1868, when Klansmen harassed two Jewish shopkeepers for allegedly overcharging their neighbors, and a year later in Marianna, Florida, where Samuel Fleischman was murdered for befriending blacks.

The 20th-century Klan movement, unlike its predecessor, was preoccupied with religion from Day One. Founder William Joseph Simmons spent 12 years as a circuit-riding preacher before Alabama's Methodist Conference defrocked him, in 1912, on charges of "inefficiency and moral impairment." In 1901, while sitting on a bench outside his home, Simmons watched the wind drive masses of cumulus clouds across the sky, and envisioned them as Klansmen. This was his inspiration to produce and copyright a constitution for the reborn KKK, which he would label "The Kloran." That autumn, when D.W. Griffith's *Birth of a Nation* opened in Atlanta, hard on the heels of the Leo Frank lynching, Simmons knew the time was ripe.

"Knights" of the KKK were pledged to support "100% Americanism" in the old Southern style, including a devotion to white supremacy and Protestant fundamentalist values, automatically excluding "alien" Catholics and Jews. The following poem, published in a Klan newsletter from 1915, is typical of the new movement's attitude:

> I'd rather be a Klansman robed in pure white
> Than a Catholic priest black as night,
> Loyal to the United States, my home,
> Rather than the dago Pope of Rome.

By the summer of 1921, close to 100,000 recruits had joined the tough-talking Klan. A sensational investigative series in the *New York World* helped Simmons in September, followed closely by Congressional hearings, from which he emerged as the star performer. From there, the Klan took off like a rocket, with standard estimates of its membership in the mid-1920s ranging from three to five million. Looking back, Wizard Simmons would declare that "Congress made us."

At the same time, there were many other factors combining to "make" the 1920s Ku Klux Klan. Black migration from the southern countryside to northern cities, coupled with disturbing rumors of an aggressive "New Negro," sparked riots and lynchings across the country. Unwanted immigrants, many of them Jews or Catholics, had "flooded" the nation by 1921, when passage of the Johnson Act rolled up the welcome mat. And, speaking of Catholics, by 1916 the Church of Rome had more than 6,000 parochial schools in America, with nearly 1.7 million students in attendance. The conspiracy was obvious to anyone with eyes to see, and those who looked most closely at such matters in the 1920s were Protestant fundamentalist clergymen.

Thousands of fundamentalist preachers signed on with the Klan, many of them bossing their local chapters in the role of "Exalted Cyclops," while others aspired to higher rank in the invisible empire. Dr. A.D. Ellis, a Protestant Episcopal minister from Beaumont, Texas, was the first "Grand Dragon" of the Lone Star State, his troops notorious for their floggings and tar-and-feather parties. Everywhere Klanwatchers turned in the 1920s, they found Protestant ministers blessing, if not actively leading, the organization that had pledged itself to maintenance of white supremacy and "100% Americanism." In bloody Williamson County, Illinois, where 20-odd persons were killed in shootouts between Klansmen and local gangsters, a minister presiding at the funeral of one martyred Kluxer prayed: "O Lord, we have put our hand to the plow and we will not turn back. Thus shall the soil and soul of Williamson County be purged and purified."

With membership declining in the Great Depression, Klan recruiters sought to boost their membership by flirting with domestic Nazi groups, stressing Jews over Catholics as the new enemy of choice. Klan publicists claimed credit for Hitler's rise in Germany, with speeches that declared: "The spark that fired Hitler and other German nationalists to build a new Germany could easily have been ignited by the example of the American Ku Klux Klan." A Miami Klansman took the notion one step further, assuring his audience that "[w]hen Hitler has killed all the Jews in Europe, he's going to help us drive all the Jews on Miami Beach into the sea." A federal tax lien finally retired the Klan in 1944, but scattered units clung to life around the country, gearing up for action with the birth of the black civil rights movement after World War II. Thousands of violent incidents resulted. A sampling would include:

- May 1951 — Rev. Joseph Mann, a black minister in Norfolk, Virginia, is kidnapped and set on fire by nightriders who tell him, "We want you to help us run some niggers out." Mann dies of his burns three days later.
- June 1951 — A Jewish community center is bombed in Miami.
- October 1951 — An unexploded bomb is found at a Miami synagogue.
- May 1955 — Rev. George Lee, a black minister active in civil rights work, is shot and killed by nightriders near Belzoni, Mississippi.
- September 1955 — Klansmen vandalize the home of Rev. Joseph DeLaine, a black civil rights activist, in Lake City, South Carolina.
- October 1955 — Arsonists burn Rev. DeLaine's church.
- January 1956 — Nightriders bomb the home of Rev. Martin Luther King, Jr. in Montgomery, Alabama.
- June 1956 — Shots are fired into a black religious meeting at Kingstree, South Carolina.
- December 1956 — Klansmen bomb the home of Rev. Fred Shuttlesworth, in Birmingham.
- January 1957 — Four black churches are bombed in Montgomery, with an unexploded bomb found at Rev. King's house; shots are fired into the home of Rev. C.K. Steele, an integrationist.
- November 1957 — Police foil the would-be bombers of a Charlotte, North Carolina, synagogue.
- February 1958 — Police defuse a bomb at a Gastonia, North Carolina synagogue.
- February 1958 — Klansmen bungle the attempted bombing of a black church in Birmingham.

- March 1958 — Synagogues are bombed in Miami and Nashville.
- April 1958 — A synagogue is bombed in Jacksonville.
- June 1958 — Klansmen bomb Rev. Shuttlesworth's home in Birmingham.
- July 1958 — Bombers strike the home of a white minister in Durham, North Carolina, identified as leader of the state's Human Relations Committee.
- August 1958 — A black church is bombed in Memphis.
- October 1958 — Synagogues are bombed in Atlanta and Peoria, Illinois.
- April 1959 — Rev. Charles Billups, a black activist in Birmingham, is abducted and beaten with tire chains.

The black civil rights movement became more aggressive after 1960, and Klansmen followed suit. As always, there were ministers beneath the sheets on both sides of the Mason-Dixon Line. In Philadelphia, Mississippi, Edgar Ray Killen combined the duties of a Baptist minister and Kleagle for the White Knights of the KKK, named by FBI investigators as the "mastermind" behind the murders of three civil rights workers in June 1964. (A federal jury was unable to decide on Killen's guilt or innocence in 1967, and the charges were dismissed six years later.) Another Mississippi clergyman, Rev. Delmar Dennis, joined the White Knights in good faith, but was quickly repulsed by their violence, shifting roles to serve as an FBI informant, later traveling as a spokesman for the John Birch Society, insisting that the Klan was run by "communists."

In neighboring Alabama, Rev. James Spears was elected to serve as the state's "Grand Dragon" in June 1966; three years later, he was one of 17 Kluxers involved in a shootout with blacks at a Klan rally in North Carolina. To the north, in Pennsylvania, Rev. Raymond Doerfler was chosen to replace one-eyed Roy Frankhouser as Grand Dragon in the 1970s, greeting an audience of Klansmen as "fellow terrorists."

And the label seemed to fit. Wherever the Klan reared its pointed head, known members or associates were linked to acts of racial violence that included arson, bombing, kidnapping, and murder. As usual, religious institutions were a favorite target of nightriding Christians. Mississippi Klansmen and their allies bombed or burned at least 38 churches between June 1964 and March 1967, with other targets including a minister's home (in McComb) and the black Baptist College in Holly Springs. By the latter part of 1967, Magnolia State kluxers turned their attention to Jews and white Catholics, bombing a synagogue and a rabbi's home in Jackson, along with the parsonage of St. Paul's Church in Laurel. Alabama Klansmen had a hard time keeping up, but they did their best in Birmingham, where a Sunday-school bombing killed four young girls in September 1963; at least 11 other churches were bombed, burned, or riddled with bullets in Anniston, Birmingham, Oxford, Elmwood, Greensboro, Ft. Deposit, and Hayneville. Three North Carolina Klansmen were jailed for attempting to burn a black church in Elm City, while the bombers of another church, in Ernul, were never identified. Georgia recorded five church-burnings in the same period, around Sasser, Dawson, Newton, and rural Twiggs County. Louisiana Klansmen torched five more, in Jonesboro, Slidell, and New Orleans. Others were bombed or set afire by "persons unknown" in Gillett, Arkansas, and in Richmond, Virginia.

Ministers who joined the civil rights crusade took their lives in their hands, on both sides of the Mason-Dixon Line. Alabama was particularly lethal for color-blind clergymen, as witnessed by the near-fatal shooting of Rev. S.D. Seay in Montgomery, the beating death of Rev. James Reeb in Selma, and the shotgun slaying of seminarian Jon Daniels in Hayneville (a Catholic priest was gravely wounded in the same attack; the killer — a part-time cop and full-time Klansman — was acquitted on a plea of "self-defense"). Within days of the Daniels shooting, a Unitarian minister was gunned down in Jackson, Mississippi. In Atlanta, Corinne Briley, wife of a minister active in civil rights, was killed when nightriders strafed her home with gunfire, following an unsuccessful attempt to burn her husband's church.

A curious development, beginning in the latter 1960s, was the effort of some Klan factions to operate as churches in their own right. California Klansman Wesley Swift set the tone, with his Church of Jesus Christ Christian, and other kluxers soon followed his lead by adopting the tenets of **"Christian Identity."** Michigan "Grand Dragon" Robert Miles, convicted of bombing school buses and flogging a high-school principal, emerged from prison as a self-ordained "Identity" minister and head of his own Mountain Kirk, which coordinated cross-burning rallies with the Aryan Nations and other neo-Nazi groups. Thom Robb and other "Identity" preachers likewise found leadership posts in the new, militant Klan, combining hatred of blacks and Jews with their commitment to the **"pro-life" movement** and oppression of homosexuals. By the early 1980s, radical factions of the new Klan were issuing declarations of war against the "Zionist Occupational Government" in Washington, setting off bombs and murdering opponents in their bid to "purify" America. **[See also: "Gay Bashing"; Terrorism]**

Lane, John

The neighbors had to know something was wrong. It started with the music, all religious tunes, blasting out of the apartment that Cynthia Palmer and her two daughters shared with John Lane in Auburn, Maine. A neighbor who came knocking, asking Lane to turn the volume down, was threatened with "the wrath of God" and took his leave. A short time later, tenants heard a banging sound, one of the Palmer children shrieking, "Daddy, let me out!" Next came the smoke, cascading from a kitchen window, with a smell like scorching hair. A second neighbor interrupted Lane and asked him what was going on.

"I'm cooking Lucifer," John Lane replied.

At last, more than an hour after the ruckus started, someone finally dialed 911. Police and firemen rallied to the scene, but they had come too late. In the electric oven, jammed shut with a kitchen chair, four-year-old Angela Palmer was already dead, her small body charred. In handcuffs, Lane babbled about the demon he had slain, pointing to the crosses he had daubed on doors throughout the small apartment. The killing order, he explained, had been delivered by a disembodied voice he knew as "Michael."

The shocking murder came as a surprise to all concerned. A social worker had come calling five days earlier, on October 22, 1985, and described what she found as "very much an average family." Now, facing murder charges and mandatory psychiatric tests, both defendants pled innocent — Lane on grounds of insanity, his girlfriend claiming he had knocked her out and tied her up before he placed her daughter in the oven.

Lane and Palmer were tried together, but with separate attorneys, in November 1985. Lane's insanity plea was crippled when he changed his story, claiming now that *he* had been unconscious on the couch, while Cynthia burned her own daughter alive. Judge Bruce Chandler rejected the fanciful story, convicting Lane of murder on November 19, handing down a sentence of life imprisonment three days later. By that time, Palmer's charge had been reduced to manslaughter, and she was acquitted on November 25, but it was the end of her luck in the courts. Eighteen months later, in May 1987, Judge John Beliveau terminated Cynthia's parental rights to custody of her surviving daughter, ruling that the child must remain a ward of the court. John Lane's conviction was affirmed by the Supreme Court of Maine in October 1987.

LeBaron, Ervil

The most notorious cult of Mormon defectors to date is the LeBaron family, which divided its time between Mexico and the United States. Patriarch Dayer LeBaron had been hounded out of Utah for espousing polygamy, back in 1924, and settled south of the border, at Colonia Juárez. His ninth child, Ervil Morrell LeBaron, was born there in February 1925. Two decades later, Dayer moved his "godly family with a special mission" 50 miles to the southwest, where they built their own desert commune and called it Colonia LeBaron. By 1950, he was on his last legs, dying of chronic lead poisoning from his years as a housepainter, and in January 1951 he named son Benjamin to lead the clan. That summer, Ervil and brother Joel decided that Benjamin was insane, defecting to join another LDS fundamentalist cult led by Rulon Allred, of Salt Lake City. In short order, the brothers had been named as bishops of Allred's new outpost, at Colonia Juárez. (Sadly, they were right about Benjamin: totally irrational by 1962, he spent the next 16 years in various mental institutions, before committing suicide in Arkansas.)

As it turned out, the new cult provided more than a simple change of scene for Joel LeBaron. In 1955, a "divine revelation" assured him that *he* was the "One Mighty and Strong Prophet" of God's true church. In April 1956, his new Firstborn Church — consisting at the time of Joel, Ervil, two other siblings, and their mother — held its first formal meeting at Colonia Juárez. By August, Joel and Ervil had finished writing *Priesthood Expounded*, a tract supporting Joel's claim to priestly authority. If Joel claimed the honors, though, Ervil was the brain behind the throne. In 1959, one early convert to the Firstborn sect complained, "We do not belong to Joel's church. We belong to Ervil's church."

One of the perks that came with power was an opportunity for Ervil to expand his private harem. Married twice in the 1950s, he had 12 wives by the end of the 1960s, with a 13th added in 1975. At the same time, he was pushing a campaign to implement "God's civil law," complete with an Old Testament-style death penalty for murder, adultery, and "treason." In 1966, two members of the Firstborn Church were killed in Mexico, and while LeBaron blamed their unsolved deaths on "Gentiles," critics in the cult would later suspect Ervil himself of the slayings.

By early 1969, a major rift had split the Firstborn Church, with "prophet" Joel denouncing "patriarch" Ervil's coercive approach to salvation. Ervil's followers responded with the first of countless threats against Joel's life, prompting Joel to strip his brother of the rank which effectively placed him above the laws of the sect. Without that elitist protection, Ervil soon found himself accused of trying to steal another cult member's wife. In May 1971, he abandoned the Firstborn Church to lead his own cult, dubbed the Church of the Lamb of God, while brother Verlan was promoted to serve as patriarch back at Colonia LeBaron.

It was the start of a religious civil war that has not ended yet. Ervil's gunmen drew first blood, in August 1972, when they assassinated Joel at his home in Los Molinos, Mexico. Verlan LeBaron promptly offered a $24,000 reward for information leading to his brother's arrest, and Ervil surrendered to Mexican police in December. A year later, convicted as the "intellectual author" of Joel's murder, Ervil was sentenced to 12 years in prison, but a higher court reversed the verdict one day later, based on technical irregularities, and Ervil was released on St.Valentine's Day 1974.

Ervil had hoped that Joel's followers would flock to his standard, once their leader was gone, but it didn't pan out. In the face of their defiance, he could only think of one response, a ritual "cleansing" of the Los Molinos compound, scheduled for the day after Christmas 1974. That night, a flying squad of "Ervilistas" raided the Firstborn community, firebombing two dozen homes and spraying the compound with gunfire. Two residents were killed in the attack, with 13 others wounded.

And the war dragged on. In January 1975, two of Ervil's wives murdered Neomi Zarate — a wife of Ervil loyalist Bud Chynoweth, suspected of "treason" to the cult — and planted her corpse in the San Pedro Mountains. Bob Simons, another self-styled LDS "prophet" from Grantsville, California, not only rejected Ervil's suggestion of a merger, but responded in April 1975 with "an open challenge to [LeBaron's] power and your authority," advising Ervil to "Do with it what you may." On April 23, LeBaron's murder squad killed Simons in the desert near Price, Utah, and buried his corpse in a pit filled with quicklime. Less than two months later, another Lamb of God — Dean Vest, a planner of the Los Molinos raid — was shot and killed by one of Ervil's many wives at a cult hideout in southern California.

The Prophet, meanwhile, had other problems on his mind. Arrested in Chihuahua, in March 1976, Ervil sat through an eight-month trial on charges stemming from the Los Molinos shootout. By October, he was getting tired of lawyers, and announced that Mexico would be destroyed by God if he was not released in 30 days. In fact, he was acquitted of all charges three weeks later, a display of power that impressed his followers no end.

Like other human beings, Ervil's lambs could not survive on prayer alone. Officially, the cult's main source of income was a string of appliance repair shops that stretched from California to Indianapolis and Jackson, Mississippi, with a special concentration around Dallas, Texas. Earning money was one thing, but Ervil's *real* work was the building of God's holy kingdom on earth, with Lord Ervil in charge, and to that end he continued preaching "blood atonement" of suspected traitors in the fold. In April 1977, his own pregnant daughter, Rebecca, was strangled on LeBaron's orders, when he feared she was considering defection from the cult.

In fact, Ervil was driven to such extremes by his own prophetic timetable, which called for his Church of the Lamb to seize control of the entire Mormon Church by May 3, 1977. Unfortunately, such a breakthrough showed no signs of happening, and Ervil blamed his leading rival, Dr. Rulon Allred, as the man behind his failure. A week after Ervil's great disappointment, on May 10, two of his trigger-women executed Allred at his Salt Lake City office. There were also plans to strafe the funeral with machine-gun fire and try for brother

Verlan, but the shooters got cold feet when they began to count police cars at the funeral home.

It was a whole new ballgame for LeBaron, after Dr. Allred's murder. He was up against a different breed of homicide investigators now, more energetic and accomplished than the talent he had dealt with back in Mexico, and Ervil's frequent rantings to his flock left many witnesses at large. Still, mere arrests did not convictions make. Wife Vonda White won a mistrial on Dean Vest's murder, in November 1978, and her conspiracy charges were dismissed. Four months later, wife Rena Chynoweth and three other Lambs were acquitted of killing Rulon Allred. By the summer of 1979, authorities in California and Utah had indicted 12 cult members on some 40 separate charges, ranging from obstruction of justice to first-degree murder, but only five defendants ever went to court, and after three trials, none had been convicted.

For all that, Ervil was the prize most coveted by lawmen, and the Mexicans had him, following a lucky break in November 1978. On June 1, 1979, Mexican authorities delivered him to American officers in Laredo, and Ervil's pleas of illegal "kidnapping" fell on deaf ears in the courts. Facing trial for Dr. Allred's murder in Utah, Ervil denied everything, but his jury was less sympathetic than the one which tried his soldiers. Members of the panel deliberated for only three hours, on May 28, 1980, before convicting LeBaron of conspiracy and first-degree murder. He was sentenced to life imprisonment, and authorities thought they had heard the last of his Lambs.

But they were wrong.

Utah prison officials knew by April 1981 that Ervil LeBaron was trying to build a new cadre of disciples on his cell block, an effort they discouraged with a transfer to solitary confinement. Ervil used his free time in the hole to finish writing *The Book of New Covenants*, and delivered it to cult member Mark Chynoweth in May. Three months later, Ervil collapsed and died while exercising in his cell, with eldest son Arturo stepping up to the plate as the new "One Mighty and Strong," pledged to carry out his father's final vision.

In essence, *The Book of New Covenants* was a rambling hit list, naming 50-odd "enemies of the faith," with specific instructions for their "blood atonement." Oddly, Mark Chynoweth was one of those listed for elimination, and a reading of the book convinced him that Ervil was either insane or possessed by the devil, but he still made several copies of the manuscript and passed them out among the faithful, thereby signing his own death warrant. Arturo LeBaron took the psycho-testament to heart with a vengeance that inspired one Utah cop to describe him as "a miserable little shit. He was arrogant, cocky and mean, and that's why Ervil made him the chief. He knew that if anyone was going to carry on his mission, it would be Arturo."

The bloodletting began in June 1983, when Isaac LeBaron — newly released from a mental institution — allegedly shot himself to death in Houston, Texas. Police ruled the case a suicide, despite two "extra" bullets fired into the ceiling and a closet door, while other members of the cult were present in the house. Across the border, meanwhile, cult defector and convicted drug smuggler Leo Evoniuk was leading a revolt against Arturo's rule, sending gunmen in all-terrain vehicles against the Lamb of God compound at Rancho La Joya, in Sonora. Several of Leo's men were killed in those raids, but they came back strong in December, ambushing Arturo and leaving him riddled with bullets.

The Book of New Covenants named Heber LeBaron as Arturo's successor, and he clinched the position in March 1984, by executing cult defector Gamaliel Ríos for his role in

Arturo's death. The slaughter continued with Raúl Ríos, fatally wounded in an ambush days after his brother was slain. Another victim, Yolanda Ríos, was Ervil's 12th wife, "tried" for disloyalty to the cult, murdered, and buried in the Mexican desert. By that time, members of the cult were running stolen cars across the border into Mexico, returning with illegal weapons and narcotics for resale in the United States, employing multiple aliases and a string of safe houses. As investigator Scott Anderson explained, "Under Heber, the Church of the Lamb was now revealed for what, in fact, it had always really been: an organized crime syndicate built along family lines, a Mormon Fundamentalist version of the Mafia."

In November 1986, Heber was cornered while robbing a bank in Richardson, Texas. He tried to shoot a policeman, but his gun misfired, and he was captured, giving his name to authorities as "William Samuel Harrison." Bail was set at $50,000 and paid by the cult three weeks later, before detectives had identified their prisoner. Heber hit the street convinced that all his family's problems could be solved if they got back to basics and resumed the "blood atonement" of traitors listed in Ervil's *Book of New Covenants*.

By that time, Leo Evoniuk had settled in California, posing as the president and "presiding prophet" of a new Millennial Church of Jesus Christ. Most of his sermons were vintage Ervil LeBaron, but it was too late to save him from the Lambs of God. On May 21, 1987, Leo disappeared forever after answering a bogus call regarding some construction work. Police found two 9mm cartridges and Leo's dentures, lying in a pool of blood beside a rural highway, near the job site he had been called to inspect. Five months later, "traitor" Dan Jordan was deer hunting with relatives in eastern Utah, when he stopped to urinate and was killed by sniper fire, bullets ripping into his head and chest.

The purge climaxed on June 27, 1988 — symbolically chosen as the 144th anniversary of Joseph Smith's lynching in Illinois. That afternoon, between 4:00 and 4:05 P.M., four targets from Ervil's 1981 hit list were "atoned" in the vicinity of Dallas, Texas. Duane Chynoweth and his eight-year-old daughter Jennifer were ambushed and shot to death after being called out to retrieve a used washer and dryer for sale in Duane's appliance shop. An identical ruse was employed to kill Eddie Marston, in nearby Irving, and Mark Chynoweth was gunned down in the office of Reliance Appliances at the same time, thus completing the sweep. Seven Lambs of God, including Heber, were jailed in Phoenix four days later, on auto theft charges, but again they made bail without being identified. Foolishly, they remained in Phoenix and were picked up again, days later, for a series of robberies. Texas police insist that Heber was responsible for the Dallas killings, along with cronies Richard LeBaron and Doug Barlow, but no charges were ever filed in the murder spree. Instead, five cultists pled guilty on auto theft charges in Arizona, with Heber and Barlow sentenced to ten years apiece.

LeGrand, Devernon

New York has long been familiar with eccentric black clergymen, but Rev. Devernon LeGrand took the cake. At age 40, in 1965, he was arrested on charges of kidnapping, assault, and firearms possession; three years later, police accused him of snatching a 23-year-old woman from her home and raping her before she managed to escape. Neither case was prosecuted, but in 1975, LeGrand was convicted of bribery and sexual misconduct with a 17-year-old girl. That same year, with his 20-year-old son Noconda, LeGrand was convicted of kidnapping and rape. He drew a sentence of five to 15 years in prison, while his son got off "easy" with an eight-year prison term.

Such conduct is not unheard of in the Big Apple, but it is peculiar for the leader of a church. Around the time of his first arrest, LeGrand had organized St. John's Pentecostal Church of Our Lord, putting down roots in the Crown Heights district of Brooklyn. His headquarters, a four-story townhouse, was occupied by 11 "nuns" and their 47 children, many of them fathered by LeGrand. According to police, LeGrand did most of his recruiting by seduction, impregnating young women, then threatening them or their children if they refused to beg for money on the streets. His black-clad "nuns" were often seen around Grand Central Station, and others had been jailed on misdemeanor charges in New Jersey. It was in the Crown Heights "chapel" that LeGrand raped his final victim, during August 1974, and authorities suspected that sexual assault was merely the tip of the iceberg.

In 1966, LeGrand's church had purchased a 58-acre spread in the Catskills, near White Sulphur Springs, converting the place to a summer retreat for the faithful. Over the next eight years, state police received steady complaints from the neighbors, alleging child abuse and health violations, wild parties and indiscriminate gunfire. Children from the camp roamed freely through the countryside, begging and stealing, while horses were cruelly beaten and left to starve. Authorities raided the camp in October 1968, seizing drug paraphernalia, photographing clogged toilets and general squalor, but LeGrand's troop returned each summer without fail, immune to public opinion.

Teenage church members Gladys and Yvonne Stewart had testified for the prosecution at LeGrand's bribery trial, but they were missing when the D.A. sought to use their testimony in the later rape case. Informants said the girls were dead, dismembered in the Brooklyn "church," with their remains transported to the Catskills for disposal. State police dug up the ranch in mid-December 1975, but they came away empty-handed. Three months later, assorted bones and bits of cartilage were found in nearby Briscoe Lake, and Brooklyn raiding parties turned up human bloodstains in the Crown Heights townhouse.

By April 1976, state police were confident that Rev. LeGrand had murdered a dozen or more victims, dumping some of them in Briscoe Lake. The list included three wives, two of LeGrand's stepchildren, the Stewart sisters, and two male employees of the church. In May, LeGrand was indicted on four counts of murder, including the Stewarts and two of his wives, slain in 1963 and 1970. LeGrand's son, 26-year-old Steven, was also charged with murdering the Stewart sisters, plus two men employed by his father as pimps. Father and son were convicted together in the Stewart case, in May 1977, and both drew prison terms of 25 years to life.

Lundgren, Jeffrey

Jeffrey Don Lundgren was born in Missouri, raised by strict parents in the Reorganized Church of Latter-Day Saints. His wife Alice, a year younger than Jeffrey, was another loyal Mormon, convinced that Satan had attacked her in her bed at summer camp in 1969, the year before they were married. Jeff joined the U.S. Navy shortly after they were married, serving four years without incident and returning to college on the G.I. Bill following his discharge. He earned straight A's in 1975, while serving as spokesman for a group of Mormon fundamentalists on campus, but his bills were piling up —

some $22,000 plus a home mortgage in 1977 — and Jeff was subsequently expelled on charges of theft.

Lundgren had been complaining since the honeymoon that Alice had lost interest in sex, a circumstance he blamed on guilt resulting from her premature pregnancy. Then again, it may have been Jeff. Alice later told police, "I discovered that Jeffrey was fascinated with his own feces. He told me that he had been using it since he was thirteen. He would smear it on himself and masturbate with it." She also described how Jeff would make her lie nude in the bathtub, while he crouched above her, defecating on her breasts. His lust for anal sex was so extreme that Alice turned to liquor as a form of anesthetic. "At first he used a lubricant when we had anal intercourse," she told authorities, "but later he decided my own blood was the best lubricant." On the side, he paid court to other women, including one who telephoned the house and spoke with Alice, describing Jeff's tutelage in the art of oral sex. It probably should come as no surprise that Jeff says Alice once attacked him with a baseball bat.

When not engaged in scatological sex, Jeff Lundgren was busy crusading for God. The Reorganized LDS Church ordained him as a priest in October 1983, but he clashed with church leaders the following spring, over their "revelation" that women could also be ordained. The messages emerging from Jeff's Sunday school class were increasingly heretical to Mormon doctrine, as when he stated that "God and Christ are the same entity." Some RLDS members were outraged, but others took Jeff's preaching to heart, and by the time his class was formally disbanded, he had a hard core of loyal disciples behind him, hanging on his every word. They were thrilled when Jeff told them about his personal conversations with God and a heavenly gift of gold tablets. "These were not the golden plates that Joseph [Smith] had been given and had already transcribed," Jeff assured his flock. "These were other plates that God had not yet revealed to mankind."

In August 1984, the Lundgrens moved from Missouri to Kirtland, Ohio, where Jeff had been accepted as a volunteer tour guide at the historic LDS temple. A house came with the unpaid position, and Jeff viewed the move as an opportunity "to be endowed with the power — just like it says in the scriptures." By the spring of 1985, disciples had begun to follow him from Missouri, some moving into Jeff's home and signing over their paychecks, gradually assuming the role of his servants. That fall, Lundgren began teaching a new Sunday school class, but he quickly ran afoul of Rev. Dale Luffman, appointed in January 1986 to supervise the RLDS church in Kirtland. When Luffman preached Christ's love, Lundgren denounced him as a liar, refuting each sermon line by line in his class. "Our God is a God of vengeance," he proclaimed, "and He expects only one thing from us — repentance. Repent, repent, repent. Those who do not repent will perish."

Jeff's gargantuan ego got another boost in early 1986, when someone remarked that his profile resembled Joseph Smith's death mask. The off-hand comment reinforced Lundgren's view of himself as the new prophet, a position jeopardized that April, when he was caught stealing from the Kirtland temple. Lundgren admitted taking the money, claiming dire necessity and that he intended to return it. A tearful confrontation finally let him keep his job, on the condition that he pay the money back. If Lundgren's followers were conscious of the scandal, they ignored it, meeting twice a week at Jeffrey's home and soaking up his rants as if they were the very words of God. That autumn, Lundgren was captivated by *Highlander*, a fantasy film about immortal swordsmen stalking one another through the centuries. Seven viewings in one weekend managed to convince him that the movie was a mirror image of his own apocalyptic visions. As he later told an interviewer, "I became convinced that God had moved the director and screenwriter of that movie. God had moved them to make it solely because he wanted Alice and me to see it. He wanted me to know that I was truly different from other men."

A short time later, Jeff claimed a personal visit from Joseph Smith, in the form of an angel, while Alice began dropping broad hints that Jeff was the church's "last seer." Dennis and Cheryl Avery were two of those who bought the weird rap, forking over $10,000 for the privilege of Lundgren's company. Within "an hour of receiving that donation, Jeff purchased a rifle and a matched pair of .45-caliber pistols, adding to the stockpile over time. With guns in hand, his message grew increasingly belligerent. "When the armies of Satan come against us," he proclaimed, "when they come to kill me and to kill you, we must be ready to fight and to die. We must be ready to shed blood." And not just a few drops, at that. "There will be lots of blood spilled," Jeffrey told his flock.

First, though, he waged a war of words against the hated Rev. Luffman, plumbing such depths by July 1987 that Luffman described their conflict as "almost demonic." Finally barred by Luffman from teaching in the Kirtland church, Lundgren continued his Sunday classes in private homes. New accusations of theft from the temple were raised, and Jeff was fired, stealing another $1,600 before he left his job. Part of that money went for rent on a five-room farmhouse and 15 acres of land, converted to a commune where everyone was expected to hold steady jobs — except for the Lundgrens, of course. "Prophets only answer to God," Alice declared, and thus were barred from working. At that, Jeff and Alice collected between $1,500 and $2,000 per week from their disciples, Lundgren preparing his flock for Armageddon by screening war movies and spinning tales of nonexistent combat missions in Vietnam. Jeff plotted a takeover of the Kirtland temple, apparently believing that his revolt would coincide with the second coming of Christ. He marked the Luffman family down for "blood atonement," as a sacrifice to Jesus, and predicted that their slayings would unleash a catastrophic earthquake in Kirtland, sparing only Lundgren's congregation.

In February 1988, Jeffrey announced that he had found a prayer that would unleash the earthquake, but he was still working out the details eight months later, when Rev. Luffman formally moved to excommunicate Lundgren. Around the same time, a thunderstorm and rainbow urged Jeffrey to accelerate his plans for human sacrifice, with a reading of *Revelation* convincing him that he had to "show blood" by April 1989. Instead of targeting the Luffman family, as planned, he shifted his sights to the Avery clan, condemning Dennis, Cheryl, and their three daughters as "wicked" for drifting away from Jeff's cult. The rest of Lundgren's followers were aware of his murder plans by March 1989, and Jeff carried them out on April 17, using one of his .45 automatics to slaughter the family of five, planting their corpses in a pit filled with quicklime. Although FBI agents and local police visited the commune a day later, they didn't know about the murder of the Avery family and left without having found any incriminating evidence. However, Lundgren's luck ran out several months later when a disgruntled disciple informed authorities about the crime. Eventually Jeff was sentenced to death as the plot's mastermind, while Alice, son Damon, and disciple Ron Luff drew prison terms ranging from 120 to 170 years. Several other Lundgren disciples pled guilty on reduced charges, to avoid the risks and rigors of a jury trial.

Lust, Gary

Thousands of workers call in sick every day, across America, but Gary Lust had a unique complaint when he walked off the job on July 28, 1983. He was possessed by the devil, Lust said, and he desperately needed an exorcism. Instead of seeking out a priest, however, the 39-year-old milkman found himself a gun, next morning, and drove to the home of his estranged wife, on the east side of Des Moines, Iowa. Linda Lust, age 35, was entertaining her 18-year-old boyfriend, Steven Harvey, when Gary arrived, and both were shot dead, Harvey in the back yard, Linda on her own front lawn. As an afterthought, Gary snatched two-year-old Jackie Johnson off the street, shoved her into his car, and sped away from the scene.

Police gave chase, topping speeds of 70 miles per hour, but the hot pursuit ended west of Altoona, on U.S. Highway 6, when Lust's car slammed into a bridge abutment. Both passengers were critically injured, but Lust would survive; Jackie Johnson, for her part, died in hospital on August 30, when her tracheotomy tube was accidentally dislodged.

Indicted on two counts of murder, Gary Lust went to trial in January 1984. In support of his insanity plea, several witnesses described his claim of demonic possession, while a psychiatrist opined that Lust could not tell right from wrong on July 29. It was a defense of sorts, but jurors were unimpressed, returning a guilty verdict on April 2, 1984. Lust faced a maximum sentence of 50 years in prison on each count.

Matthews, Robert Jay: See "Christian Identity" Movement

Meinholz, Henry

September 15, 1990 was an ordinary Saturday in small-town Kingston, Massachusetts. Nothing seemed out of place when 13-year-old Melissa Benoit left a friend's house that afternoon, headed home, but she never arrived. Her widowed mother checked with friends and neighbors on the block, but no one could remember seeing Melissa pass by. Finally, in desperation, Mrs. Benoit reported her child's disappearance to the Kingston police station, across the street from her home.

A full-scale search was underway by Monday, when Kingston's only detective, Richard Arruda, routinely stopped at the home of 52-year-old Henry Meinholz, a neighbor of Melissa's and a Bible School instructor at a local church. Meinholz told the detective that he had been watching TV sports on Saturday, and had not seen Melissa. Later, when FBI agents conducted a house-to-house search with tracking dogs, the canines recoiled from Meinholz's freshly painted garage.

Frustrated, the G-men asked residents along Melissa's presumed homeward path to take polygraph tests. Meinholz was tested on September 25 and failed, his physical response to certain questions indicating that he had, indeed, observed Melissa on the day she disappeared. At first, Meinholz blamed the incriminating test results on illness, promising to try again next day, but in the pre-dawn hours of September

26, he telephoned FBI agent Tom McGeorge with a startling confession. He had failed the polygraph, Meinholz now said, because he sometimes fantasized about molesting little girls. In fact, he had been known to follow school buses, masturbating in his car as girls emerged, and more than once he had tried to pick young children up, for oral sex.

FBI dog-handlers returned to the Bible teacher's home that afternoon, this time invading his basement, where Melissa Benoit's rotting corpse was found beneath a tarp-covered pile of mixed dirt and coal. Relatives identified the girl from her distinctive fingernail polish, and while decomposition ruled out any finding on the cause of death, police were clearly dealing with a homicide.

In custody, Meinholz admitted raping and killing Melissa. He had been smoking a cigarette in front of his house, he said, when Melissa passed by, and a disembodied voice told him: "You're not a man unless you have her. Do it!" Meinholz had lured the girl into his garage, asking her to "help get something," then locked her in and raped her several times before the same voice ordered him to "Kill her!" With that order ringing in his ears, Meinholz quickly smothered Melissa with a blanket and hid her body in the cellar.

Meinholz's trial opened on November 15, 1991, and jurors returned a verdict eight days later, ignoring the insanity defense to convict him of first-degree murder. Judge Cortland Mathers delivered the maximum sentence of life without parole, but he could not resist a parting comment to the killer. "It is said," the judge intoned, "that my predecessors in Colonial times had a gallows erected on the green in front of this courthouse and summarily sent defendants convicted, as you have been, to be hung. I truly regret that option is not open to me in this case."

Menéndez de Avilés, Pedro

The New World's first Protestants were Huguenots, members of a French Calvinist sect severely persecuted in their own land until the Edict of Nantes rescued them in 1598. They had no such protection in 1562, when a Huguenot party settled at Port Royal, South Carolina, but the colony failed on its own, before the Spanish troops of King Philip II could intervene. Two years later, though, the Huguenots returned and built Fort Caroline, at the mouth of the St. Johns River, in Spanish Florida. This time, they intended to stay.

When the news reached Madrid, King Philip wasted no time in retaliating. He negotiated a contract with Pedro Menéndez de Avilés, a Spanish trader in America and sometime commander of the Indies fleets, to expel the Protestant intruders and establish a permanent settlement in Florida. De Avilés arrived in August 1565, erecting a fort on the site he called St. Augustine, now America's oldest occupied city. That done, he marched his soldiers overland by night, to strike Fort Caroline on September 21. The garrison was captured, and De Avilés ordered the execution of all Huguenot men, mutilating the corpses by having their eyes cut out. In defense of the barbaric action, he declared: "I do this not unto Frenchmen, with whom my king is at peace, but unto heretics." Eight days later, De Avilés captured two bands of shipwrecked Huguenots who had been traveling to reinforce Fort Caroline. Their slaughter brought the total body count to something like 900 in America's first instance of religious conflict.

The Huguenots retaliated in August 1567, when a strike force led by Dominic de Gourgues captured the Spanish garrison at San Mateo, near the ruins of Fort Caroline. The Spaniards were held prisoner until May 1568, when De Gourgues hanged them en masse, proclaiming: "I do this not as unto Spaniards or mariners, but as unto traitors, robbers, and murderers."

Michel, Josef and Anna

At age 23, Anneliese Michel was in most respects an ordinary college student. She was conscientious and considerate, a pious child of devout Roman Catholic parents, but things changed suddenly in 1973. She papered the walls of her dorm room with pictures of saints, hung crucifixes everywhere, and prayed incessantly. She also raged at relatives and classmates without cause, spouted obscenities, and lapsed into convulsions. A physician diagnosed epilepsy, but Josef and Anna Michel were unconvinced, suspecting that their daughter's condition stemmed from demonic possession. Their parish priest confirmed that diagnosis, sending them on to Germany's most famous exorcist.

Eighty-year-old Father Adolf Rodewyk was a renowned Satanologist from Frankfurt, and while he agreed that Anneliese was certainly possessed by multiple demons, he declined to perform the exorcism ritual himself. The Michels were referred to a pair of younger practitioners, Fathers Erns Alt and Arnold Renz, who assured Josef and Anna of their daughter's eventual recovery.

Not that cleansing Anneliese would be a snap, by any means. The exorcists believed she was possessed by half a dozen evil spirits, and no minor demons at that: the list included Lucifer, Nero, Judas Iscariot, Cain, Adolf Hitler, and Father Helgar Fleischman (excommunicated and hanged for killing his mistress back in 1563). It was a formidable opposition team, but Alt and Renz felt equal to the task.

Beginning on September 14, 1975, the holy duo performed a series of exorcism ceremonies, conducted both at Anneliese's dorm and at her parents' home. Over time, her seizures returned with a vengeance, accompanied by Hitler's shouts of "Heil!" and blasphemous outbursts from Der Führer's demonic sidekicks. At one point, exorcists and parents alike reported the appearance of bloody stigmata on Anneliese's hands and feet. The young woman stopped eating around Easter, and she was down to a hideous 62 pounds when she finally died, lashed to her bed, on June 30, 1976. The family physician was summoned to sign a hasty death certificate, but he called police instead. A German court found Josef, Anna, and the two priests guilty of negligent homicide, but their prison sentences were suspended in favor of three years probation for all four defendants. Convictions notwithstanding, Josef Michel continues to blame Satan for his daughter's death, reporting that his home in Klingenberg is now haunted by swarms of demonic flies and mice.

Miller, Benjamin Franklin

Between 1967 and 1971, black residents of Stamford, Connecticut were intimidated by a string of murders claiming female victims, four of whom were strangled with their own brassieres. Police reported that some of the victims were junkies, and three were known prostitutes, but the killer's apparent selectivity did nothing to calm a community under siege. By the summer of 1971, black citizens were ready to accuse police of negligence — or worse — in their long-running search for the elusive strangler.

Rose Ellen Pazda, age 29, had been the first to die, reported missing on August 4, 1967, her skeletal remains recovered during April 1969. Donna Roberts, 22, was found on May 3, 1968, the day after her disappearance from Stamford. The third victim, 21-year-old Gloria Conn, was strangled to death on September 7, 1968, with her body recovered the next day, 200 feet from the spot where Roberts was found.

The killer took three years off before strangling 19-year-old Gail Thompson, on July 10, 1971. Six weeks later, on August 22, he returned to claim the life of 34-year-old Alma Henry, her body discarded like so much rubbish.

Thus far, all the victims had died or been found within a quarter-mile radius of the Riverbank-Roxbury Road overpass. Four of the five were from Stamford, with one reported missing from nearby Mount Vernon, New York, and police found evidence of a car backing into the places where bodies were found, indicating that the killer hauled his victims in the trunk.

Accumulated evidence put homicide investigators on the trail of Benjamin Miller, a Darien post office clerk and self-ordained street preacher who spent most of his time with black congregations after his own church expelled him for disruptive behavior. Described by his former pastor as "almost a fanatic," Miller had moved to Connecticut from Illinois at 18 years of age, in 1948. Employed at the post office for ten years, he talked religion on the job but otherwise ignored his fellow workers, keeping to himself whenever possible.

Committed to Norwalk's Fairfield Hills Hospital on February 17, 1972, Miller found detectives waiting when he checked out a month later. Arrested on March 17, he was charged and ultimately convicted in all five of the Stamford "bra murders," his apprehension restoring a measure of peace to the troubled community.

Mormons

Joseph Smith, Jr., was born in Vermont, two days before Christmas in 1805. His family soon moved to western New York, where Christian revivalism had whipped the population's interest in things spiritual to a fever pitch. Joe Senior made a meager living as a dowser, hunting water for his neighbors with a twisted "magic" stick, and Joseph's mother was a religious dilettante, drifting from one church to another in New York's "burned-over district," passing the transient zeal on to her son. Joe Junior began his "religious" career as a necromancer for hire, most frequently consulting the departed on behalf of neighbors who were seeking buried treasure. Sadly, his success — or lack thereof — encouraged paying clients to denounce him as a fraud. In 1826, at 21, Smith was indicted as a "disorderly person and an imposter *[sic],"* convicted on his own testimony that he used mystic spells and incantations to achieve results. The hitch, according to his angry patrons, was that Joseph never *got* results; he simply pocketed their cash and gave a helpless shrug when things went wrong, blaming "guardian demons" for his repeated failure.

Around that same time, Smith was courting Emma Hale, in Harmony, Pennsylvania, but Isaac Hale refused to countenance his daughter's marriage to a con man. Smith and Hale hashed out their differences in September 1827, Joseph agreeing to give up his spooky career and move to Pennsylvania, where Isaac promised to set the newlyweds up on a farm of their own. It was a decent offer, but Joe Junior couldn't hack the tedium of tilling fields, and he was soon back in New York, his bride in tow, looking for another way to cash in on offbeat religion.

Sometime before the spring of 1830, Joseph found his hook. According to the story he would later publish, it had been a well-kept secret for a decade. Back in 1820, Smith explained, he had been praying in the woods when he "saw a pillar of light exactly over my head, above the brightness of the sun, which descended gradually until it fell upon me." In the midst of that light were two figures, and "One of them spake unto me, calling me by name and said, pointing to the other — This is my beloved Son, Hear Him!" The second figure, presumably Jesus, warned Smith to steer clear of the various sects in the neighborhood, since they were all corrupt and "an abomination in my sight." That wrapped it up for Joe's first audience with God, and while the visitation didn't stop his swindling neighbors in the years to come, at least Smith kept his vow to stay away from the competing churches in New York.

Perhaps he was already waiting for the chance to lead his own.

Joe Junior's next brush with divinity came in September 1823, when an angel beamed into his bedroom on two successive nights. "He called me by my name," Smith later wrote, "and said unto me that he was a messenger sent from the presence of God to me and that his name was Moroni; that God had work for me to do." Not far from Joseph's house, the angel said, there was a certain "Hill Cummorah," where a set of golden tablets had been buried, with accessories. The tablets, said Moroni, were engraved with "an account of the former inhabitants of this continent, and the sources from whence they sprang." Next morning, Smith rushed off to find the holy treasure trove, unearthing the tablets, along with a sword, a breastplate, and two "peeping stones" — the oddly named "Urim" and "Thummim" — designed to help Smith translate his important find. Before he could begin that work, however, fickle Moroni reappeared and warned him off, pronouncing Joe Junior unfit to receive the new gospel. Smith was instructed to leave the treasure where he found it, and return in exactly one year, for updated instructions. According to Smith, the big tease continued until September 1827, when Moroni finally pronounced him ready to don a prophet's robes.

Translating previously undiscovered scripture is a full-time job, and Joseph needed help, someone to jot the message down as it revealed itself to him, along with cash to let him concentrate on God's work, rather than the tedium of toiling for his daily bread. As luck would have it, Smith found a disciple who met both needs at once. Martin Harris was an affluent farmer and religious gadfly from Palmyra, New York, who agreed to pay Smith's bills and take dictation while Joe Junior used his "peeping stones" to translate holy hieroglyphs.

The process of translation was unusual, to say the least. Smith typically sat with his face buried in a hat, or else with a blanket draped over his head, while "reading" the divine message to Harris. As pronounced by Smith, the new gospel described an early voyage to America, by settlers who sailed from the Red Sea some 600 years before Christ. Their leader was a man named Lehi, whose family was split by dissension over God's calling to the distant "promised land." Once they were safe ashore on North America, Lehi died, and his sons were divided by a bitter quarrel, Nephi standing loyal to their father's vision, while Laman and Lemuel defected to start their own tribes. A thousand years of bloody conflict ensued between the Nephites and Lamanites, the latter cursed by God with reddish skin, emerging as progenitors of the American Indians. For all their opposition to Almighty God, the Lamanites finally overwhelmed their Nephite adversaries in a climactic battle near the Hill Cummorah. Only one Nephite — Moroni, son of Mormon — survived the massacre, to hide the sacred tablets and look forward to the later coming of a prophet who would share their message with the world.

By February 1828, Martin had heard enough of Smith's story — and enough complaints from his skeptical wife —

that he was moved to ask if he could see the tablets. Smith refused, but did provide a brief handwritten transcript of the symbols he was "translating." It was illegible to Martin, so he went in search of help, beginning with Professor Charles Anthon, at Columbia University. Anthon reported that the weird symbols belonged to no known language, adding his suspicion that the tale of golden tablets was a hoax. Dr. Samuel Mitchell, vice president of Rutgers University, agreed with that assessment, but Smith dismissed the problem by explaining that the tablets were inscribed with "reformed Egyptian characters *[sic]*" unknown to modern science. His rap was so convincing that Martin began telling his friends that Professor Anthon had *confirmed* Smith's translation, a tale which Anthon denounced as "perfectly false," blasting Smith's story as "a hoax upon the learned" and "a scheme to cheat the farmer [Martin] of his money."

Secular criticism seldom stands a chance against "divine inspiration," and Joe Junior's con game was no exception to the rule. In March of 1830, Smith published his *Book of Mormon*, paying the printer's bill with money from a mortgage on the Harris farm. Sluggish sales left Harris unable to pay his debt, and the bank eventually foreclosed, but Harris never seemed to hold a grudge against Joe Junior. How important was a house, when they were dealing with eternal questions of salvation?

Critics attacked the *Book of Mormon* from day one, ridiculing characters with names like "Shiz" and "Aha," calling for hard evidence to support Smith's revision of history. Mark Twain devoted a whole chapter of *Roughing It* to Joe Junior's work, highlighting clumsy plagiarism from the King James Bible, finally dismissing the *Book of Mormon* as "an insipid mass of inspiration" and "chloroform in print." The so-called "Anthon transcript" vanished when Smith's book was published, and when critics asked to see the golden tablets, Smith told them that Moroni had reclaimed his property. Smith *did* produce two groups of men, who swore that they "beheld and saw the plates, and the engravings thereon," but his witnesses were less than persuasive. The first three — Martin Harris, David Whitmer, and Oliver Cowdery — claimed to have seen both the plates and an angel, while another group of eight men — all but one blood relatives of Smith or Whitmer — said that they had seen the plates alone. (Ironically, Harris and Cowdery were later excommunicated by Smith, while Whitmer left the fold on his own. Joe Junior's rift with Harris was so bitter that he called his one-time confidant "too mean to mention," claiming that God himself had branded Harris "a wicked man.")

The first formal meeting of Joe Junior's cult convened on April 6, 1830, at the home of Peter Whitmer, in Fayette, New York. Six disciples were present as Smith sketched the outlines of his new Church of Jesus Christ of Latter-Day Saints (LDS), better known to friends and enemies alike as "Mormons." The turnout was sparse, but they deserved a leader with a title to be proud of, Smith proclaiming that he should henceforth be known as "a seer, a translator, a prophet, an apostle of Jesus Christ, an elder of the church through the word of God the Father, and the grace of our Lord Jesus Christ." It was a mouthful, and his message sounded more than slightly off-the-wall, but Smith knew salesmanship. From six believers huddled in a cabin, he increased the fold to more than 30,000 in a decade, doubling again by 1850, and topping 80,000 in 1860. Clearly, from the converts' point of view, Joe Junior and the Mormons must have been doing something right.

The Mormon message was a key to Smith's success, and it was no coincidence that he christened his followers "latter-day" saints. Like William Miller, Smith believed — or professed to believe — that the end of the world was at hand, Christ's second coming an imminent prospect. Unlike other Christian churches, though, Smith's Mormons offered hope for sinners who had died before they heard The Word. By means of retroactive baptism, with live disciples standing in for the deceased, *anyone* could be saved from hellfire, while other rituals "sealed" children to their parents forever, providing an iron-clad guarantee of reserved seats in heaven. Best of all, the Prophet told his flock, there would be different levels of reward in the Celestial Kingdom, with top honors saved for the most deserving, those slated to become gods themselves. For Joseph's personal benefit, there was the "Law of Consecration," under which believers signed over title in all of their property to the church, becoming "stewards" of their own belongings. Any surplus they produced would be held by the church, presumably for distribution to the poor.

Mainline churches wasted no time in attacking the latter-day saints. Some wondered how the *Book of Mormon*, ostensibly buried in New York from 420 A.D. till September of 1823, could possibly contain long passages lifted verbatim from the King James Bible (published in 1611). Defecting Mormon William McLellin raised hoots of derision with his report that Smith claimed personal ordination to the priesthood from John the Baptist, and that Smith had translated his *Book of Abraham* from a papyrus "taken from the bosom of an Egyptian mummy." Critics recalled Smith's criminal conviction, from 1826, and a similar indictment in the very year he organized his church, accusing him of using the sacred "Urim" and "Thummim" in a new fortune-hunting racket. In

1834, investigative journalist E.D. Howe interviewed Smith's New York neighbors, publishing their descriptions of him as a liar and religious con man, and the giggle factor was only increased by Smith's occasional "Words of Wisdom," such as the 1833 proclamation admonishing his followers to shun alcohol, tobacco, and "hot drinks" (later interpreted to mean tea and coffee).

Smith and company stood firm in the face of the storm, Joe Junior discarding false modesty to describe his own *Book of Mormon* as "the most correct of any book on earth." His grand-nephew, Joseph Fielding Smith, would later write that "Mormonism must stand or fall on the story of Joseph Smith. He was either a prophet of God, divinely called, or he was one of the biggest frauds the world has ever seen." For faithful disciples such as Brigham Young, the carpenter-turned-evangelist who would later succeed Smith as president of the church, the choice was obvious: "Every spirit that confesses that Joseph Smith is a Prophet, that he lived and died a Prophet and that the *Book of Mormon* is true, is of God. Every spirit that does not is anti-Christ." If anyone missed the point, Young was willing to elaborate, proclaiming that any church outside the LDS denomination was "an abomination in God's eyes."

In June 1831, God told Joe Junior that his saints should pull up stakes and settle in Jackson County, Missouri, described in heavenly revelation as the "new Jerusalem." It is anyone's guess as to why Smith stopped along the way, planting a Mormon colony in northeastern Ohio, but the Lord is said to move in mysterious ways. In any case, it was an unfortunate choice for the latter-day saints. Their nonbelieving neighbors — dubbed "Gentiles" in Mormon godspeak — accused the new settlers of various crimes, with saints responding that their accusers were "enemies of the Lord." The truth was probably somewhere in between, but Ohio was still close enough to the frontier, in those days, for hard men to settle their feuds without recourse to courtrooms. In March of 1832, Joe Junior and a sidekick, evangelist Sidney Rigdon, were beaten, tarred and feathered by a Gentile mob in Hiram, Ohio, some twenty miles south of the Mormon outpost at Kirtland.

While Smith was thus distracted in Ohio, his advance party was busy putting down roots in Missouri, where their welcome from Gentiles was no less pacific. A mob in Independence trashed the LDS newspaper and raided several homes in July 1832, leaving two saints with a fresh coat of tar and feathers, warning the rest to move on with all deliberate speed. Mormons, for their part, responded with an armed demonstration three days later, flaunting their defiance with the creation of a militant troubleshooting squad, called "Danites," who would defend the colony (and, incidentally, keep dissident Mormons in line). Still, Gentile raids continued through that autumn, with an LDS store demolished at Independence, and Mormons driven from their homes at gunpoint around Big Blue. An estimated 200 homes had been torched, with some 1,500 Mormon settlers driven from the county, by the time Danites clashed with Gentile nightriders on November 4, leaving two men dead and several others wounded.

Back in Ohio, meanwhile, Joe Junior was doing his best to replicate Zion on earth. In 1831, he issued an order for single Mormons to find Indian wives — a "dark, and loathsome, and filthy people" — in the hope that interbreeding with saints would make them "fair and delightsome." According to Smith, this remedy for skin-sin dated back to prehistory, when God cursed the rebellious Lamanites with "a skin of blackness," allowing them to suffer for 500 years before intermarriage with the favored Nephites put them back in the pink. Four years later, Smith received another revelation from the Lord that would cause no end of trouble for his saints, long after he was gone.

The trouble began with Smith's hormones and a pretty, 17-year-old servant girl named Fannie Alger, who moved in with Joseph and his wife in 1835. Joe Junior wanted Fannie, but the road to connubial bliss had two major stumbling blocks: Emma Smith, and a passage from the *Book of Mormon* that declared "There shall not be any man among you have save it be one wife; and concubines he shall have none; for I, the Lord God, delight in the chastity of women." Another message from God, beamed to Smith some time in 1831, had re-emphasized the point, with an order that "Thou shalt love thy wife with all thy heart, and shalt cleave unto her and none else." It was unthinkable for Smith to tamper with the scriptures, but he still might bed young Fannie, if the Lord would only change *his* mind about the ban on plural mates. Joe Junior prayed about it and, amazingly, he got the answer he desired, in 1836:

> Verily, thus saith the Lord ... if any man espouse a virgin, and desire to espouse another, and the first give her consent, and if he espouse the second, and they are virgins, and have vowed to no other man, then he is justified; he cannot commit adultery for they are given to him.

In case Smith's wife missed the point, God added a personal post script: "And let my handmaiden, Emma Smith, receive all those that have been given unto my servant Joseph." Even with God on his side, however, Joseph was afraid to face Emma's wrath. He sent his brother Hyrum to deliver the news and receive the inevitable tongue-lashing. Emma was so furious, in fact, that she burned God's written declaration in the fireplace, but she later came around, accepting Fannie Alger as the first of Joe Junior's 48 additional wives.

Rumors of Mormon polygamy spread like wildfire around Kirtland, Ohio, but Smith and his disciples kept up a bold face of denial, Joe Junior declaring that Gentile neighbors were ill-equipped to swallow the "strong meat" of "celestial marriage," demanding that their preliminary instruction should be confined to the "first principles" of Mormonism. Critics from the press and mainline churches were referred to verses in the *Book of Mormon* which denounced polygamy as fornication, but the truth was difficult to hide from prying eyes. Between polygamy and their practice of primitive communism, the latter-day saints invited condemnation from their more conservative neighbors, but it was Joseph's love of money that brought their Ohio colony to grief, in the end.

Ever watchful for opportunities to line his pockets, Joe Junior had opened the Kirtland Safety Society Bank in 1836. He had no cash to speak of, at the time, but lured depositors by filling strongboxes with sand and scrap metal for weight, sprinkling a thin layer of half-dollar coins on the top, for appearance's sake. As one contemporary noted, "The effect of those boxes was like magic. They created confidence in the solidity of the bank, and that beautiful paper money went like hot cakes. For about a month, it was the best money in the country." In the meantime, Joe Junior was spending the *real* money hand over fist, on real estate, hoping for a windfall profit if and when the railroad came along to buy it back. The bubble burst in 1837, when Joseph's bank ran out of silver and was forced to close its doors. Ohio's legislature fined Smith $1,000 for operating an unchartered bank, but the state had to get in line behind furious depositors and their attorneys. On January 12, 1838, Smith and Sidney Rigdon fled Ohio in the middle of the night, Joe Junior later claiming the nocturnal move was necessary "to escape mob violence, which was about to burst upon us under the color of legal power to cover the hellish designs of our enemies."

They ran all the way to Missouri, but found their prospects little better in the Show-Me State. Missouri settlers feared that Mormons were agitating local Indians with their Lamanite rap, and they were understandably nervous when Joe Junior began to sermonize about "consecrating the riches of the Gentiles unto my people." Continued rumors of polygamy added spice to the broth of hostility, and election-day violence flared at Gallatin, that August, with riotous Gentiles blocking Mormons from the polls. By autumn, Missouri's Governor Lilburn Boggs had instructed his militia that "The Mormons must be treated as enemies and must be exterminated or driven from the state, if necessary, for the public good. Their outrages are beyond all descriptions."

Thus motivated, a strike force of 300 Gentiles, armed with everything from muskets to cannon, attacked the LDS settlement at Dewitt, Missouri, on October 6. Danite gunmen retaliated by raiding Gallatin and looting shops, dispersing to the countryside where they burned at least 150 Gentile homes in two counties. On October 24, four persons were killed and seven wounded, when Danites raided a militia camp at Crooked River. Six days later, the militia struck back at Haun's Mill, murdering 17 unarmed Mormons, including several children. By the time militia units were dissolved, in late November, Missouri authorities estimated that 40 Mormons had been killed, against losses of one "citizen" dead and 15 wounded. And the surviving saints were fleeing for their lives.

They ran to Illinois, where a sympathetic state legislature offered land and relative freedom of worship to the harried fugitives. The saints built their settlement near Commerce, on the Mississippi River, and Joseph named the place Nauvoo, informing his gullible flock that the word was Hebrew for "beautiful plantation." By any name, the new community was a success, ranking as the second largest Illinois city by 1844, its population of 12,000 souls nearly equal to Chicago's.

With a grant of near-total autonomy from the state of Illinois, Joe Junior began to spread his theological wings. Polygamy was still hush-hush, as far as Gentiles were concerned, but Smith soon elevated "celestial marriage" to the status of a religious "duty," with individual sanctity judged by the number of wives a man possessed. Since only God's elect were favored with multiple spouses, it stood to reason that men with numerous wives were more blessed than those with only one or two. The former rule of wedding only virgins was abolished at Nauvoo, so that even married women could be "sealed" to worthy saints, but Smith retained the final say on who should marry whom. An entry in Smith's diary, dated October 5, 1843, describes how he:

> gave instructions to try those persons who were preaching, teaching, or practicing the doctrine of plurality of wives; for according to the law, I hold the keys of this power in the last days, for there is never but one on earth at a time on whom the power and its keys are conferred; and I have constantly said no man shall have but one wife at a time unless the Lord directs otherwise.

At the same time, Smith was busy "inventing" new temple rituals for his flock to observe, most of them lifted — often verbatim — from the rituals of the Masonic lodge. Mormons would heatedly deny any link to Freemasonry in years to come, but there is no avoiding the fact that Joe Junior became a Mason in 1842, barely two months before the new rituals were "revealed" to him in a vision from God, while the Masonic square and compass appeared on the breast of the loose-fitting "garments" Mormons were obliged to wear beneath their normal clothes. There was also time for settling old scores, as in May of 1842, when Missouri's Governor Boggs was shot and wounded by a sniper at his home, in Independence. Danite gunman O.P. Rockwell was tried for the crime and acquitted for lack of hard evidence, after which he freely boasted of his guilt.

In 1841, God ordered the construction of a hotel in Nauvoo, dictating financial arrangements that placed the property and most of its income in Joe Junior's hands. Before long, he owned most of the commercial ventures in town, using his wealth to support his ever-growing harem of wives, some as young as 15. The prophet was not without detractors, however, including John Bennett, the mayor of Nauvoo and a general of the "Nauvoo Legion," who defected to write a scathing exposé of Smith in 1842. Around the same time, Smith organized a new Council of Fifty to expand LDS political power, with the ultimate goal of placing Joe Junior in the White House. As Smith told his followers, "I calculate to be one of the instruments of setting up the kingdom of Daniel by word of the Lord, and I intend to lay a foundation that will revolutionize the whole world." By 1844, the group was ready to go public, but Smith's candidacy met immediate opposition from the dissident *Nauvoo Expositor*. So heated were its editorials, blasting Smith as a religious fraud and would-be dictator, that he dispatched a mob to wreck the paper's press and office on June 7, 1844.

The official response was immediate and emphatic. Arrest warrants were issued for Smith, brother Hyrum, and other Mormon leaders, on charges of inciting a riot. Still defiant, "Lieutenant General" Smith brandished a saber before his disciples and ranted, "I call God and angels to witness that I have unsheathed my sword with a firm and unalterable determination that this people shall have their legal rights, and be protected from mob violence, or my blood shall be spilt upon the ground like water, and my body consigned to the silent tomb." In fact, the Smith brothers fled Illinois five days later, decamping in the middle of the night, and only tearful pleading by Joe Junior's wives convinced them to return, on June 26. A day later, vigilantes came for Joe and Hyrum at the jail where they were housed, in Carthage, and both men were killed without trial.

The Mormon church was shattered by Smith's death. Joe Junior had named a son — Joseph Smith III — as his successor to the role of Prophet, Seer, etc., but high-ranking saints were reluctant to vest so much authority in an 11-year-old child. Six different factions briefly vied for power in Nauvoo, before Brigham Young — a Vermont native and one of Joe Smith's earliest converts — managed to consolidate five groups behind his leadership. The sixth and smallest faction, calling themselves "Josephites" or the "Reorganized Church of Latter-Day Saints," moved back to Missouri, where they publicly renounced polygamy and established perpetual rule by direct descendants of Joseph Smith. The Josephites would try to press their claim against the parent church in years to come, but all church records were retained by Brigham Young and company, purged of any reference to young Joseph's anointing by his father.

Brigham Young seemed the perfect man to lead the wounded church through the bitter days ahead. Described by his daughter as a "Puritan of the Puritans," Young seized control of the Mormon empire by direct, ruthless action. When Sidney Rigdon made a bid for leadership, Young had him tried for heresy, defrocked, and abandoned to "the buffetings of Satan." Other contenders for the Mormon throne were horsewhipped, threatened with economic ruin, or "whittled" out of town by Danites brandishing Bowie knives, whittling sticks within inches of the subject's face. Rumors spread that stubborn dissidents were falling prey to the tactic of "greasing and swallowing" — that is to say, being thrown into the Mississippi River with a boulder tied around their necks.

Modern Mormons deny any suggestion of murders committed by the church, but history records a strong propensity for violent talk — and action — on the part of ranking saints that dates back to the spring of 1839. Joe Junior was reportedly engrossed in conversation with St. Peter, when he mentioned his ongoing problems with dissenters in the church. According to Smith, St. Peter replied that he — Peter — had personally "hung Judas for betraying Christ," and that Smith should do likewise with his enemies. Brigham Young refined the concept of lethal retribution, declaring that "There are sins that men commit for which they cannot receive forgiveness in this world, or in that which is to come, and if they had their eyes open to see their true condition, they would be perfectly willing to have their blood spilt upon the ground, that the smoke thereof might ascend to heaven as an offering for their sins." When squeamish Mormons denounced the policy as too harsh, Young replied, "I know, when you hear my brethren telling about cutting people off from the earth, that you consider it a strong doctrine, but it is to save them, not to destroy them. I know that there are transgressors who, if they knew themselves the only condition upon which they can obtain forgiveness, would beg of their brethren to shed their blood."

Thus, we see the origins of Mormon "blood atonement," the nearest thing to church-sanctioned human sacrifice in the western hemisphere since the Aztecs were conquered by Spain in the 16th century. Sinners were to be saved by ritual slaughter for a list of crimes that ranged from theft and murder to taking the Lord's name in vain and criticizing leaders of the Mormon church. Nor was plain killing enough to satisfy the code; rather, an offender should have "his throat cut from ear to ear, his tongue torn out by its roots, his breast cut open and his heart and vitals torn from his body and given to the birds of the air and the beasts of the field, and his body cut asunder in the midst and all his bowels gush out." Under terms of the blood atonement doctrine, ritual murder was both a sacred duty and a *favor* to the chosen victim, as Brigham Young explained:

> All mankind love themselves, and let the [blood atonement] principles be known by an individual, and he would be glad to have his blood shed. That would be loving themselves, even unto eternal exaltation. Will you love your brothers and sisters likewise, when they have committed a sin that cannot be atoned for without the shedding of their blood? Will you love that man or woman enough to shed their blood? This is loving our neighbor as ourselves; if he needs help, help him; if he wants salvation and it is necessary to spill his blood on the earth in order that he be saved, spill it.... That is the way to love mankind.

If anyone believed Young's rhetoric was simply tough talk to impress a hostile world, they could have asked the relatives of Phineas Wilcox, a Mormon knifed to death and secretly buried at Nauvoo on September 16, 1845, on suspicion of spying for the Gentiles. Wilcox was not the first saint "blessed" with blood atonement, and he would not be the last.

Purging dissenters was one thing, but holding armed Gentiles at bay was a tougher proposition. LDS nightriders shot up an anti-Mormon meeting at Green Plain, Illinois, in September 1845, but the raid only encouraged retaliation, vigilantes torching homes and barns, flogging or shooting Mormons wherever the opportunity presented itself. In September 1846, when 2,000 Gentiles packing field artillery besieged Nauvoo, the reigning Prophet received his first urgent message from God.

It was time to move on.

Brigham Young was vague about their destination when the Mormons started drifting westward, offering the sage advice that "I will know the place when I see it." Still, he *was* the self-proclaimed voice of God on earth, and who were his followers to question that kind of authority? In July 1847, gazing over the arid valley of the Great Salt Lake, Young recognized his promised land and named it "Deseret." In time, Deseret — or the "Great Basin Kingdom" — would spread from Salt Lake, as far south as Las Vegas, Nevada, and westward to the region of modern San Bernardino, California.

The Mormons had arrived, and it was a tremendous luxury to have a "nation" of their own, where they were free of persecution and the saints made all the rules. Prophet Young set the tone for his regime in 1848, with a publication entitled *The Kingdom of God.* As defined by Young:

> The Kingdom of God is an order of government established by divine authority. It is the only legal government that can exist in any part of the universe. All other governments are illegal and unauthorized. God,

> having made all beings and worlds, has the supreme right to govern by His own laws, and by officers of His appointment. Any people attempting to govern themselves by laws of their own making, and by officers of their own appointment, are in direct rebellion against the kingdom of God.

Of course, God only spoke to Brigham Young, so *he* made up the laws of Deseret and chose divinely sanctioned officers — inevitably wealthy Mormons who agreed that Young should have complete control of everything that happened in the "kingdom." Absolute submission was the price of living safe and sound in Deseret. "It is necessary," Brigham told his flock, "that every citizen should cultivate such a character and disposition as shall be pleasing to their King. Whenever the King shall give advice or counsel upon any subject, they should, without any hesitation, adhere strictly to that advice or counsel."

One bit of advice from King Brigham, in 1852, was the first public admission of Mormon polygamy. Elder William Clayton got the ball rolling, with his announcement "that the doctrine of plural and celestial marriage is the most holy and important doctrine ever revealed to man on the earth, and without obedience to that principle no person can ever attain to the fullness of exaltation in celestial glory." Elder Orson Pratt proclaimed that "God the Father had a plurality of wives... by whom He begat our spirits as well as the spirit of Jesus His first born." Monogamy was derided as the "source of prostitution and whoredom," not to mention a public health hazard. As Heber Kimball told the *Deseret News:* "I have noted that a man who has but one wife, and is inclined to that doctrine, soon begins to wither and dry up, while a man who goes into plurality looks fresh, young, and sprightly."

Even so, there were logistical problems when it came to choosing plural wives. The men of Deseret were running short of prospects by the latter 1850s, their shortage compounded by roving evangelists who "sealed" the best-looking women on sight. As Elder Kimball explained, "The brother missionaries have been in the habit of picking out the prettiest women for themselves and bringing only the ugly ones to us. Hereafter you have to bring them all here [i.e., to Salt Lake City] before taking any of them, and let us all have a fair shake."

The pleasures of polygamy aside, by the mid-1850s, King Brigham sensed a slackening of righteous discipline among his subjects. Some saints had become dangerously independent in their thinking, "contaminated" by the steady flow of Gentile travelers who passed through Deseret, some lingering to put down roots. Young was worried enough, by September 1856, that he announced a new campaign to purify the church, renowned historically as the "Mormon Reformation." *Inquisition* might have been a better label for the project, as LDS elders went from door to door with a catechism of 26 questions, conducting personal interrogations and recording "sins." The questions included subjects as diverse as tithing and personal hygiene, but the most ominous asked if anyone in the household had ever criticized Mormon principles, revelations of the Prophet, or "the Presidency of the Church as now organized." In theory, transgressors were safe if they repented and were rebaptized; in fact, the grilling provided a perfect vehicle for blackmail and a settling of old scores, marking "enemies of the faith" for elimination by King Brigham's "Avenging Angels."

Modern Mormons avoid discussion of the Reformation whenever possible, dismissing a "handful" of violent incidents as the work of individual fanatics, executed without official sanction, but the truth is rather different. In fact, the Prophet's own remarks not only justified, but *demanded* execution of "sinners," albeit for their own good, and his call for Mormons to "love" their neighbors by spilling their blood was published in the official LDS *Journal of Discourses* on the very day Young's Reformation was announced. One documented victim was Rosmo Anderson, condemned in 1857 for the "crime" of adultery. Danite assassin John Lee — himself convicted and ultimately executed for mass murder — described how Anderson was seized by church elders in Cedar City, allowed to pray beside his open grave, before they cut his throat and held his body up to let the blood spill out. Even moving out of state could bring a visit from the homicidal Danites, as William Parrish learned, when he announced his plan to take his family from Springville, Utah, to the greener fields of California. Parrish and his sons were gunned down on orders from LDS elders, their bodies carted off in a wagon. When William's body was found, days later, his throat had been slashed, his torso stabbed 48 times. As his wife later reported, "There had been public preaching at Springville, to the effect that no apostates would be allowed to leave; if they did, hogholes would be stopped up with them."

So busy were the Danite murder squads, in those days, that subsequent expansion of Salt Lake City provided no end of embarrassment for the church, construction crews constantly turning up skeletons from shallow graves in vacant lots. The "Avenging Angels" were so flagrant and brutal, that their notoriety reached all the way to London, where Sir Arthur Conan Doyle used them as villains in his first recorded case of Sherlock Holmes, but nothing they inflicted on the faithful would make headlines like the Mountain Meadows massacre.

179

It was September 7, 1857, when a wagon train of 140 emigrants bound for California was attacked by Indians at Mountain Meadows, five miles south of modern Enterprise, Utah. Seven travelers were killed before they got the wagons circled and beat off the first attack, digging in for a protracted siege. Three emigrants slipped out to go for help, but two of them were killed by Indians, the third gunned down by a Mormon who resented Gentiles traveling through Deseret. As time wore on, the Indians asked Mormon bishop John Lee for his help, and Lee — concerned about the bad publicity that would accrue from the preceding murders — summoned 50 Danite gunmen to the battleground. They hatched a plan to lure the emigrants from cover with a flag of truce and promise of protection from the savages. Lee described the action in his memoirs, 20 years after the fact:

> The women and children were hurried right on by the troops. When the men came up they cheered the soldiers as if they believed that they were acting honestly. Higbee then gave the orders for his men to form in single file and take their places as ordered before, that is, at the right of the emigrants... Just as we were coming into the main road, I heard a volley of guns at the place where I knew the troops and emigrants were... Our teams were then going at a fast walk. I first heard one gun, then a volley at once followed.
>
> McMurdy and Knight stopped their teams at once, for they were ordered by Higbee, the same as I was, to help kill all the sick and wounded who were in the wagons, and to do it as soon as they heard the guns of the troops. McMurdy was in front; his wagon was mostly loaded with the arms and small children. McMurdy and Knight got out of their wagons; each

> one had a rifle. McMurdy went up to Knight's wagon, where the sick and wounded were, and raising his rifle to his shoulder, said: *"O Lord, my God, receive their spirits, it is for thy Kingdom that I do this."* He then shot a man who was lying with his head on another man's breast; the ball killed both men.
> [Emphasis in the original.]

A total of 120 men, women, and children were slaughtered in the Mountain Meadows massacre, their deaths blamed on hostile Indians until a dissident saint spilled the beans. Even so, it was 1877, a full 20 years after the crime, before Bishop John Lee was convicted of multiple murder and executed at the original massacre site.

The butchery at Mountain Meadows was particularly inconvenient for Brigham Young, coming as it did in the midst of his all-out war with the United States. Utah had applied for statehood in 1849 and was granted territorial status a year later, precipitating Young's demotion from king to governor, but the legislature still rubber-stamped his every whim. As governor, Young also had the power to appoint state judges, thereby guaranteeing that Mormons were rarely convicted of crimes against Gentiles, while non-Mormons found it virtually impossible to sue a saint. Federal soldiers stationed in Utah were openly despised by the Mormons, and largely confined to their camps. Joseph Smith had once warned Young "that there would be one danger to beset him, and that would be his love of wealth," but Smith was buried back in Illinois, his heirs cut off from wielding any power in the church. (When Smith's mother published a history of her family, promoting the Reorganized LDS church, Young ordered that all copies in Utah should be "gathered up and destroyed, so that no copies should be left.") With no one to restrain him, serving both as governor of Utah territory and trustee of the LDS church, Young claimed most of the Great Basin's timber land for himself, seized exclusive grazing rights to the best prairie land, and named himself director of the Greater Salt Lake Water Works Association. On the side, he also owned or dominated all commercial links to the outside world, including railroads, telegraph, and mail transport companies.

It was a situation ripe for conflict with the feds, and Congress found its opening in 1852, when Young went public with the doctrine of polygamy. By that time, the king-turned-governor had at least 20 wives of his own, and Congress seized the opportunity to put him in his place by condemning plural marriage in the territories. Passing a resolution was one thing, however; enforcing it 2,000 miles from Washington was something else. In August 1856, Surveyor General David Burr reported a near-fatal assault by Mormons on one of his aides, in Salt Lake City, and the "Mormon War" was on.

It was a struggle of attrition, rather than pitched battles, with LDS guerrillas holding the traditional advantage of an army fighting on its own home ground. They murdered six emigrants suspected as "federal spies," near Kayesville, in May 1857 and pulled off the Mountain Meadows massacre in September; by October, they were raiding federal supply trains, holding U.S. troops at gunpoint in one incident and forcing them to burn 350,000 pounds of food. An associate justice of the territorial government fled Utah, in fear of his life, and reported to Washington that LDS leaders were bent on destroying the "illegal and unauthorized" federal government by any means, fair or foul. President James Buchanan dispatched a new governor to Utah, with an escort of 2,500 soldiers, but the army bogged down in Wyoming for the winter, harassed by Danite commandos and their scorched-earth campaign. Governor J.W. Dawson finally took office in

Utah, but he ruled in name only. Evacuating the territory in January 1862, he was ambushed at Weber Canyon and suffered "shocking and almost emasculating injuries" at the hands of Danite assailants who were later killed while resisting arrest.

Mormons welcomed the onset of America's Civil War, praying earnestly for a Confederate victory. When the Gentile conflict was settled, Young told the faithful, "We are bound to become a sovereign state in the union or an independent nation by ourselves." His hopes were dashed, however, by Washington's passage of the Morrill Anti-Bigamy Act — which also called for disincorporaiton of the church and placed a $50,000 limit on church-owned real estate. Completion of the transcontinental railroad, in 1869, brought further pollution from Gentiles settling in Utah, but the LDS establishment was stubborn. Official sanction for "blood atonement," in the form of a statute allowing condemned prisoners to choose decapitation over hanging or the firing squad, remained in force until 1888, and polygamy was not officially renounced until 1890. Utah finally became a state in 1896, with both sides anxious to forget about the "Mormon War." **[See also: LeBaron, Ervil; Lundgren, Jeffrey; Rachal, David; Singer, John]**

Mountain Kirk: See Ku Klux Klan

"Move": See American Christian Movement for Life

Nation of Islam

In the summer of 1930, a mysterious peddler turned up in Detroit's ghetto, working the streets with a religious rap he used to sell the goods he advertised as "African." His race and nationality were indeterminate — some thought he was an Arab — but the culture-hungry locals welcomed him into their homes as one of their own. Mrs. Lawrence Adams recalls:

> He came into our houses selling raincoats, and then afterwards, silks. In this way he could get into people's houses, for every woman was eager to see the nice things the peddlers had for sale. He told us that the silks he carried were the same kind that our people used in their home country, and that he was from there. So we asked him to tell us about our own country.

Soon, the stranger was holding religious meetings in private homes, relating his own experiences in foreign lands, adding dietary admonitions and health tips for those who cared to listen. Mrs. Adams, soon converted to the peddler's brand of Islam as Sister Denke Majied, described his approach:

> He would eat whatever we had on the table, but after the meal he began to talk. "Now don't eat this food, it is poison for you. The people in your own country do not eat it. Since they eat the right kind of food they have the best health all the time. If you would just live like the people in your home country, you

> would never be sick any more." So we all wanted him to tell us about ourselves and about our home country and about how we could be free from rheumatism, aches, and pains.

As he flew in the face of well-documented African famine and disease, so the stranger used a Bible to teach Detroit blacks of the "true religion" — not Christianity, but the religion of tribesmen in Africa and Asia. Most American blacks knew no other religious text than the Bible, and the peddler explained that it would do for now, albeit with careful interpretation, until they had a chance to study the Koran. Over time, his lectures became increasingly bitter toward whites, and he "began to attack the teachings of the Bible in such a way as to shock his hearers and bring them to an emotional crisis."

Even then, no one knew much about the stranger in their midst. He liked to call himself Mr. Farrad Mohammad or Mr. F. Mohammad Ali, but he would also answer on occasion to the names Professor Ford, Mr. Wali Farrad, and Wallace D. Fard. One early convert recalled his introduction to the man Detroit blacks were already calling "The Prophet": "My name is W.D. Fard, and I come from the Holy City of Mecca. More about myself I will not tell you yet, for the time has not yet come. I am your brother. You have not yet seen me in my royal robes."

From that deliberate mystery, various legends grew around the stranger in Detroit. Some said he was the black Jamaican son of a Syrian Moslem father, while others swore he was a Palestinian or a wealthy descendant from the tribe of Koreish, which gave the world Muhammad. Yet another tale said that Farrad had trained in London for a diplomatic career, for his native "kingdom of Hejaz," but he had sacrificed his future to bring "freedom, justice, and equality" to the "black man in the wilderness of North America, surrounded and robbed completely by the Cave Man." Under questioning by Detroit police, Farrad identified himself as "the Supreme Ruler of the Universe," and at least some of his followers called him a god in human form. At the other extreme, a Chicago newspaper once described him as "a Turkish-born Nazi agent [who] worked for Hitler in World War II."

Whatever his point of origin, Farrad told blacks that he had come to rouse his "uncle" — the "Black Nation" — to its full potential in a world temporarily controlled by "blue-eyed devils." Thousands of ghetto blacks responded to his message that the North was merely a subtle, dishonest version of Dixie, where racists held power without the legal trappings of Southern segregation. White officials, from beat cops to social workers, became targets of intense race hatred from Farrad's "Black Nation." One recruit, Robert Harris, planned to sacrificc two white welfare workers as "infidels." When the women learned of his plan and informed the police, Harris confirmed for detectives that he would, indeed, have killed the two "no-good Christians" if he had only been able to find them in time.

Farrad's house-to-house visits ended after he established his first temple in Detroit, but his sermons continued to borrow freely from the Bible, the Koran, and Freemasonry as he sought to give blacks an expanded "knowledge of self." Converts were encouraged to purchase radios, so that they could listen to Joseph Rutherford, of the Jehovah's Witnesses, and the fundamentalist rantings of J. Frank Norris, in Texas. Farrad warned the faithful that whites should never be taken literally, since they are incapable of speaking truth. Instead, all white speech and writing was "symbolic," requiring skilled interpretation... by Wali Farrad. Despite their evil ways, the "blue-eyed devils" were tools of Allah, from whom blacks could learn their own history in roundabout fashion, if studied with care. It was, in short, a racist message dressed up in religious trappings, custom-tailored for appeal to any black who had been slighted or insulted by Caucasians. It was Allah who commanded them to hate; the "prophet" simply acted as his voice.

By 1933, Farrad had constructed such an effective organization that he could step back from most of the active leadership duties, leaving them in other hands. He had a "University of Islam" — in fact, a combined elementary and high school — where black children were drilled in astronomy, "higher mathematics," and techniques for the "ending of the spook civilization." On the side, he also founded a Muslim Girls Training Class, to produce properly submissive wives and mothers. Finally, his fear of the police and other enemies drove Farrad to organize the Fruit of Islam, a paramilitary unit led by captains and instructed in the use of firearms.

Among the earliest converts to Farrad's "Nation of Islam" — better known as Black Muslims — were the three Poole brothers, transplanted from Georgia to Detroit in the 1920s. Somehow, they neglected to inform Farrad that they were related, and when it was time to replace their "slave names" with "original" African names, "despite his omniscience, the prophet gave [them] the surnames of Sharrieff, Karriem and Muhammad." When the snafu was discovered, Farrad explained that he had "divine knowledge" of their "proper" names. Indeed, Elijah Poole — henceforth Elijah Muhammad — was such a zealot that he swiftly rose through the ranks to become Farrad's chief lieutenant, named Minister of Islam in early 1934, to preside over the church despite opposition from more moderate spokesmen.

In June 1934, shortly after Elijah Muhammad's promotion, Wali Farrad vanished without a trace, never to be seen again. His disappearing act sparked as many unsubstantiated rumors as his first appearance in Detroit. Some disciples said he had been murdered by police, white racist vigilantes, or dissident Muslims; one story placed him "aboard a ship bound for Europe," while others named Elijah Muhammad as a suspect in the mystery. The Black Muslims were 8,000 strong when Farrad went up in smoke, but they soon lost much of their aggressiveness, declining in numbers and influence once The Prophet's guiding hand had been removed. Internal quarrels went public, with moderate Muslims ousting Elijah Muhammad from Detroit to Temple No. 2, in Chicago, where he established a new headquarters and began reshaping the Nation of Islam in his own militant image. In short order, he assumed Farrad's title of "Prophet," adding "Messenger of Allah" for good measure.

Even as he started empire building, though, the self-styled prophet was beset by legal problems. In 1934, Muhammad was sentenced to six months probation for contributing to the delinquency of a minor, after he refused to move his child from the "University of Islam" to a public school. Eight years later, he was one of 80 blacks arrested by federal agents for allegedly conspiring with Japan against America. Chicago's FBI chief told the press that "no definitive connection had been found by his men between Negro organizations and Japanese activity in this country," but indictments were returned on grounds that the Black Muslims and two other militant groups were "alleged to have taught Negroes that their interests were in a Japanese victory, and that they were racially akin to the Japanese." U.S. Attorney J. Albert Woll linked the defendants to statements "as vicious as any ever uncovered by a grand jury," and Muhammad was convicted of sedition, serving four years in federal prison. Ironically, his plight inspired the Nation of Islam to new growth under long-distance leadership, as the movement hailed its first authentic "martyr."

As outlined by Wali Farrad and amplified by Elijah Muhammad, Black Muslim racial theories present a strange mirror image of Christian Identity beliefs, almost a photographic negative, with black and white reversed. In Muslim theology, "Original Man" as created by Allah was "none other than Black Man." Black Man, in turn, created all other races — including whites, for whom he invented "a special method of birth control." Thus, blacks "came with the earth" as the "tribe of Shabazz," when a huge explosion severed earth and moon some "66 trillion years ago," but whites have only existed for 6,000 years. All blacks are Muslims, whether they know it or not, and "the Black Man by nature is divine." Jesus himself was a Muslim prophet and a black man, yet Christianity somehow became a white man's religion, serving pallid mutants who were "grafted from the Original Black Nation, as the Black Man has two germs (two people) in him. One is black and the other brown. The brown germ can be grafted into its last stage, and the last stage is white. A scientist by the name of Yakub discovered this knowledge... 6,645 years ago, and was successful in doing the job of grafting after 600 years of following a strict and rigid birth control law." The unfortunate result of that experiment was a world overrun with "blue-eyed devils" who subjugated Original Man, since humanity had been "grafted" out of them, along with their "divine" pigmentation. While denying all charges of racism, Black Muslims insist that "The human beast — the serpent, the dragon, the devil, and Satan — all mean one and the same; the people or race known as the white or Caucasian race, sometimes called the European race." Furthermore, "Since by nature they were created liars and murderers, they are the enemies of truth and righteousness and the enemies of those who seek the truth."

For reasons unknown, these pale-skinned demons were given 6,000 years to rule the earth, theoretically ending in 1914, but they were to maintain control for another seventy "years of grace" — that is, until 1984 — while the chosen of Allah were resurrected from slavery and ignorance. The Bible is reviled by Muslims as a "poison book," dedicated to a white man (King James), which conceals the role of Moses, Christ, and other Muslim prophets, while slandering God with a charge of adultery (for impregnating Joseph's wife, Mary). Black Muslims observe strict dietary laws and adopt an ultrapuritanical view of sex — with conspicuous exceptions for the Minister of Allah — with philanderers subject to punishment by the Fruit of Islam's goon squad. At the bottom line, though, they preach racial hatred every bit as virulent as any proffered by the **Ku Klux Klan** — and by the early 1970s, those twisted teachings would cause blood to flow in city streets from coast to coast.

The Nation of Islam boasted some 50,000 members by 1964. Black Muslims had been involved in sporadic violence from the cult's beginning, and the pattern continued through the early 1960s. In Los Angeles, during April 1962, Muslims assaulted two patrolmen outside their mosque, responding with gunfire when police reinforcements rushed to the scene. When the smoke cleared, 1 Muslim was dead and 11 others wounded, with 8 officers included on the list of casualties. If they despised white police, however, the Muslims were equally disdainful of black "Uncle Toms," and some of the faithful expressed their antipathy for Dr. Martin Luther King by pelting his car with eggs when he went to give a speech in Harlem, in June 1963.

At the same time, Muslim leaders showed a curious affinity for the company of white racists. In June 1961, minister Malcolm X (born Malcolm Little) met with leaders of the **Ku Klux Klan** in Atlanta, Georgia, to discuss a "nonaggression pact" and seek cooperation from the KKK in forging dual, racially separate societies, assuring Klansmen that Muslims believed "the Jew is behind the integration movement, using the Negro as a tool." Over the next year, George Lincoln Rockwell and his American Nazis were welcomed at Muslim conventions in Chicago and Washington, D.C., while KKK "Grand Dragon" Calvin Craig returned the favor in 1964, introducing minister Jeremiah X at a Klan rally in Atlanta's Hurd Park.

Malcolm X would later blame the racist conclaves on direct orders from Elijah Muhammad, citing the flirtation with white fascist groups as one reason for his leaving the Nation of Islam. In fact, tension had been brewing for some time between Elijah and his most famous disciple, climaxing in Malcolm's 1963 suspension, after he described President Kennedy's assassination as a case of "chickens coming home to roost." Malcolm was also put off by Elijah's flagrant womanizing and the fact that he had fathered numerous illegitimate children. Over the next few months, as Malcolm drifted steadily toward true Islam, moving farther away from Elijah's brand of sci-fi weirdness, he became an object of scorn to loyal Muslims. In July 1964, while traveling in Egypt, Malcolm fell suddenly ill and was rushed to the hospital, where a stomach pump saved his life; friends still insist that he was poisoned, on orders from Elijah Muhammad in Chicago. Five months later, on Christmas day, Muslim defector Leon Ameer, now loyal to Malcolm, was ambushed and severely beaten by members of the Boston mosque. He lay comatose for three days, before regaining consciousness. Boston, in fact, was a hotbed of Muslim antipathy toward Malcolm, with minister Louis X — later Louis Farrakhan — penning editorials for *Muhammad Speaks* which challenged Malcolm to "face the music," strongly implying that his days were numbered if he should return to the United States.

In fact, if Malcolm's later writings are correct, the first attempt to kill him came even before he left the Nation of Islam. A Muslim with experience in demolition was allegedly recruited to plant a bomb in Malcolm's car, but he ran to Malcolm instead, prompting Malcolm to write that "[t]he first direct order for my death was issued through a Mosque Seven official who previously had been a close assistant." New York police and federal agents dismissed that report as a crass publicity stunt, and they were nowhere to be seen when knife-wielding strangers tried to ambush Malcolm near his home, in 1964. Next came the Cairo poisoning, if such it was, and the internecine action heated up in early 1965. Malcolm's home was firebombed on the night of February 14, and one week later, to the day, he was assassinated by black gunmen while delivering a speech at the Audubon Ballroom, in Harlem. The four men finally convicted of his murder were all New Jersey Muslims, loyal to their Chicago "prophet." As triggerman Talmadge Hayer — a.k.a. Mujahid Abdul Halim — later said, "I had a lot of love and admiration for the Honorable Elijah Muhammad, and I just felt like this is something that I have to stand up for. That is what I believe. So that led to me getting involved to the extent that — you know, I would go all the way."

(Louis Farrakhan is plagued to this day by suspicions that he may have been involved in Malcolm's death, but no such evidence has ever been produced, and Farrakhan blames all such rumors on "the establishment media," flatly denying any role in the crime. In 1995, Malcolm's daughter was briefly detained on suspicion of plotting Farrakhan's death, presumably in retaliation for her father's assassination, but she was released without trial, and no further prosecution is anticipated. For the record, it appears that the final plot to kill Malcolm originated with Muslims in New Jersey and New York, while Farrakhan was in charge of the Boston mosque. There is also evidence that both federal and local police authorities had advance knowledge of the assassination plan.)

Malcolm's death did not resolve the violent rift within Elijah Muhammad's Nation of Islam; quite the opposite, in fact. Within two days of Malcolm's murder, Muslim mosques were burned by arsonists in New York and San Francisco, both presumably by followers of Malcolm who were looking for revenge. February 1971 witnessed street fighting between Muslims and Black Panthers in Atlanta, as the two "black nationalist" groups clashed over rights to sell their newspapers on a specific street corner. In May 1973, a Muslim named Hakim Jamal was gunned down in front of his wife and children, allegedly for "loose-lipped" criticism of Elijah Muhammad. That September, Newark minister James Shabazz was publicly assassinated, and 14 members of the rival New World of Islam were charged with conspiracy in his death. A month later, two Black Muslims were found decapitated at the site of his murder, their heads discarded four miles away from the scene.

The most violent internecine conflict raged between loyal followers of Elijah Muhammad and members of the rival Hanafi Muslim sect, led by Hamaas Abdul Khaalis, who regarded Elijah as a false prophet and defiler of Islam. Khaalis openly denounced Elijah in 1973, and soon began receiving threats against his life. Before the end of the year, Khaalis and his son-in-law were beaten by Muslims in Washington, D.C. In January 1974, seven Hanafis were slaughtered in a Washington house once owned by basketball star Kareem Abdul-Jabbar. The victims included five children, four of whom were drowned in a bathtub. A lucky survivor identified the killers as a hit team from the Nation of Islam. Five Black Muslims were charged with murder in the case, and all were convicted.

Fratricidal mayhem did not stop the Muslims from continuing their history of violent clashes with white authority figures, however. In August 1965, two days after the Watts riot ended, a shoot-out between Muslims and cops at the L.A. mosque sent 4 persons to the hospital and 59 to jail. In January 1968, Muslims invaded Brooklyn's Junior High School No. 17, assaulting the principal and two teachers. Four persons were injured, with one Muslim arrested, blaming his actions on "mistreatment" of black students at the school. Atlanta saw more violence in May 1969, when Muslim demonstrators assaulted four policemen in retaliation for the arrest of some disorderly picketers. Still in Georgia, Sgt. Hiram Watson was shot and killed while trying to arrest a Black Muslim in Cordele, during October 1970. January 1972 witnessed the worst violence yet, when gunfire erupted at a Black Muslim rally in Baton Rouge. When the smoke cleared, two blacks and two policemen were dead, with another 31 persons wounded. Mayor W.W. Dunn blamed the shooting on "Black Muslims from Chicago who had boasted they were taking over Baton Rouge," and while Elijah Muhammad denied any knowledge of the incident, 13 Muslims were convicted of inciting a riot. Three months after that explosion, five policemen and three civilians were injured after a brawl and gunfight broke out at a Muslim mosque in Harlem. Nine months later, in Brooklyn, four Sunni Muslims were caught in a shoot-out with police after looting a gun store; all four received prison terms of 25 years. In May 1974, three Sunnis robbed a Cleveland apartment of $2,000 and fled with a hostage. Cornered by police in a nearby house, they held nine more hostages in a 90-minute siege that left six cops and two civilians wounded.

For sheer ferocity, it is difficult to match the "Death Angels" cult, a Black Muslim splinter group founded in California during late 1969 or early 1970. Members accepted the standard Black Muslim philosophy — that whites are "beasts" and "grafted devils" spawned in an ancient genetic experiment — but these cultists carried their beliefs into action, seeking to exterminate Caucasians. On joining the Death Angels, recruits were photographed, earning their "wings" — drawn on the snapshot with a ballpoint pen — after killing a specified number of whites. Based on a point system geared to emotional difficulty, candidates were required to kill four white children, five women, or nine men. Murders were verified through media reports, eyewitness accounts by fellow Angels, or the collection of Polaroid snapshots.

(As reported by author Clark Howard in *Zebra*, one Death Angel candidate flew to Chicago — "New Mecca" in Muslim parlance — with a collection of grisly photographs, seeking promotion to the non-existent rank of lieutenant in the cult. His unexpected visit puzzled members of the headquarters staff and might have been disastrous, if he had not been intercepted by a leader of the secret group, who "counseled" him and sent him home.)

By October 1973, the killer cult had at least 15 accredited members, their winged photos displayed on an easel at covert gatherings. Together, these 15 were theoretically responsible for killing 135 men, 75 women, 60 children, or some combination of victims sufficient to earn their "wings." The California State Attorney General's office had compiled a list of 45 similar murders, committed with cleavers, machetes, or close-range gunshots, involving white victims and black assailants, with known suspects invariably linked to the Nation of Islam. Attacks had been recorded in San Francisco, Oakland, Berkeley, Long Beach, Signal Hill, Santa Barbara, Palo Alto, Pacifica, Los Angeles, and San Diego, plus rural areas in the counties of Alameda, Contra Costa, Los Angeles, San Mateo, Santa Clara, and Ventura.

By January 28, 1974, when California law enforcement personnel convened a secret conference on the problem, 64 persons were known to have died in ritualistic racial attacks, and three more deaths were recorded by March. A rare survivor, Thomas Bates, was thumbing rides near the Bay Bridge at Emeryville, north of Oakland, when two black men pulled up in an old model Cadillac. Rolling down the window, the passenger grinned at Bates, said, "Hello, devil," and then opened fire with a pistol at point-blank range, wounding Bates in the hip, stomach, and arm. Bleeding profusely, Bates managed to reach a nearby motel, where employees phoned for police and an ambulance.

By early 1974, San Francisco was paralyzed with fear at the sudden rash of "Zebra" murders, committed on random white targets by black assailants, claiming 15 dead and eight wounded over a six-month period. Eight suspects were arrested in May 1974, and while four were later released for lack of evidence, four others were prosecuted in a trial lasting from March 3, 1975 to March 9, 1979. Three of the four defense attorneys were hired by the Nation of Islam, in a show of solidarity with the mass murderers. At the end of those marathon proceedings, jurors needed barely 18 hours to convict all defendants on all counts, and the four were sentenced to life imprisonment.

As for the Death Angels, their existence has never been publicly acknowledged by American law enforcement, and the results of confidential investigations into the cult remain classified. None of the 15 "accredited" Angels were charged in the San Francisco case, which bagged only prospective members, still short of their tally for final qualification. The others are presumably still at large. Still hunting.

"Nativist" Movement

Protestant hatred of Catholics was transplanted to the New World with the first British settlers, in the early 17th century. Jesuits were widely suspected of inspiring and supporting Indian attacks on early British colonies in North America, and settlements controlled by Puritans passed laws proscribing Roman Catholics, along with Quakers, Jews, and witches. Even colonial Maryland, established as a refuge for Catholics in America, was not safe from conflict. Two years of bloody **religious wars**, pitting Catholics against Puritans, resulted in a Protestant's installation as proprietary governor, and while the Toleration Act of 1649 granted religious freedom to all Christians (still excluding Jews and other "infidels"), Catholics would be viewed with suspicion for centuries to come.

Despite their minority status, many Protestants still believed that Catholics, directed from the Vatican, conspired to rule the world, and that belief brought many members to the so-called "nativist" movement, driving self-styled patriots to brutal acts of violence. In 1829, Boston Protestants spent three days rioting in the streets, stoning and looting Irish Catholic homes, but another five years would elapse before the real outbreak of mayhem began. In the meantime, rabid nativists were going back to school, collecting "evidence" against the immigrants they feared.

The 1830s witnessed a rash of anti-Catholic "disclosures," published in book or pamphlet form, which professed to be the memoirs of ex-priests and "escaped nuns." Martha Britt Sherwood led the pack, in 1835, with publication of *The Nun*, alleged to be the personal narrative of "a devoted Papist" who described convents riddled with trapdoors and secret passageways, leading to Medieval dungeons where inmates were shackled and tortured for penance. The heroine finally escapes, aided by the handsome brother of a murdered nun, with whom she lives happily ever after as a "complete woman." *The Nun* was still selling briskly to Protestant readers when a similar work, titled *Six Months in a Convent*, was unleashed on the public by author "Rebecca Theresa Reed." Yet another nativist broadside was released in 1836, under the ponderous title *Awful Disclosures of Maria Monk*. Monk's narrative rehashed the usual complaints, but also added charges of infanticide, alleging that nuns and novices in Montreal were regularly impregnated by lustful priests, their offspring born secretly, smothered at birth, and buried in the convent's cellar. The charge was serious enough to warrant an investigation, conducted by an ad hoc committee which found numerous discrepancies in "Monk's" report, finally announcing that "Maria Monk is an out and out impostor, and her book in all its essential features is a tissue of calumnies." In August 1837, media reports alleged that Monk had been abducted by a flying squad of priests, and sequestered at a Catholic sanitarium in Philadelphia. Dr. W.W. Sleigh, a Philadelphia physician and self-described "sterling Protestant conscientiously opposed to the views of the Catholic Church," investigated the stories and pronounced them false, describing

Monk for the record as a mentally unbalanced woman "at present incapable of taking care of herself."

Deranged or not, nativist authors had a major impact on their audience. Brawling erupted between Protestants and Catholics at a Baltimore nativist rally, in March 1834, and worse clashes were reported from Manhattan a month later, on election day. The year's worst anti-Catholic violence, however, was perpetrated in Charlestown, Massachusetts, that August.

The trouble began with a quarrel between Catholic laborers at Charlestown's Ursuline convent and Protestant workers from a nearby brickyard. Following a scuffle, some of the disgruntled Protestants spread rumors reflecting adversely on "the moral purity of the convent's inmates." On the night of August 11, a howling mob attacked the convent, burning it to the ground. A Catholic church on Franklin Street was menaced by a second mob, on August 12, before authorities regained control of Charlestown's streets. Thirteen rioters were arrested, eight charged with capital arson for burning the convent, but all were acquitted. Twenty years after the fact, a committee of the Massachusetts legislature called for reparations in the case, but no money was ever paid.

Nativist agitation increased dramatically after Charlestown, fueled by the unexpected collaboration of Samuel F.B. Morse, inventor of the telegraph. The son of a Charlestown Congregationalist minister who hated other faiths, and Catholics in particular, Morse visited Rome in 1829, professing furious amazement at the Catholic religious ceremonies he observed. When revolutionary violence rocked France a year later, Morse saw an illusory link between those incidents and a supposed Catholic plot to undermine American freedom. Specifically, he blamed Jesuits, "an ecclesiastical order, proverbial through the world for cunning, duplicity, and total want of moral principle." In 1834, writing as "Brutus," Morse convinced the *New York Observer* to publish his rant on the supposed "Foreign Conspiracies Against the Liberties of the United States," released in book form a year later, under Morse's own name. The windy diatribe, which called for creation of a national "Anti-Popery Union," remained in print for years. A new edition was released by the American and Foreign Christian Union in 1841, becoming a fixture of Sunday schools and public libraries over the next decade.

By the time of Morse's call for an Anti-Popery Union, several American cities already boasted chapters of a political organization calling itself the Native Party, whose primary goal in those early days was a move to expand mandatory residence prior to naturalization from five to 21 years. Aside from running candidates for office, the Native Party also resorted to mob violence. A partial list of incidents includes the following:

- ✞ February 17, 1835 — Protestants and Catholics brawl at a nativist rally in New York City.
- ✞ June 26, 1835 — more sectarian rioting in New York leaves one person dead and dozens injured.
- ✞ July 4, 1835 — Nativists and Catholics battle in the streets of Detroit on Independence Day.
- ✞ September 5, 1835 — Protestant rioters attack Catholic immigrants in Florida.
- ✞ January 22, 1836 — Nativist mobs assault Catholic immigrants in Indiana.
- ✞ August 1836 — Protestants riot outside a new Catholic church in Boston, riddling a statue of Bishop Benedict Fenwick with bullets.

- ✞ September 1836 — A nativist street demonstration in Boston includes wild gunfire directed at an effigy of the pope.
- ✞ September 5, 1837 — Catholic rioters in Pennsylvania respond to nativist attacks by trashing a Lutheran church.
- ✞ August 30, 1839 — Ten persons are shot by Pennsylvania militiamen as authorities suppress rioting between German Protestants and Irish Catholic laborers on the Chesapeake and Ohio Canal.
- ✞ October 2, 1840 — One person is killed, with scores injured, during nativist riots in St. Louis.
- ✞ December 8, 1840 — Anti-Catholic rioting erupts at a meeting of New York City's Public School Society.
- ✞ February 16, 1841 — A nativist orator is mobbed by Irish Catholics.
- ✞ April 12, 1842 — Protestant rioters stone the home of a Roman Catholic bishop in New York City, afterward pursuing Irish immigrants through the streets.

The Native Party scored its first significant victory in New York City's 1843 mayoral campaign, with the election of friendly candidate James Harper, and while it would seldom carry another election in the Empire State, the party remained influential for years to come. Elsewhere, the call to arms from nativist orators was more likely to send Protestant bigots racing for the cartridge box than to the ballot box.

Philadelphia was a prime case in point, where the Native Party chose a heavily Irish neighborhood for its street demonstration on May 3, 1844. The march was broken up, but nativists returned three days later, only to be scattered by rain. They adjourned to the nearby Washington Market, where fistfights and shooting broke out in the crowd. At least one person was killed, with over 50 wounded, before the mob besieged a Catholic school. Defenders in the schoolhouse opened fire, killing two rioters and wounding several more in a fusillade that finally scattered the mob. Rioting resumed the next day, with eight killed and 16 wounded after nativists stormed the Irish Kensington neighborhood, torching homes and shops. Two Catholic churches and a parochial school were burned on May 8, before contingents of cavalry and U.S. Marines arrived to clear the streets for good.

At that, Philadelphia's truce was short lived. On July 5, members of the Nativist Party began spreading rumors that muskets were being stockpiled at the Church of St. Philip de Neri. A mob ransacked the church, and while they found no weapons, random violence against Catholics continued for the next two days. Troops were called up a second time on July 8, restoring a semblance of order after skirmishes that left two soldiers dead and 26 wounded, with the untabulated civilian toll substantially higher.

The Native Party ultimately faded from the scene, but its demise signaled no end to the flood tide of anti-Catholicism. More than half a million Irish Catholics immigrated to the States in three years, from 1847 through 1849, and their arrival prompted the creation of yet another "anti-popery union." Organized in 1852, the new secret society called itself the Grand Council of the United States of North America, but its members were better known as "Know-Nothings," for their refusal to divulge the group's secrets. Founder Edward Judson had the right credentials for the job, including an 1849 conviction for inciting riots in New York, which cost him a $250 fine and one year in jail. Back on the streets, unrepentant and ready to fight, Judson published numerous fiery editorials under the pen name of "Ned Buntline." In 1854, the Know-Nothings won a public endorsement from Samuel F.B.

Morse, who praised them for "resisting aggression of foreign influence and its dangerous assaults on all that Americans hold dear." Two years later, the Grand Council claimed chapters in every state, with membership restricted to native-born Protestants with Protestant parents. Its constitution declared that "The purpose of this organization shall be to resist the insidious policy of the Church or Rome, and the foreign influence against the institutions of our country by placing in all offices in the gift of the people, or by appointment, none but native-born Protestant citizens."

To that end, the Know-Nothings rolled up a record of riotous violence surpassing that of the Native Party. Driven to a frenzy by President Franklin Pierce's appointment of a Roman Catholic as U.S. Postmaster General, the Grand Council recruited "Father" Alessandro Gavazzi, a defrocked priest from Italy, to help fan the flames in America. Gavazzi claimed that Pierce himself was a closet "Romanist," collaborating with "Satanical Jesuits" in a plot to overthrow the Constitution. On a swing through Canada, in June of 1853, Gavazzi's fiery speeches touched off rioting in Montreal, where 13 persons died. It was a decent start, but the Grand Council was far from finished. Their final tab includes:

- March 1853 — Know-Nothing rioters, agitated by false rumors of a Protestant child being kidnapped, menace the Catholic church where she is allegedly confined.
- May 1854 — Riots erupt from a nativist street demonstration in Boston.
- May 28, 1854 — Nativist demonstrators march on New York's City Hall, assaulting Irish Catholics along the parade route.

- June 1854 — Know-Nothing rioters attack Catholic homes in Nashua, New York.
- June 4, 1854 — A mob of 20,000 Protestants in Brooklyn, led by a spearhead of 200 Know-Nothings, riot against Catholic immigrants for several hours before national guardsmen restore order.
- June 11, 1854 — Irish Catholics in Brooklyn lob stones at two nativist orators — Rev. John Booth, of the Primitive Methodist Church, and J.S. Orr (a.k.a. "The Angel Gabriel") — touching off another riot by 10,000 Protestants.
- July 1854 — Know-Nothing bombers destroy Catholic churches in Dorchester, Massachusetts, and Sidney, Ohio.
- July 3, 1854 — Rioters storm a Catholic church and destroy several homes in Manchester, New Hampshire.
- July 6, 1854 — Nativist rioters burn a Catholic church at Bath, Maine.
- July 7, 1854 — Another Catholic church is burned, this one at Palmyra, New York.
- July 8, 1854 — Arsonists in Bath, Maine, destroy their second Catholic church in three days.
- July 11, 1854 — Know-Nothings riot in Lawrence, Massachusetts, wrecking 20 Catholic homes, after false rumors spread that an Irish man has defaced an American flag.
- July 13, 1854 — Irish Catholics brawl with Know-Nothings at a nativist street rally in Buffalo, New York.
- August 1854 — Nativist rioters battle to free a Know-Nothing agitator from jail in Charlestown, Massachusetts.
- August 6-7, 1854 — Two days of Know-Nothing riots, precipitated by elections in Louisville, Kentucky, leave 20 persons dead and many others wounded.

August 7-8, 1854 — False rumors of an arsenal at St. Patrick's Church spark two days of rioting in St. Louis, with 10 persons killed, scores injured, and 60 Catholic homes destroyed.

September 8, 1854 — Armed members of the "U.S. Protestant Association" vandalize St. Mary's German Church in Newark, New Jersey, fatally wounding a Catholic bystander.

October 1854 — Nativist rioters take to the streets of Boston on three successive Sundays.

October 25, 1854 — Father John Bapst is stripped, beaten, tarred and feathered, and run out of Ellsworth, Maine, on a rail for advising local Catholics to protest expulsion of their children from local public schools.

November 1854 — Know-Nothing rioters in Williamsburg, New York, menace a Catholic church and terrorize Irish immigrants on election day.

November 15, 1854 — Protestant mobs threaten a Catholic church in New York City.

December 11, 1854 — Know-Nothing thugs surround the home of New York City's mayor, forcing the release of a nativist agitator from jail.

March 20, 1855 — Nativist rioters, spurred by rumors of "captive women" held at Catholic church in Providence, Rhode Island, nearly demolish the chapel before armed Irishmen drive them away.

September 1855 — Know-Nothing bombers score their second hit on a Catholic church in Sidney, Ohio.

September 1855 — Father John Bapst is tarred and feathered again, this time in Bangor, Maine.

- April 27, 1856 — A Roman Catholic church in Ellsworth, Maine, stoned on several previous occasions, is burned to the ground by Know-Nothing arsonists.
- October 8, 1856 — Armed Know-Nothings bar Catholics from the polls in Baltimore, beating several would-be voters, while police watch idly from the sidelines.

Still, it was not all fun and games for the Grand Council, in its bid to save America from creeping popery. Organized as the "American Party" for electoral purposes, Know-Nothings scored sweeping victories where their nativist forebears had recorded only indifferent results. In its first campaigns, during 1854, the American Party elected governors in nine states, along with 62 U.S. senators and 104 members in the House of Representatives, plus many state legislators. Massachusetts was a particular stronghold of bigotry, where Know-Nothings held every elective state office, every seat in the state senate, and all but two of 378 seats in the state house of representatives. At least 24 of the newly elected state legislators were Protestant ministers, and similar gains were seen in neighboring Connecticut. In 1855, the American Party swept state legislatures in Rhode Island, New Hampshire, Maryland, and Kentucky, with strong showings in Virginia, Tennessee, Georgia, Alabama, Mississippi, and Louisiana.

By 1856, Know-Nothings were ready to run for the White House, nominating Millard Fillmore as their candidate in a campaign marred by unmitigated bigotry against Catholics. The Democratic Party, massed behind James Buchanan, took a leaf from the Know-Nothing play book and smeared fledgling Republican hopeful John Fremont by branding him a Jew. When that preposterous assertion failed, the Democrats regrouped and started damning Fremont as a Jesuit! (In fact, he had been raised Episcopalian, but maintained no church affiliation in adulthood.) Caught up in the mudslinging, American Party spokesmen ironically accused Democrats of kissing up to nativist voters, thus poaching on the AP's anti-Catholic preserve. The final vote that November was a grave disappointment to militant Protestants: while polling some 900,000 popular votes nationwide, the American Party won only eight votes in the vital electoral college, watching their man go down to defeat. Four years later, with civil war looming on the horizon, the Grand Council found its strength spent, unable to field a single candidate for office. Anti-Catholicism would return to plague the land, in years to come, but for the moment, there were other menaces to think about. **[See also: Ku Klux Klan]**

Nemeto, Hiroshi: See Eto, Sachiko

Norris, J. Frank

Texas firebrand J. Frank Norris — named by *Christian Century*, in 1924, as "probably the most belligerent fundamentalist now abroad in the land" — was the forefather of modern televangelists, haranguing a national radio audience from his home base in Fort Worth. Roman Catholics and advocates of women's suffrage were among his favorite targets, and Norris was also an ardent Creationist, declaring that "Evolution has our schools by the throat ... destroying the faith of young people in the faith of their Fathers." As pastor of Fort Worth's First Baptist Church, Norris was chastised and barred from Baptist conventions for his public performances, which, in the words of one observer, "had turned a staid church into a Barnum and Bailey circus." Never one to take criticism lying down, Norris fired back at his detractors with both barrels:

> Should the Devil have all the best tunes? Should Beelzebub have all the applause? Why shouldn't people applaud in church? It proves that they are alive. What's the difference between a lot of deacons and preachers in the Amen corner shouting their "Amens" and allowing the congregation to express their "Amens" by clapping their hands? They don't like my sensational methods. They want a nice quiet mealy-mouthed preacher who hasn't the guts to hit sin hard and fight the gang. Join my church. We've got a great fight on here now. But we've got the enemy on the run. They're licked but they're still kicking.
>
> They talk about dignity and solemnity. Poppycock! Too many preachers think that the church should be like a graveyard. By all means, go to the graveyard if you want dignity and solemnity. I prefer life! Sensation is life. Lack of sensation is stagnation! A lot of preachers are so dignified they are petrified. J. Frank Norris will never preach to empty benches. I'll have a crowd if I have to start a dog fight.

And the crowds followed Norris: 6,000 and up in the flesh, for a sermon; 65,000 subscribers to his *Searchlight* tabloid; untold thousands more tuning in to his radio broadcasts. On one occasion, claiming that his enemies had tried to wreck the First Baptist radio station, Norris posted armed guards on the property, with "shoot-to-kill" orders.

Norris's most visible enemies were members of the Fort Worth establishment led by Mayor H.E. Meacham, a Roman Catholic. Rev. Norris, for his part, was an outspoken friend — if not a dues-paying member — of the Rome-hating **Ku Klux Klan**, constantly attacking the Fort Worth municipal government as a cesspool of "graft, Romanism and taxation."

When the city purchased land from the Catholic Church to widen an alley, Norris blasted Mayor Meacham for "pandering" to Rome, but his real gripe seemed to be the city taxes levied on rental income from real estate Norris had tried to hide under the church's tax-exempt umbrella. Finally, on the afternoon of July 17, 1926, Norris was accosted at his church by Elliott Chipps, a 49-year-old lumber dealer and friend of Mayor Meacham. Norris claimed that Chipps threatened his life and reached for a gun, but it was Chipps — unarmed — who wound up dead, drilled with four bullets from Norris's pistol.

Fort Worth's police chief found Norris "just as cool as a cucumber" in the wake of the shooting. "He was the coolest fellow you ever saw." Indicted for murder, Norris stuck by his self-defense story and produced a friendly witness who described Chipps reaching for his empty hip pocket, as if to draw a weapon. As for Chipps, Rev. Norris declared, "It was the hand of God that killed him." Jurors deliberated 45 minutes before acquitting Norris, and he wept with gratitude at the verdict, declaring, "Mine is a sorrow — a Gethsemane — that will go with me to the end of my days." He seemed to have recovered nicely, though, two Sundays after the shooting, when Lloyd Bloodworth, Texas "Grand Dragon" of the KKK, appeared at First Baptist to shake Norris's hand and thank God for his ongoing campaign against Catholics.

Nourani, Sayeed: See Bashir, Mohammed

Nuske, Matthew

Ralph Vollmer was a man with problems in January 1993. Raising hogs in the Australian outback was hard enough on the 55-year-old rancher, but the real trouble came from his wife Joan, six years his junior. Many men complain about their wives, but Ralph could put them all to shame. Joan Vollmer was possessed by demons, he averred, which made her shout obscenities and gambol in the fields stark naked, in full view of passing cars and school buses.

At first, Ralph tried to cope with Joan's behavior on his own. He lashed her to the bed, but she escaped. Next time, he left her in the basement, with a heavy armchair pinning down the trap door, but she raised such hell downstairs that Vollmer could not sleep. Most people, in that situation, would consult a psychoanalyst, but farmer Ralph turned to his Bible. Chapter nine of *Matthew* described Jesus casting devils out of two possessed unfortunates, projecting the evil spirits into swine.

The pig farmer knew what he had to do.

Leah Clugston, age 77, was Antwerp, Australia's resident exorcist — or one of them, at any rate. With several of her cronies, she had been expelled from Rev. Roger Atze's Lutheran Church months earlier, for diagnosing "possession" in cases that ranged from mental illness to the common cold. Since then, she had organized her own Charismatic Church, instructing her disciples in the art of exorcism and conducting numerous such rituals herself.

As luck would have it, Clugston was recuperating from a particularly rigorous exorcism when Ralph Vollmer called her for help, on the night of January 21, but she alerted two of her surrogate demon-fighters, 31-year-old Lisa Reichenbach and 29-year-old David Klinger. The pair were veterans of some two dozen "cleansings," and they agreed with Vollmer that his wife was possessed — by ten different demons, in fact. They prescribed prayer and paddling, but when a week of beatings failed to drive the demons out of Joan, they called for backup.

Matthew Nuske, 23 years old, made an unlikely savior. He worked full-time at a slaughterhouse, in nearby South Warandyte, when he wasn't saving souls from Satan, but exorcism was his true calling. One look at Joan Vollmer, and he ordered her bound to the fireplace, nude, while he sent Ralph out to purchase olive oil and all the Glad Wrap he could find. The oil, Nuske explained, was to anoint God's chosen warriors, while the Glad Wrap should be strung around the outside of the house in layers, "to protect us from evil."

What followed was a tragicomic exercise in lunacy. Joan Vollmer raved and sang "ungodly songs" until she lost consciousness from being kicked and beaten by her saviors. When Nuske and Ralph had exhausted themselves, they telephoned Leah Clugston for advice, receiving her assurance that "You've got them on the run. You're nearly there." To finish off the rite, Clugstons sent David Klinger and Leanne Reichenbach back to the pig farm, all four of them kicking Ralph's wife, Vollmer himself slamming a heavy Bible into her face. When she finally died, Nuske consulted his exorcist's handbook and declared, "This condition is quite normal." Winded but winning, the quarter resumed "kicking for the Lord," convinced by Nuske's promise that "a renewed wife will arise from this corrupted, bloody body within two days."

Unfortunately for the lot of them, no resurrection was forthcoming. Leah Clugston visited the farm on February 1, but there was nothing she could do; decomposition had begun, and lifeless Joan defied the "laying on of hands," complete with solemn orders to "arise and walk." Clugston performed the rite three times, without success, before she spied an angel in the corner, warning her to leave the farm as rapidly as possible.

The next call went to Rev. Atze, who viewed the grisly scene and promptly called police. Ralph Vollmer and his four would-be saviors were charged with manslaughter in September, but a local magistrate — perhaps influenced by Clugston's one-sided conversations with God on the witness stand — found insufficient grounds to hold the five for trial. The public prosecutor's appeal of that judgment was upheld with respect to Vollmer, Nuske, Reichenbach, and Klinger. Tried before Judge Thomas Crossley, in October 1994, the four exorcists were convicted and sentenced to prison.

Order, The: See "Christian Identity" Movement

Order II, The: See "Christian Identity" Movement

Order of the Solar Temple

Luc Jouret made an unlikely messiah. Born of emigrant parents in the Belgian Congo, in 1947, he returned to Belgium as a young man and served in the army, before going on to medical school at the Free University of Brussels. Jouret earned his medical degree in 1974, and while he first planned to specialize in obstetrics, an unexpected change of heart directed him into homeopathic medicine. On the side, he dabbled in mysticism, developing a special fascination with the Knights Templar. **[See: Inquisition]** Jouret went so far as to join an occult group, the Renewed Order of the Temple, which mingled neo-Nazi racism with muddled Templar philosophy. Rising through the ranks of the Renewed Order,

Jouret was near the top when a power struggle in the mid-1980s led him to defect.

Moving to Switzerland with a small band of disciples in tow, Jouret founded his own International Chivalric Order Solar Tradition — known as the Solar Temple, for short. The new group soon absorbed a smaller mystical society, the Foundation Golden Way, run from Geneva by aging millionaire Joseph DiMambro. Pooling their resources, Jouret and DiMambro produced a new theology of sorts, with chapters in Switzerland, France, and Canada. They seemed to worship nature, waxing eloquent about man's rape of the environment, but cult doctrines leaned heavily on submission and paranoia. Recruits paid heavy dues, ranging from $50 per week at the lowest level, to $150 for the middle-ranking "Club Arcadia," and $150 weekly for members of the ultimate "Golden Circle."

Temple rituals were admittedly peculiar, including sessions wherein members wore plastic bags over their heads, while confessing their sins against Mother Nature, but the group still drew an upscale group of recruits, including affluent businessmen and a handful of government employees. Jouret was tapped for a series of inspirational lectures to Quebec businessmen in 1988 and '89, but time was already running out for the latter-day Templars.

It was in Quebec, spawning ground of **Roch Theriault** and his "Ant Hill Kids," that the Solar Temple first ran afoul of the law. Joe DiMambro had served six months for a Canadian fraud conviction, back in 1972, but that indiscretion was long since forgotten. Now, in 1993, Quebec authorities had the Solar Temple under surveillance for suspected weapons violations, capped by an arrest involving silencers, in which Jouret pled guilty and paid a $750 fine. There were other complaints, as well — including one from a defector who declared that he had given half a million dollars to the cult before he split, reporting that "Jouret thinks he's Christ." Increasingly, authorities were interested in Temple bank accounts — reportedly hoarding some $90 million in several European countries — and Jouret lectured his disciples endlessly upon the coming persecution. Letters to the press complained of "relentless" government investigations, while Jouret and DiMambro hinted at the possibility of a suicide solution, à la the **People's Temple** in Guyana. "Death," Jouret advised his captive audience, "can represent an essential stage of life."

The end came on October 5, 1994. The first alarm was raised by a farmer at Cheiry, 50 miles northeast of Geneva, when he noticed flames leaping on a hilltop near his home. Firefighters burst into the house to find its owner, 72-year-old Albert Giacobino, shot dead on the floor. Inside a nearby barn, untouched by flames, they found a chapel done up all in red, with a mystic pentagram on the floor and a huge, Christ-like portrait of Luc Jouret overlooking the pulpit. Sprawled out on the floor, in a tidy starburst pattern, were 23 lifeless members of the Solar Temple, including ten men, 12 women, and a 12-year-old girl. Roughly half the dead had plastic bags over their faces, several had their hands tied, and all had been shot repeatedly in the head — some as many as eight times. Three rifles were found at the scene, but all 52 shell casings had been fired from a .22-caliber pistol, nowhere to be found. In a final macabre touch, empty champagne bottles were scattered around the chapel, and in an adjacent room with mirrored walls.

Four hours later, an explosion rocked the Swiss village of Grangessur-Salvan, 50 miles southeast of Cheiry. A mile outside town, three adjoining ski chalets were engulfed in flames. The smoking ruins contained another 25 corpses, five of them children, most found dead in their beds. None had been shot, as at Cheiry, but tranquilizers and hypodermic needles were much in evidence — as was the pistol missing from the Cheiry massacre. Days later, two of the charred corpses were identified from dental records as Luc Jouret and Joseph DiMambro.

And still, the carnage was not done. Across the Atlantic, in another ski chalet 50 miles northwest of Montreal, another explosion and fire lit the night. Inside, Canadian police found corpses of two adult couples and a three-year-old girl — the latter with a wooden stake through her heart. Interrogation of surviving Temple members indicated that the girl, whose parents also died at the chalet, had been killed days earlier, in a kind of ritual sacrifice, after cult members mistook her for the infant anti-Christ.

In the wake of the mass murder-suicides, Swiss newspapers and cult investigators received a series of letters explaining why the bloodshed had been "necessary." Some of the dead had not gone willingly, the anonymous writer admitted, and they had to be "gently" killed — for their own good, of course. The letters were signed "Mr. Depart."

The Solar Temple cult was not wiped out in 1994, nor did the transatlantic suicides drive its surviving members from the fold. Reportedly convinced that self-inflicted death would send them to a paradise called "Sirius," in outer space, another 16 cultists took their own lives in December 1995, their corpses found in the smoldering remains of a burned-out house near Grenoble, France. Fifteen months later, outside the rural village of Saint Casimir, Quebec, 37 miles southwest of Quebec City, five more Solar Temple devotees went up in flames, their house rigged with exploding propane tanks. Authorities responding to the fire found three dazed teenagers, apparently drugged, staggering around the yard, close by the blazing funeral pyre. Inside the house, their parents lay dead, along with three other adults. Four of the bodies were laid out on an upstairs bed, arranged perpendicular with their feet touching, to form the sign of a cross.

Otomo, Yoko: See Eto, Sachiko

Park Soon Ja

Thirty-two people, including several children, were found dead in a Seoul, South Korea, factory on August 29, 1987, police declaring their suspicions of a suicide pact linked to a religious cult. The factory's owner and identified leader of the nameless cult, Park Soon Ja, was among the dead. As it happened, police had been searching for Park beforehand, in connection with charges that she had swindled $8.7 million from several of her followers. Traces of poison were found in some of the bodies, and most of the victims were found with their hands and feet tied, suggesting that their deaths may not, in fact, have been voluntary.

Peiris, Matthew George Frederic

Matthew Peiris was born in Ceylon — now Sri Lanka — and moved to England as a young man, training for the Anglican priesthood. Ordained in 1952, he soon became a deacon at St. Albans, then a full-fledged priest at the church of St. Francis of Assisi, finally rising to the post of curate at Hatfield Hyde, in Hertfordshire. It was, if not a meteoric rise, at least respectable... but there was something strange about

Father Peiris, all the same. When preaching, Peiris said, he had a way of lapsing into a trance at will, once displaying stigmata on his palms which, in his words, "make me a saint." Peiris also claimed the divine power to heal and cast out evil spirits, incorporating stylized exorcisms as a regular after-hours service.

Conservative Anglicans caught a break when Father Peiris pulled up stakes and moved back to Sri Lanka, at age 60. There, he soon met attractive, 27-year-old Darlene Ingram, desperately job-hunting since husband Russell had been laid off, in 1976. Father Peiris hired her as a secretary, and soon made her his mistress as well. He went even farther, helping Russell Ingram find work at a local newspaper. Both Ingrams attended St. Paul's, where Peiris was the vicar, and they often turned up at Peiris's regular Thursday-night exorcisms.

In addition to his healing powers, Father Peiris soon displayed an aptitude for predicting the future. In April 1978, he announced that Russell Ingram appeared to be ill, although the man in fact felt fine. Two months later, when Russell collapsed at his home, Darlene chose Father Peiris to care for him, rather than consulting qualified physicians. Ingram was ill for 17 days, and unconscious for 20 hours, before Father Peiris took him to the hospital, and even there he tried to interfere with treatment, advising doctors not to give Russell any glucose injections, since "sugar is bad for him." Ingram recovered enough to go home with Darlene and Father Peiris on July 14, but he was back in the hospital four days later, dead within three hours of arrival. His passing was attributed to hypoglycemia (unnaturally low blood sugar) causing irreversible brain damage.

On January 31, 1979, Father Peiris's wife lapsed into a coma at home, and hypoglycemia was again diagnosed. Peiris lied to the doctors, neglecting to inform them that his spouse had been ill for several days before he brought her in. There was no helping her at that point, and she died on March 19, without ever regaining consciousness.

The game had gone too far, by then. Peiris's adult son recalled his father buying large numbers of Euglucon tablets — then available without prescription — which are used, in small doses, to reduce excess blood sugar levels. Taken in excess, Euglucon is fatal, and Russell Ingram's father now remembered watching Peiris feed his son a handful of pills, explaining that they were prescribed by a doctor. It was yet another lie, and all detectives needed to file murder charges against Peiris and Darlene Ingram, in May 1979.

The trial, beginning after much delay in December 1983, was something of a sideshow, Father Peiris resplendent in his white cassock and large crucifix, while his lover wore a stylish white sari. The proceedings dragged on for 163 days, a panel of three judges finally convicting both defendants on murder charges and sentencing both of them to hang. Appeals of the conviction were rejected, but their sentences were later commuted to terms of life imprisonment.

"People's Temple"

The charismatic leader of America's most deadly cult to date was Indiana born in 1931, the son of an alcoholic Ku Klux Klansman and a self-styled mystic fortune teller. Jim Jones learned racism early on, from his old man, but he was equally entranced by his mother's fanciful tales of imagined meetings with African pygmies and South American headhunters. Somewhere along the way, he also became obsessed with religion, learning to quote long Bible passages from memory by age eight; at 12, he was already preaching to congregations of younger children, spicing the services up with "faith healing" of stray animals. Married by age 18, to a nurse four years his senior, Jones fathered a son in 1959 and named him Stephen Gandhi Jones. Years later, in defiance of his upbringing, he would adopt a black child and two Asians.

It was a rocky road for Jim Jones, starting off as a Methodist minister in conservative Indianapolis. His white congregation objected to the number of blacks he was converting, and some were frankly skeptical of his alleged meeting with God on a train ride to Philadelphia. Defrocked by the Methodists in 1954, Jones opened his own Community National Church in an abandoned synagogue, later renamed the People's Temple Full Gospel Church. His flock was poor, but "Father" Jones made up the difference, selling imported monkeys at $29 a head to support a soup kitchen, a thrift shop, and two nursing homes. On the side, he also joined the Communist Party, but kept that news under his hat when his church merged with the larger Disciples of Christ.

The new affiliation with one of America's largest denominations, coupled with his popularity in the ghetto, won Jones an appointment to Indy's Human Rights Commission in 1961. He paid lip service to Martin Luther King, Malcolm X, and the anti-war movement, and made a pilgrimage to Father Divine's Peace Mission in Philadelphia. There, he studied at the feet of the master, learning to "heal" in the grandiose style that soon had supplicants coughing up chicken livers and claiming they were cured of cancer. Working his "cash crop" to the hilt, Jones hired makeup artists to age young mothers, then brought them to his church in wheelchairs, nursing infants they had allegedly borne in old age, through "Father's" blessing.

By 1965, Jones was ready for a larger audience. His black Cadillac led a caravan of cars and minibuses west to California, where he eventually put down roots in San Francisco's depressed Fillmore district. Within a decade, his flock had grown to the point that Mayor George Moscone took notice, appointing Jones to a seat on the city's housing board. Jones used his post to dole out jobs among the faithful, reinforcing his image as a divine provider, tightening his grip on a congregation that doubled, then tripled in size.

At the same time, "Father's" antics were increasingly bizarre. He reeled off angry sermons, sometimes brandishing a Bible overhead, then dashing it to the floor as he shouted, "Too many people are looking at *this*, and not at me." In April 1968, when Dr. King was killed, Jones staged a fake attempt upon his own life, staggering to the pulpit one morning with chicken blood smeared on his face and clothes, claiming he'd been shot, then feigning a "miraculous" recovery while his audience wept and cheered. In 1973, Jones was arrested due to charges levied by an undercover police officer in a porno theater, but the charges were subsequently dismissed in a dispute over the arrest's legality. By that time, he was also snorting coke behind the scenes, demanding sexual abstinence from his flock while he collected a personal harem of nubile young girls — always white. Married members of the congregation needed "Father's" approval for sexual intercourse, and children were kept from their parents as much as possible, by Jones's order. Would-be dissenters were shadowed by an elaborate spy system within the People's Temple, while Jones employed a cosmetician to enhance his imagined resemblance to Elvis Presley.

Still, for all the weirdness and sexual shenanigans, the People's Temple continued to prosper. Jones spent half a million dollars to renovate an old synagogue in the Fillmore district, and continued courting the press. With some 3,000 members in his cult, he claimed an inflated 20,000, and the local media often parroted his figure without troubling to check the facts. Those kind of numbers translate into muscle at the polls, and Jones was considered a force to be reckoned with in northern California, rating a dinner with Rosalyn Carter during the 1976 presidential campaign.

And then, within a few short months, it all began to fall apart. One of "Father's" Caucasian disciples, Tim Stoen, had invited Jones to impregnate Stoen's wife, "with the steadfast hope that the said child will become the devoted follower of Jesus Christ and be instrumental in bringing God's kingdom here on earth, as has been his wonderful father." Jones was happy to oblige, and an affidavit was signed by Stoen acknowledging Jones' paternity, but after all was said and done, the Stoens had second thoughts and filed a lawsuit to affirm their custody. Around the same time, *New West* magazine was preparing an exposé on the cult, and a midnight burglary of the editor's office failed to stop the piece from running in August 1977. It was all too much for Jones, and two weeks later, he decided it was time to seek another Promised Land.

This time, he led his people to Guyana, where the government leased 27,000 jungle acres near the Venezuelan border to the People's Temple. Jones started with 380 pioneers, their ranks soon swelling to 1,000 as the land was cleared and "Jonestown" sprouted from the earth. With all restraints thrown off, Jones gave free rein to his psychosis. By early 1978, the once-friendly *San Francisco Chronicle* was blasting Jonestown as a "jungle outpost" where "the Rev. Jim Jones orders public beatings, maintains a squad of fifty armed guards, and has involved his 1,100 followers in a threat of mass suicide." Jones ordered "white night" drills, in preparation for a raid by "CIA mercenaries," while haranguing his flock with reminders that death was preferable to slavery. That summer, when concerned relatives of the cultists began to call for an investigation, Jones issued a statement that "We will resist actively, putting our lives on the line" to defend

Jonestown. "This has been the unanimous vote of the collective community."

It was mid-November when California congressman Leo Ryan led a fact-finding mission to Jonestown, and the rest is history. During a brief tour of the compound, Ryan's party was approached by 15 cultists who desired to leave. Jones made a show of letting them go, but gunmen were waiting at the airstrip, and all hell broke loose. When the shooting stopped, Ryan, three newsmen, and one cult defector were dead; 11 other persons had been wounded. Back at Jonestown, "Father" called his final "white night" exercise, aides doling out poisoned Fla-Vor-Aid and shooting those members who tried to escape. At the end of their night's work, 914 persons lay dead in the camp, including 276 children.

Phineas Priesthood: See "Christian Identity" Movement

Piper, Thomas W.

The sexton of Boston's Warren Avenue Baptist Church was an odd duck, by any criteria. He always dressed in black, complete with flowing cape, and sometimes twirled his thick mustache as if he were the villain in a low-rent melodrama. He was also fond of liquor laced with laudanum, but kept that vice a secret from the other members of the church. They knew him mainly as the bell-ringer who summoned them to Sunday services and greeted them with smiles as they arrived. None guessed that Thomas Piper also had a deadly, darker side.

His private demon surfaced for the first time on December 5, 1873. That afternoon, a pedestrian in suburban Dorchester spied a curious black-clad figure, long cloak flapping, as he capered in some bushes, acting like a madman. As the passerby approached, the strange man fled, but what he left behind was grim enough. Young Bridget Landregan, a servant girl, had been beaten and strangled to death, her caped assailant interrupted before he could ravish the corpse.

Mary Sullivan was the next to die, ambushed and clubbed to death. Again, witnesses described her killer vaguely, as a man dressed all in black. Another Mary, Tynan, was the stalker's third target, bludgeoned and severely mutilated in her bed. She survived for a year, in an asylum, but never regained sense enough to describe her assailant.

Boston was verging on panic when the caped stalker claimed his last victim, but this time he was caught in the act. Piper lured five-year-old Mabel Young into the belfry of Warren Avenue Baptist, promising to show her his pet pigeons, but all the girl saw was a baseball bat, slamming into her skull. Unknown to Piper, Mabel's aunt had seen him with the child, and she wasted no time in rounding up a makeshift posse. Piper tried to elude them, jumping out an upstairs window and casually strolling back into the church, but would-be rescuers had already forced the belfry door, discovering Mabel's corpse and Piper's blood-stained bat.

In custody, the 26-year-old defendant confessed all four murders, then recanted prior to trial in Mabel's case. The change of tune did him no good, and he was sentenced to die. While awaiting execution, he once more confessed his crimes, this time to Boston's police chief. When he was asked to write the details down, however, Piper turned stubborn. "I'll be hanged if I will," he replied... and so, he was, in 1876.

Posse Comitatus: See "Christian Identity" Movement

"Pro-Life" Movement

There is no mention whatsoever of abortion in the King James Bible. Fundamentalist John Rice, whom Jerry Falwell calls his mentor, freely admits in his book *Abortion* that only one Biblical text (*Exodus* 21:22-25) even refers to the death of an unborn child, that caused when a pregnant mother is accidentally injured by two men fighting. And yet, since the U.S. Supreme Court's decision on *Roe v. Wade*, in 1973, abortion has become the "litmus test" and single-minded focus of religious zealots in America, compelling some to lapse from simple prayer and civil disobedience to brutal acts of terrorism and assassination. On the fringe, indeed, a weird subculture has evolved, where black is white and "pro-life" murders are described as Godly acts, ordained by Jesus Christ.

The so-called "right-to-life" crusade is a rare point of agreement between Protestant fundamentalists and leaders of the Catholic church, for whom abortion is the sin to end all sins, worse even than the use of condoms during intercourse. A National Opinion Research Center poll from 1984 suggests that leaders of the Roman church are out of step with their parishioners — 86% of whom approve abortion if the mother's health is seriously threatened, while 76% approve it in the case of rape and 34% regard abortion as legitimate in *every* case. (This compares to overall ratings of 90%, 80% and 39% on the same three questions for Americans at large.) Nonetheless, Boston's Cardinal Bernard Law declared abortion the "critical issue of this campaign" in 1984, and mobilized the church to force its teachings on the nation as a whole. In 1982 and '84, Philadelphia's Cardinal Krol and Virginia's Bishop Thomas Welsh involved their parishioners in campaigns to defeat several pro-choice candidates, with Pennsylvania congressman Robert Edgar marked as a special target. Bishop Welsh, formerly from Allentown, had set a diocesan precedent by launching voter-registration drives in Catholic churches. When the media inquired about his interest in the ballot box, Welsh said, "Politics is the way we do things."

But not the only way. There have been lawsuits, too, including a bizarre case on Long Island, where relatives of a comatose woman sought to improve her chances of survival by terminating her pregnancy. Outraged "right-to-life" crusaders promptly barged into the family's private business with a legal claim of "fetal guardianship," forcing multiple court appearances and significantly delaying the abortion — which, when finally performed, did lead to the comatose woman's revival. Aside from driving an innocent family to the brink of financial ruin, the zealots achieved nothing on Long Island — except, of course, for reaping the publicity they crave.

Heartless harassment, in fact, is a central feature of the "pro-life" campaign — and one which has resulted in some telling legal setbacks for the zealots' cause. In Michigan, when pickets at a Livonia women's health-care clinic advertised the names of female patients on their placards, they were slapped with a lawsuit for invasion of privacy and saw their defeat upheld on appeal. Dallas physician Norman Tompkins and his wife won a judgment of $8.6 million in damages against Operation Rescue, two other "pro-life" groups, and ten individuals who spent a year harassing them with picket lines, poison-pen letters, and telephone threats. A month later, in November 1995, the U.S. Supreme Court refused to let Operation Rescue off the hook for another $99,000 in legal fees owed to a women's health-care clinic in Sacramento, California. In another Dallas lawsuit, filed against Operation Rescue by Planned Parenthood, the Christian crusaders saw their computers and office furniture confiscated to satisfy a $1 million judgment. The stakes are even higher in Oregon, where Planned Parenthood has filed a $200 million lawsuit against the Portland-based American Coalition of Life Activists and Advocates, alleging a wide pattern of harassment including "WANTED" posters, seeking an injunction against such behavior by two groups and 14 individuals.

Lawsuits aside, abortion is the issue that has driven right-wing zealots to abandon prayers and civil disobedience in favor of all-out terrorism. Between 1977 and 1994, American clinics which perform abortions reported at least 1,624 incidents of violence and harassment, including three murders, two attempted murders, two kidnappings, 35 burglaries, 144 bombing or arson attacks, 66 attempted bombings or arsons, 91 assaults, 178 death threats, 192 stalking incidents, 137 clinic invasions by armed or abusive individuals, and 568 incidents of vandalism. Arson and bombing attacks in 29 states resulted in 51 arrests and 44 convictions, while 23 other cases were closed under the statute of limitations. Nationwide, 52% of America's clinics which perform abortions reported incidents ranging from death threats to bombings and shootings in 1994. The pattern continued in 1995, with three California clinics burned in one week of February, and a Jackson, Wyoming, clinic damaged by arsonists in September.

Vociferous opponents of abortion swear that these attacks are unconnected, individual attempts to halt the "modern holocaust," and yet their rhetoric gives aid and comfort to the snipers, bombers, arsonists, and vandals who appear to think that Christian values — like Mao Tse Tung's definition of political power — issue from the barrel of a gun. Some prominent leaders of the "pro-life" movement include:

- Randall Terry, founder of Operation Rescue in 1987, who has called upon his followers to obey a "higher law" than man's in wiping out abortion clinics. Serving federal prison time for his activities as this is written, Terry claims that he opposes violence, while comparing the "pro-life" campaign to America's revolt against England in 1776. "It meant that real men fired real bullets at other real men who shed real blood," he writes, with a notation that those on the receiving end "died excruciating, real deaths." That's fine with Terry, who believes that "Real confrontation and conflict, real courage and sacrifice, real blood, sweat and tears are needed to restore liberty." In a newspaper column written from prison, Terry described a series of "pro-life" murders in Florida as "deplorable" but "inevitable," adding: "God only knows what horrors await us if we do not bring a swift end to the murder of innocent children *[sic].*"

- Rev. Michael Bray, pastor of the Reformation Lutheran Church in Bowie, Maryland, who named one of his children after a convicted clinic bomber doing time in Texas. As editor of the *Capitol Area Christian News*, Bray raised money by selling bumper stickers that read EXECUTE ABORTIONIST-MURDERERS. His book, *A Time to Kill?,* justifies vigilante action against clinics which perform abortions, and he has supported convicted murderer Paul Hill's declaration of all-out war on abortionists by saying, "I defend the position ... as distinct from advocating it." In fact, Bray is on record as saying that "[a]nyone who truly believes that the slaughter of children is what we have with abortion could go out and shoot an abortionist." Pressed for an answer as to whether *he* would kill a doctor on his own, Bray said, "I can never say I never would, but I have no plans to. The only legitimate reason not to do it is lack of the call." He *would* bomb clinics, though, and served nearly four years in prison during the 1980s, on a conviction for conspiracy to bomb ten targets in Maryland, Delaware, Virginia, and the District of Columbia. One issue of Bray's newspaper carried the following item: "Grand Rapids, Mich. One week following a stink bomb attack, the Planned Barrenhood office in this city was sprayed with gunfire. About fifteen shots from a handgun brought $20,000 in damages. Now $20,000 divided by fifteen equals $1,333.33 per bullet. We commend the stewardship of resources."

◆ Rev. David Trosch, a Catholic priest from Mobile, Alabama, suspended by the church for his extremist views in 1993, who declares that murderer Paul Hill "deserves a medal of honor" for shooting a physician and his bodyguard in Florida. He also lied to the press about knowing Hill, denying an acquaintance when they had, in fact, protested at clinics together. As founder of the ironically named Life Enterprises Unlimited, Trosch finds the murder of abortionists "not only justifiable, but morally obligatory." "If one hundred doctors were killed," he declares, "it would put the abortion industry out of business." Nor is his field of targets limited to doctors who perform the surgery in question. Rather, Rev. Trosch predicts that anyone who *advocates* abortion, including the U.S. President and his staff, "will be sought out and terminated as vermin are terminated." Of course, such statements should not be construed as part of a conspiracy. "There's no plan," Trosch insists. "This is a very strictly personal moral issue with everyone who has acknowledged that abortion is murder." In 1993, around the time of his suspension from the church, Trosch made national news when his cartoon of a doctor with a gun at his head, captioned "JUSTIFIABLE HOMICIDE" was rejected by the *Mobile Press Register*. A Mobile abortionist was murdered by persons unknown six months later, but detectives blamed a bungled burglary. Defiant in his exile from Catholicism, Trosch proclaimed that full-scale war might be required to rid the county of clinics which perform abortions. "It doesn't end," he said. "Not until the Constitution is revised to protect the unborn from the moment of conception. Morally, it cannot end."

- Donald Spitz, a one-time field director for Operation Rescue and leader of Pro-Life Virginia, who gained national attention after signing assassin Paul Hill's petition describing the murder of abortionists as "justifiable homicide." Spitz was converted to radical Christianity in the late 1960s, while strolling through San Francisco's Tenderloin district, when he heard a voice "which I perceived to be the voice of God." Spitz was one of the first "pro-life" activists to voice support for double-murderer John Salvi, declaring that if Salvi gunned down Massachusetts clinic workers "to defend the lives of unborn babies, it's justifiable, it's moral, it was a righteous act." Furthermore, in Spitz's view, Salvi's rampage represents "an evolution of consciousness to the realization that babies are dying ... and writing your congressman is a waste of time." To Spitz, any "pro-life" activists who denounce the killing of doctors "are cowards who are condemning the babies." Despite such tough talk, however, Spitz is prone to weasel in the crunch. "I have no intention of doing any illegal activities," he told the press in 1995. "It's never crossed my mind."
- William Cotter, spokesman for Operation Rescue in Boston and another supporter of crazed gunman John Salvi. In Cotter's view, "The blame [for Salvi's murder of two clinic employees], if it belongs anywhere, belongs with those who deny the truth about abortion."

- Andrew Burnett, co-founder of the American Coalition of Life Activists, organized for zealots willing to "at least consider more aggressive action than the tactics of civil disobedience." In January 1995, the ACLA staged a "March for Life" in Washington, D.C., where activists passed out a "Deadly Dozen" list of targeted abortionists, complete with addresses and phone numbers. Of course, Burnett denies it was a hit list. "We're asking people to call, write, and pray for these men," an ACLA field director told reporters, "that they would turn away from killing unborn people." Not that Burnett opposes killing doctors, mind you. As a signer of Paul Hill's "justifiable homicide" petition, he has declared that, "Violence isn't always wrong. It isn't always wrong to kill." Arrested more than 50 times at various clinics, by 1995 Burnett owed an estimated $1 million in damages to those he has harassed. In his spare time, he publishes a magazine, *Life Advocate*, along with Rev. Bray's manifesto for murder, *A Time to Kill?*
- Michael Dodd, a Kansas "pro-life" activist jailed in 1991, for his leadership role in riotous protests at clinics in Wichita, and another signer of Paul Hill's "justifiable homicide" petition. Lacking the courage of his convictions, Dodd waffles on the nature of his association with Hill. "He got my number from someone," Dodd told reporters in 1994. "He was looking for strategically placed leaders in the pro-life movement. I said, 'Hey, I'll make the sacrifice.' " Dodd still denies any threatening intent, however. "I've been telling people it's a statement of belief rather than an endorsement," he proclaims. "I would never consider doing anything like that myself."
- Dave Leach, proprietor of a Des Moines music store and publisher of a modest "pro-life" newsletter, whose signa-

ture also found its way onto Paul Hill's petition. "Somehow I got on his list," Leach recalls, "and he asked if I would allow my name to be added. If you'll look at how carefully crafted the sentences are, the logic is irrefutable. As disturbing as the conclusion is, I could not justify turning him down." All in the name of Christian brotherhood, of course.

- Rev. Matthew Trewhella, a convicted arsonist, cofounder of Missionaries to the Preborn, and a national committee member of the extremist U.S. Taxpayer's Party (USTP), described by spokesmen for Planned Parenthood as part of a nationwide conspiracy to terrorize clinics which perform abortions. In May 1994, Operation Rescue's Randall Terry appeared at a USTP rally in Wisconsin, where video cameras captured his proposal for a special training school to "raise up militant, fierce, unmerciful men and women — particularly men." Trewhella followed Terry to the pulpit with a suggestion that individual Christian churches should form their own "militias" for paramilitary action. "This Christmas," he declared, "I want you to buy each of your children an SKS rifle and 500 rounds of ammunition." In case anyone missed the point, another speaker at the meeting, radio "personality" Jeffrey Baker, warned the audience that "patriotic Christian men and women" must abandon "the policies of appeasement, as opposed to standing up and saying abortionists should be put to death." A month after that gathering, Trewhella and 20-odd members of his "ministry" were observed participating in firearms training at the rural farm of disciples Robert and Mary Briedis.
- Rachelle ("Shelley") Shannon, an Oregon "pro-life" activist sentenced to ten years in prison for the August 1993 attempted murder of Dr. George Tiller in Wichita, Kan-

sas. From jail, she wrote to clinic gunman Michael Griffin, in a Florida prison, proclaiming that "I know you did the right thing. It was not murder. You shot a murderer. It was more like anti-murder." In October 1994, Shannon was hit with 30 more felony counts, based on her role in a conspiracy to burn women's health-care clinics in California, Idaho, Nevada, and Oregon. That case was settled with her guilty plea on six arson counts, in June 1995.

- John Burt, a former leader of the **Ku Klux Klan** in Florida, now state director of Donald Treschman's Rescue America, who claims presently to reject "the Klan's violence and racial bigotry." Still, in Burt's view, "fundamentalist Christians and those people [the KKK] are pretty close, scary close, fighting for God and country. Some day we may all be in the trenches together in the fight against the slaughter of unborn children." Asked what he would do to close clinics which perform abortions in America, ex-Klansman Burt replies, "Whatever it takes."

Indeed, the merger of "pro-life" forces with groups of the paramilitary racist fringe is neither recent nor surprising. One of the movement's favorite intimidation tactics, issuance of "WANTED" posters in the name of prominent abortionists, began with North Carolina's White Patriot Party (formerly the Confederate Knights of the KKK) in 1985, when the following item was published in *The Confederate Leader*:

> Jew abortion king, Bernard Nathanson, of New York City, was tried, convicted, and sentenced to death by hanging by a fair and unbiased judge and jury of the White Patriots on May 19 at Siler City, North Carolina. Nathanson was convicted of 55,000 counts of first-

> degree murder, treason against the United States of America, and conspiracy to commit genocide against the White Race.

Further west, the Aryan Nations' computerized "Liberty Net" advises that "Periodic disruptions of these murder parlors can only slow down the real holocaust!!!!!" Aryan Nations members are urged to join the "pro-life" movement with the advice that "It's part of our Holy War for the pure Aryan Race." Operation Rescue's Randall Terry is quick to allege that Jewish doctors perform a disproportionate number of abortions in America, while Nazi Tom Metzger is more direct. "Almost all abortion doctors are Jews," Metzger claims. "Abortion makes money for Jews. Almost all abortion nurses are lesbians. Abortion gives thrills to lesbians. Abortion in Orange County is promoted by the corrupt Jewish organization called Planned Parenthood... Jews must be punished for this holocaust and murder of white children along with their perverted lesbian nurses." Members of the neo-Nazi skinhead American Front have joined Operation Rescue and the Advocates for Life Ministries in their clinic blockades, while Dixie's Christian Knights of the Ku Klux Klan describe "Jewish-engineered legal abortion" as "one of many tools used to destroy the white race." In Florida, during August 1994, the militant Templar Knights of the KKK organized a rally in support of clinic murderer Paul Hill.

The Florida scenario, in fact, is especially instructive as to how "pro-life" zealots cooperate in acts of terrorism while denying any part in a conspiracy. Don Treschman's Rescue America published its first WANTED poster on Pensacola abortionist Dr. David Gunn in 1992, including Gunn's photograph, home address, telephone number, and daily itinerary. A short time later, John Burt recruited would-be activist Michael Griffin into the Florida chapter of Rescue America and put him to work as a volunteer at "Our Father's House," Burt's home for unwed mothers. On Sunday, March 7, 1993, Burt and Griffin went to church together, Griffin praying aloud "that [Dr. Gunn] would give his life to Jesus Christ." Three days later, Griffin ambushed Dr. Gunn outside the Pensacola Women's Medical Services clinic, pumping three bullets into his back and killing him instantly. (The clinic had twice been bombed, in 1984 and '86, with another foiled attempt in 1988. The first bomb was accompanied by a note, calling it "a gift to Jesus.") Griffin's attorneys tried for an insanity defense, over their client's objections, claiming John Burt had driven Griffin mad with his harangues and graphic photos of aborted fetuses. Unimpressed jurors convicted Griffin of first-degree murder, but Burt remained optimistic. "No babies will die for the next three or four weeks," he told newsmen, in the wake of Dr. Gunn's murder. "It's something good coming out of something bad."

In fact, Burt and company were already working overtime to target Dr. Gunn's successor. One member of the Rescue America surveillance team was Paul Hill, ex-minister of the Presbyterian Church in America and the Orthodox Presbyterian Church, whose writing credits included a pamphlet titled *Should We Defend Born and Unborn Children with Force?* In the wake of Dr. Gunn's murder, Hill organized a group called Defensive Action and joined Rev. Michael Bray in composing the now-infamous "Defensive Action Declaration." That document, ultimately signed by 30-odd "pro-life" crusaders nationwide, described Dr. Gunn's slaying as "justifiable homicide" and further proclaimed: "We the undersigned declare the justice of taking all godly action necessary to defend innocent human life, including the use of force... We proclaim that whatever force is legitimate to defend the life of a born child, is legitimate to defend the life of an unborn child."

Back in Pensacola, that meant stalking Dr. John Bayard Britton, who was filling in for Dr. Gunn. As soon as Britton was identified, Rescue America produced another WANTED poster, with the alleged aim of "exposing him for the butcher that he is." In February 1994, Dr. Britton found a note at his house, asking, "What would you do if you have five minutes left to live?" Rev. David Trosch joined Paul Hill in demonstrations at Dr. Britton's clinic (while denying that the two of them had ever met), but such action was too mild for Hill. On July 29, 1994, this "man of God" was waiting with a shotgun when 69-year-old Dr. Britton left the Ladies Center clinic, accompanied by his wife and a male bodyguard. Firing into their car, Hill murdered Dr. Britton and retired U.S. Air Force Lt. Col. James Barrett, age 74; 68-year-old June Britton was cut by flying glass, but otherwise uninjured in the shooting. At his trial, Paul Hill advanced an absurd defense of justifiable homicide, but jurors saw through the ruse and recommended the death penalty.

"Pro-life" activists, including some in Florida, also share responsibility for the December 1994 rampage of John Salvi III, an anti-abortion fanatic who went on "camping trips" with a right-wing Florida militia group in 1992. On December 30, 1994, the would-be hairdresser and self-described devout Catholic raided two Brookline, Massachusetts, clinics, shouting, "This is what you get! You should pray the rosary!" That said, he opened fire with a semiautomatic weapon, killing two receptionists and wounding five other victims before he fled the area. Unsatisfied with his achievement in the Bay State, Salvi then drove to Norfolk, Virginia, where he fired 23 shots into a clinic often picketed by members of Don Spitz's Pro-Life America faction. At Salvi's arrest on New

Year's Eve, police found him in possession of literature from both Spitz's group and Father Paul Marx's Human Life International, a global organization formed in 1981 with Vatican approval. It came as no surprise, in the wake of Salvi's arrest and indictment, when Don Spitz stepped up to praise him as a Christian patriot. "Why," Spitz asked the press, "is the life of a receptionist worth more than the lives of fifty innocent human babies?" Other zealots camped out on the sidewalk fronting Salvi's jail cell, bearing placards which described him as a "Prisoner of War" and a "Protector of Life." One clergyman, equipped with a megaphone, called out to Salvi, "Thank you for what you did in the name of Jesus." At his trial, defense attorneys claimed that Salvi was insane, obsessed with fears of an impending "economic holocaust" against American Catholics, but Salvi's own Manson-like outbursts in court convinced some observers that he was "obviously playing to the camera." In March 1996, he was convicted and sentenced to life without parole. Salvi died in prison in late 1996, an apparent suicide.

There is no shortage of fanatics in America, where Cal Thomas, one-time public relations director for Jerry Falwell's Moral Majority, declared in 1982 that "if the abortion problem is not solved by legal means, it will be necessary to take some form of radical action." Thousands of zealots have heeded that call in the past 14 years, apparently including Oklahoma "prophet" Willie Ray Lampley, jailed with his wife and associate John Dare Baird in November 1995, on federal charges of plotting to bomb women's health-care clinics, gay bars, and the anti-Klan Southern Poverty Law Center. Another suspect in the same case, still at large as this is written, allegedly told an August 1995 meeting of the Tri-States Militia, held in South Dakota, that "God won't be mad at us if we drop four or five buildings. He will probably reward us."

Q

Quakers: See Capital Punishment

R

Reichenbach, Leanne: See Nuske, Matthew

Religious Wars

Warfare fueled by religious hatred has claimed countless millions of lives throughout recorded history. Extensive volumes could (and have) been written about the wholesale slaughter perpetrated by true believers. The space available permits no more than a brief chronology of holy wars and their combatants, spanning some 2,500 years. (Granted, religion may not have been the sole or even the most important motive in at least some of these conflicts, nonetheless I have compiled this list in good faith and to the best of my ability.) They include:

- ✝ First Sacred War (590 BC) — Greeks battle over the shrine of Apollo at Delphi
- ✝ Second Sacred War (449-448 BC) — Spartan troops join the ongoing struggle for control of Delphi
- ✝ Third Sacred War (355-346 BC) — Thebans and Thessalonians attack Phocis for cultivating fields sacred to Apollo
- ✝ Fourth Sacred War (339-338 BC) — Fighting resumes over sacred land in Greece

- ✞ Revolt of the Maccabees (168-143 BC) — devout Jews in Syria violently resist government efforts to make them adopt paganism
- ✞ Jewish Conquest of Idumea (135 BC) — John Hyrcanus, priest-king of independent Judea, conquers neighboring Idumea and forcibly imposes Judaism on the vanquished Idumeans
- ✞ First Jewish Revolt (AD 66-73) — ultra-orthodox Jewish zealots rise against Roman rule in Syria and Judea
- ✞ Siege of Masada (AD 72-73) — 900+ Jewish zealots defy Roman legions before committing mass suicide to avoid capture
- ✞ Second Jewish Revolt (AD 115-17) — Jewish zealots rebel against Greeks and Romans alike in Cyrenaica (eastern Libya), Egypt, Cyprus, Asia Minor, Judea and Mesopotamia
- ✞ Bar Cocheba's Revolt (AD 132-35) — Jewish insurrection against repressive Roman rule in Judea
- ✞ "Yellow Turban" Rebellion (AD 184-204) — Taoist rebels challenge the Hab emperor in China
- ✞ Mecca-Medina War (AD 624-30) — Muhammad, founding prophet of Islam, leads troops against the pagan Qurayshite natives of Meccas
- ✞ First Byzantine-Muslim War (AD 633-42) — Muslims vs. the Byzantine Empire
- ✞ Muslim Conquest of Persia (AD 634-51) — disciples of Muhammad expand from Arabia to invade the Byzantine and Sassanid Persian empires
- ✞ Second Byzantine-Muslim War (AD 645-56) — religious slaughter resumes as Emperor Constans II tries to recoup losses from the previous conflict

- ✞ Muslim Revolt (AD 656) — internecine warfare between rival Muslim sects in Mesopotamia
- ✞ Muslim Civil War (AD 657-61) — bitter Muslim fighting in Syria creates two rival sects, the Shi'ites and Sunnis
- ✞ Third Byzantine-Muslim War (AD 668-79) — new Muslim invasion of the Byzantine Empire
- ✞ Muslim Civil War (AD 680-92) — Ummayyad Muslims vs. the dissident Kufan sect in a struggle for control of Mecca
- ✞ Fourth Byzantine-Muslim War (AD 698-718) — sporadic fighting drags on between new generations of religious enemies
- ✞ Muslim Revolt (AD 699-701) — Muslim troops battle Afghan rebels in the caliphate's eastern provinces
- ✞ Muslim Conquest of Spain (AD 711-18) — Muslim invaders from northwestern Africa seize territory in Christian Spain
- ✞ First Frankish-Moorish War (AD 718-32) — Spanish Muslims push north of the Pyrenees into Christian France
- ✞ First Iconoclastic War (AD 726-31) — Byzantine Emperor Leo III vs. Pope Gregory II over Leo's opposition to idol-worship
- ✞ Second Frankish-Moorish War (AD 734-59) — Muslim raids into France continue for another quarter-century
- ✞ Fifth Byzantine-Muslim War (AD 739) — Byzantine troops defeat a renewed Muslim attempt at conquest
- ✞ Second Iconoclastic War (AD 741-43) — Byzantine Emperor Constantine V increases persecution of icon worshipers
- ✞ Sixth Byzantine-Muslim War (AD 741-52) — 11 more years of religious carnage

- ✞ Muslim Civil War (AD 743-47) — Abbasids and Shi'ite rebels oppose the ruling Ummayyads in Syria, Mesopotamia, Arabia, and Persia
- ✞ Abbasid Revolution (AD 747-50) — Muslim civil war in Persia
- ✞ Revolt of Muqanaa (AD 775-78) — Shi'ite Muslim rebels rise against the orthodox caliphate
- ✞ Charlemagne's Invasion of Northern Spain (AD 777-801) — France's Christian king assaults Spanish Muslims with such ferocity that some Basque Christians are moved to oppose him
- ✞ Seventh Byzantine-Muslim War (AD 778-83) — Muslim invaders suffer thousands of casualties in a series of annual raids
- ✞ Eighth Byzantine-Muslim War (AD 797-98) — Muslim forces launch new attacks and demand tribute payments
- ✞ Ninth Byzantine-Muslim War (AD 803-9) — Emperor Nicephorus I breaks a standing treaty with his Muslim enemies
- ✞ Muslim Civil War (AD 809-13) — Muslim dissidents rebel against the ruling Abbasid caliphs
- ✞ Shi'ite Rebellion (AD 814-19) — Shi'ite Muslim extremists rise against the dominant Sunnites, effectively dividing the Islamic world into rival armed camps
- ✞ Khurramites' Revolt (AD 816-38) — members of the Kurramite sect attack Muslim forces in Persia and Mesopotamia
- ✞ Tenth Byzantine-Muslim War (AD 830-41) — another series of annual raids by Muslims into Byzantine territory
- ✞ Muslim Sack of Rome (AD 846) — Spanish Muslims loot and burn the holy city of Christendom

- ✞ Eleventh Byzantine-Muslim War (AD 851-63) — constant Muslim raids provoke a new Byzantine offensive
- ✞ Muslim Civil War (AD 861-70) — inclusion of Turks in the ruling caliphate sparks Muslim rebellions in Persia, Turkestan, Mesopotamia, Arabia, and Egypt
- ✞ Paulician War (AD 867-72) — Muslim Byzantine rulers strive in vain to suppress the dualistic Paulist Christians
- ✞ Twelfth Byzantine-Muslim War (AD 871-85) — Byzantium extends its eastern frontier, while Muslims fight among themselves
- ✞ Karmanthian Revolt (AD 899-906) — the Shi'ite Muslim Karmanthians rebel against orthodox rule in lower Mesopotamia
- ✞ Spanish Christian-Muslim War (AD 912-28) — contending religions clash in southern Spain
- ✞ Sack of Mecca (AD 930) — heretical Muslims of the Karmanthian sect loot Islam's holiest city
- ✞ Muslim Civil War (AD 936-44) — Muslim dissidents fight to liberate Syria from a weakened caliphate
- ✞ Muslim Civil War (AD 945-48) — Syrian Hamdanid Muslims resist invading Ikhshidites from Egypt
- ✞ Thirteenth Byzantine-Muslim War (AD 960-76) — Nicephorus II launches a counteroffensive to foil new Muslim incursions
- ✞ Muslim Civil War (AD 976-77) — Hamdanids and Karminthians unite in a futile attempt to defeat Fatimid Muslims in southern Syria
- ✞ Spanish Christian-Muslim War (AD 977-97) — the struggle between Spanish Moors and Christians continues
- ✞ Jewish Revolt in Ethiopia (AD 980) — Gudit, a Jewish tribal chieftaness, leads the seizure of power from the Christian ruling dynasty

- ✞ Fourteenth Byzantine-Muslim War (AD 995-99) — Syrian Hamdanids request Byzantine aid against invading Fatimids from Egypt
- ✞ Spanish Christian-Muslim War (1001-31) — Muslims fight to suppress Christian opponents in Cordoba and Castile
- ✞ Ardoin's Revolt (1002) — Lombards vs. the Holy Roman Empire in Italy
- ✞ Byzantine-Muslim Naval Wars (1030-35) — Muslim pirates ravage Byzantine shipping and provoke military retaliation
- ✞ Hungarian Pagan Uprising (1046) — Slavic peasants violently resist forcible conversion to Christianity
- ✞ German Civil War (1077-1106) — King Henry IV vs. Pope Gregory VII in a struggle for the church in Germany
- ✞ First Holy Roman Empire-Papacy War (1081-84) — deposed German King Henry IV continues his struggle against Pope Gregory VII
- ✞ Bogomil's Revolt (1086-91) — Bulgarian "heretics" are annihilated for resisting the Byzantine Empire
- ✞ Almoravid Conquest of Spain (1086-94) — Berber Muslims vs. Spanish Christians
- ✞ Crusader-Turkish Wars (1100-46) — Muslims and Christians kill time, and each other, in Turkey between the First and Second **Crusades**
- ✞ Muslim Civil War (1102-08) — Seljuk Turks battle rival Muslim groups in Syria and northern Mesopotamia
- ✞ Almohad Conquest of Spain (1146-72) — internecine warfare between opposing sects of Berber Muslims
- ✞ Wars of the Lombard League (1167-83) — Holy Roman Emperors battle Pope Alexander II for religious and political supremacy in Italy

- ✞ Conquests of Muhammad of Ghur (1175-1206) — a founding father of Muslim rule in India suppresses Hindus and Buddhists
- ✞ Saladin's Holy War (1187-89) — Egypt's Muslim sultan launches a jihad to evict Christian Crusaders from Jerusalem
- ✞ Latin Empire-Byzantine Empire War (1204-22) — power struggles in the Balkans and Asia Minor erupt in the wake of the Fourth **Crusade**
- ✞ Danish-Estonian War (1219-27) — Livonian Christians launch a crusade against Estonians of the Eastern Orthodox persuasion
- ✞ Second Holy Roman Empire-Papacy War (1228-41) — struggle for power between Emperor Frederick II and Pope Honorius III
- ✞ Spanish Christian-Muslim War (1230-48) — King Ferdinand III launches a crusade to overthrow Moorish rule
- ✞ Third Holy Roman Empire-Papacy War (1243-50) — Frederick II continues his feud with a new enemy, Pope Innocent IV
- ✞ Crusader-Turkish Wars (1272-91) — Feuding Muslim Turks and pagan Mongols join forces to attack Christian outposts in the Holy Land, Palestine and Syria
- ✞ War of the Eight Saints (1375-78) — Florence leads a coalition of eight Italian states in revolt against Pope Gregory XI, when he attempts to move the Papacy from France to Rome
- ✞ Vijayanagar Conquest of Madura (1378) — Hindu vs. Muslim in India
- ✞ Crusade of Nicopolis (1396) — Pope Boniface IX raises an army to expel Ottoman Turks from the Balkans

- ✞ Portuguese Conquest of Ceuta (1415) — Christian Portuguese oust Muslim Moors from a port on the Straight of Gibraltar, rolling on to suppress Muslim rebellions in Morocco, Algeria, and Tunisia
- ✞ Hussite Wars (1419-36) — persecuted Hussite Protestants take up arms against Catholic oppressors in Bohemia
- ✞ Hussite Civil War (1423-34) — internecine slaughter between Protestant disciples of John Huss, as radical Taborites battle "moderate" Utraquists in Bohemia and Moravia
- ✞ Hungarian-Turkish War (1441-44) — Turks vs. Slavs and Magyars over Hungary's support for a "false Mustafa"
- ✞ Bohemian Civil War (1448-51) — Hussite Protestants vs. the ruling Hapsburg dynasty
- ✞ Portuguese-Moroccan War (1458-71) — Christian kings of Portugal and Castile launch a crusade against Muslims in Morocco
- ✞ Hungarian-Turkish War (1463-83) — the Pope unites Hungary and Venice to oppose Ottoman conquests in Serbia
- ✞ War of the Monks (1465) — internecine struggle between Japanese Buddhist sects
- ✞ Bohemian Civil War (1465-71) — Bohemia's ruling Catholics crush the Hussite Protestants
- ✞ Bohemian-Hungarian War (1468-78) — Pope Paul II and Bohemian Catholics vs. King George of Podebrad
- ✞ Spanish Christian-Muslim War (1481-92) — peace breaks down again between Spanish Christians and Moors
- ✞ Ferrarese War (1482-84) — Pope Sixtus IV incites Venetians to attack rebellious citizens of Ferrara

- ✞ Hungarian-Turkish War (1492-94) — Holy Roman Emperor Maximilian I repels Ottoman invaders from contested territory
- ✞ Portuguese Conquests in India and the East Indies (1500-45) — Catholic Portugal expands its influence in an effort to drive Muslims from the spice trade
- ✞ Spanish Conquests in North Africa (1505-11) — King Ferdinand II launches a crusade against Muslim "infidels"
- ✞ Spanish Conquest of Puerto Rico (1508-11) — Juan Ponce de Leon "civilizes" Arawak natives
- ✞ Portuguese Campaigns against Diu (1509-47) — Catholic Portugal seeks to wrest control of the Arabian Sea from Egyptian Muslims
- ✞ Vijayanagar Wars (1509-65) — Muslims reassert their dominance over Hindus in India
- ✞ War of the Holy League (1510-14) — Pope Julius II organizes a league of Italian states to evict French occupation forces
- ✞ Ferrarese War against the Papal State (1512) — the Duke of Ferrara seeks revenge for his excommunication by Pope Julius II
- ✞ Spanish Conquest of Mexico (1519-20) — Hernan Cortes effectively destroys Aztec civilization
- ✞ Hungarian-Turkish War (1521-26) — Persia and the Holy Roman Empire unite to foil Ottoman advances in the Balkans
- ✞ Knights' War (1522-23) — royal supporters of the Lutheran Reformation battle loyal Catholics in Germany
- ✞ German Peasants' War (1524-25) — Protestant rebels pillage pre-Reformation Germany
- ✞ Spanish Conquest of Yucatán (1527-46) — Cortés and Francisco de Montejo suppress the native Mayan culture

- ✞ First Kappel War (1529) — Catholic vs. Protestant in Switzerland
- ✞ Second Kappel War (1531) — Swiss religious mayhem resumes after a brief truce
- ✞ Spanish Conquest of Peru (1531-33) — Francisco Pizarro crushes Inca opposition to win new converts for Christianity
- ✞ Count's War (1533-36) — Catholic nobles vs. Lutheran burghers and peasants in Denmark
- ✞ First Mogul War against Gujarat (1535-36) — India's Muslim ruler battles Hindu dissidents
- ✞ Spanish Conquest of Chile (1540-61) — Christian *conquistadors* forcibly subjugate more native "heathens"
- ✞ Dacke's War (1542-43) — Swedish peasants rebel against the harsh anti-Catholic policies of King Gustavus I
- ✞ Schmalkaldic War (1546-47) — nine German states form a Protestant alliance against the Holy Roman Empire
- ✞ Portuguese War against Ternate (1550-88) — Catholic Portugal wrests control of the Molucca Islands from Muslim natives
- ✞ Scottish Uprising against Mary of Guise (1559-60) — Scottish Catholics vs. Protestants for ultimate supremacy
- ✞ First War of Religion (1562-63) — French Catholics vs. Protestant Huguenots, sparked by a massacre of Protestants at Vassy
- ✞ Second War of Religion (1567-68) — French Protestants rise against the threat of an "international Catholic conspiracy"
- ✞ Third War of Religion (1568-70) — royal repression of Calvinism sparks more violence between Catholics and Protestants

- ✞ Second Mogul War against Gujarat (1572-73) — the Muslim emperor expands his domain into Hindu-controlled territory
- ✞ Fourth War of Religion (1572-73) — sectarian bloodshed in France resumes following the massacre of 3,000 Protestants on St. Bartholomew's Day
- ✞ Fifth War of Religion (1575-76) — French Protestants gain ground as religious warfare resumes
- ✞ Sixth War of Religion (1576-77) — French King Henry III leads a new crusade against Protestants
- ✞ Portuguese-Moroccan War (1578) — Catholic King Sebastian launches a new crusade against Moroccan Muslims
- ✞ Seventh War of Religion (1580) — sporadic fighting continues between French Catholics and Protestants
- ✞ First Ottoman-Druse War (1585) — Druse Muslims battle Shi'ites and others in Lebanon
- ✞ Eighth War of Religion (1585-89) — Catholics and Protestants divide in support of rival contenders for the French throne
- ✞ Ninth War of Religion (1589-98) — French Catholics enlist Spanish aid against Protestant King Henry IV
- ✞ Druse Rebellion (1600-07) — Druse Muslims and Maronite Christians unite against the Ottoman government
- ✞ Second Ottoman-Druse War (1611-13) — infighting continues between rival Muslim sects in Lebanon
- ✞ Bohemian-Palatine War (1618-23) — Protestant nobles in Bohemia resist imposition of Austrian Catholic rule
- ✞ Thirty Years' War (1618-48) — Protestant forces in France, Sweden, Denmark, the Netherlands, and England oppose the Catholic Hapsburg Empire, based in Austria

- ✞ First Bearnese Revolt (1621-22) — French Catholics vs. Protestant Huguenots
- ✞ Second Bearnese Revolt (1625-26) — violence between French Catholics and Protestants continues
- ✞ Third Bearnese Revolt (1627-29) — continued bloodshed between French Catholics and Huguenots
- ✞ Portuguese-Mogul War (1631-32) — Indian Muslims and Hindus resist expansion of the slave trade by Christian colonists
- ✞ Shimbara Revolt (1637-38) — Japan's Tokugawa shoguns expel Christian missionaries
- ✞ First Bishop's War (1639) — Scottish Presbyterians resist Anglican incursions
- ✞ Second Bishop's War (1640) — Anglican King Charles resumes battle with Scottish Presbyterians
- ✞ Great Irish Rebellion (1641-49) — Catholic natives resist oppression by Protestants concentrated in Ulster
- ✞ Maryland's Religious War (1644-46) — Puritans vs. Catholics in the days before the Toleration Act of 1649
- ✞ First Maratha-Mogul War (1647-65) — oppressed Hindus vs. autocratic Muslim rulers in India
- ✞ Cromwell's Irish Campaign (1649-50) — Protestants vs. Catholics, with Britain eventually seizing two-thirds of the country
- ✞ First Villmergen War (1656) — Catholics vs. Protestants in post-Reformation Switzerland
- ✞ First Covenanter's Rebellion (1666) — Scottish Presbyterians attack Edinburgh to oppose restoration of the Anglican episcopacy
- ✞ Second Maratha-Mogul War (1670-80) — Hindu rebellion against dominant Muslims resumes in India

- ✞ First Mogul-Sikh War (1675-1708) — Muslims vs. Sikhs in northern India
- ✞ Rajput Rebellion against Aurangzeb (1679-1709) — Hindus clash with orthodox Muslim rulers in India
- ✞ Second Covenanter's Rebellion (1679) — repressive measures against the Presbyterian church spark more violence in Scotland
- ✞ Third Maratha-Mogul War (1681-1705) — sectarian bloodshed continues between Indian Muslims and Hindus
- ✞ Third Covenanter's Rebellion (1685) — Scottish Presbyterians rise once again, this time against rumored Catholic incursions
- ✞ Camisard's Rebellion (1702-10) — French Protestants revolt against denial of religious freedom by a Catholic king; persecution continues until 1750
- ✞ Fourth Maratha-Mogul War (1709-16) — India's Mogul emperor recruits Sikh allies against rival Hindu Marathas
- ✞ Second Villmergen War (1712) — strife resumes between Swiss Protestants and Catholics
- ✞ Polish Civil War (1768-73) — Catholic nobles oppose Russian demands of equality for Protestants and Orthodox believers
- ✞ Cretan Rebellion (1770) — Christians on Crete revolt against Muslim occupation
- ✞ Spanish-Algerine War (1775) — Morocco's Muslim sultan fights to expel Spanish Christians
- ✞ Brabant Revolution (1789-90) — conservative Catholics in the area of modern Belgium and Holland rebel against clerical reforms imposed by the Hapsburg Holy Roman Emperor
- ✞ Wars of the Vendee (1793-1832) — a series of five uprisings by Catholics in western France

- ✞ White Lotus Rebellion (1796-1804) — Buddhist dissidents rebel against the ruling Manchu hierarchy
- ✞ Tripolitan War (1800-05) — the American navy retaliates against Muslim pirates in the Barbary States
- ✞ First War of Abd el-Kader (1808-34) — Muslim vs. Christians in Algeria
- ✞ Egyptian War Against the Wahabis (1811-18) — Wahabi Muslims in Saudi Arabia battle Egyptian invaders
- ✞ Cretan Rebellion (1821-22) — Turkish Janissaries slaughter Christians on Crete, prompting violent counterattacks
- ✞ Padri War (1821-37) — Dutch colonists vs. Muslim rebels in Sumatra
- ✞ Irish Tithe War (1831) — Catholics rebel against laws mandating tithes to the Anglican Church
- ✞ First Carlist War (1834-39) — conservative clergy supports Don Carlos in his bid for the throne against Queen Isabella II
- ✞ Second War of Abd el-Kader (1835-37) — renewed Muslim-Christian conflict in Algeria
- ✞ Third War of Abd el-Kader (1840-47) — continued Muslim-Christian bloodshed in Algeria
- ✞ First Sikh War (1845-46) — British colonial troops strive to suppress Sikh opposition in the Punjab
- ✞ Second Sikh War (1848-49) — the British complete their subjugation of Sikhs in India
- ✞ Taiping Rebellion (1850-64) — millions die as Manchu imperial troops seek to suppress Taoist zealots in China
- ✞ Crimean War (1853-56) — Turkish Muslims violently resist Tsar Nicholas I's attempt to "protect" Orthodox Christians in the Ottoman Empire

- ✞ Tukulor-French Wars (1854-64) — Muslim natives clash with French colonial forces in the Senegal River valley
- ✞ "Bleeding Kansas" (1855-61) — Conflict over slavery which preceded the American Civil War, including massacres by religious fanatic **John Brown**
- ✞ Utah War (1857-57) — federal troops suppress polygamy in the face of Mormon **terrorism**
- ✞ Spanish-Moroccan War (1859-60) — Muslim raids on Spanish possessions prompt a declaration of war
- ✞ Muslim Rebellion in China (1863-77) — Muslim tribes in Chinese Turkestan rise against their Manchu overlords
- ✞ Russian Conquests in Central Asia (1865-81) — Tsars Alexander I and Nicholas I subjugate Muslim Turkestan, while opposing native sects fight among themselves
- ✞ Cretan Uprising (1866-68) — Religious mayhem continues between Christian natives and Turkish occupation forces on Crete
- ✞ Tientsin Massacre (1870) — rebellious Chinese kill 18 Christians at a French-run monastery; 16 Chinese are executed in reprisal
- ✞ Second Carlist War (1873-76) — more religious mayhem in Spain after Queen Isabella is deposed
- ✞ Achinese War (1873-1907) — Muslim natives vs. Dutch Christians in northern Sumatra
- ✞ Serbo-Turkish War (1876-78) — Christian inhabitants of Bosnia and Herzegovina rebel against their Muslim Turkish rulers
- ✞ Sudanese War (1881-85) — devout Muslims launch attack on Egyptian puppets of the British in Sudan
- ✞ Ugandan Religious Wars (1885-92) — King Mwanga launches attacks to expel Catholic, Protestant, and Islamic missionaries

- ✞ Italo-Ethiopian War (1887-89) — Sudanese Muslim fanatics, the Mahdists, lead a revolt against Italian colonists
- ✞ Rif War (1893) — Muslim Berbers menace territory held by Christian Spaniards in Morocco
- ✞ Sudanese War (1896-99) — a British-Egyptian expeditionary force expels Muslim resistance fighters from Sudan
- ✞ Holy Wars of the "Mad Mullah" (1899-1920) — puritanical Sufi Muslims seek to expel "infidel Christian" colonists from Somalia
- ✞ Moro Wars (1901-13) — Muslim Moro tribesmen terrorize the Philippines' Christian majority
- ✞ Sanusi Revolt (1915-17) — Sunni Muslim natives oppose French and Italian expansion in northern Africa
- ✞ Rif War (1919-26) — Moroccan Muslims continue their efforts to expel Spanish Christians
- ✞ Druse Rebellion (1925-27) — Druse Muslims rebel against French occupation forces in Syria
- ✞ Indian Civil War (1947-48) — Hindu vs. Muslim in the newly liberated subcontinent
- ✞ Indo-Pakistani War (1947-48) — Pathan Muslims revolt against oppressive Kashmiri Hiny landowners
- ✞ Arab-Israeli War (1948-49) — Allied Arab and Muslim states vs. Israel's new Jewish regime
- ✞ Achinese Rebellion (1953-59) — Muslim rebels vs. the ruling Indonesian government
- ✞ Algerian War (1954-62) — Muslim natives opposing colonial rule by French Christians
- ✞ Sinai War (1956) — Egypt vs. Israel for the Suez Canal
- ✞ Chadian Civil War (1965-90) — Arab Muslims from northern Chad, sometimes assisted by Libyan troops, battle Bantu Christians and pagans from the south

- ✞ Irish "Troubles" (1968-) — sectarian slaughter between Catholics and Protestants highlights a nationalist effort to expel British forces from Northern Ireland
- ✞ Ceylonese Rebellion (1973) — Hindu Tamil minority vs. Ceylon's Buddhist Sinhalese majority, ending with suppression of the rebels and inauguration of a new state (Sri Lanka)
- ✞ Yom Kippur War (also Ramadan War) (1973) — Israel vs. five Arab states
- ✞ Lebanese Civil War (1975-91) — Druse, Sunni, and Shi'ite Muslims wage guerrilla war against the dominant Christian Phalangists
- ✞ Iranian Revolution (1979) — Ayatollah Khomeini's Muslim fundamentalists evict the Shah and institute a strict theocracy
- ✞ Siege of the Sikh Golden Temple (1984) — some 600 persons die in fighting between Indian troops and Sikh extremists in Amritsar
- ✞ "Ethnic Cleansing" in Bosnia (1992-96) — "Christian" Serbs rape and slaughter thousands of their Muslim neighbors; Muslims and Catholic Croats also commit numerous atrocities

[See also: Biblical Bloodshed; Crusades; Mormons; Terrorism]

Renz, Arnold: See Michel, Josef

"Sacrifice Church"

Between January 1911 and April 1912, a night-prowling killer or killers invaded a dozen homes in Louisiana and Texas, attacking black families in their sleep, killing 49 victims with an axe or hatchet. In every case, the murdered sleepers were mulattos or black members of a family with mulatto children, and investigators quickly fastened on a theory that the victims were selected for their "tainted" blood. White racists were never suspected of the crimes, perhaps because the raids were too well-planned and thought out in advance. A black woman, Clementine Bernabet, was jailed on suspicion of murder following the fourth massacre, in Lafayette, Louisiana, but she was still in jail when the next raid occurred, whereupon she was freed by police.

Thus far, the only clue available to homicide investigators was a matter of geography: the killer(s) had been moving westward, from Louisiana into Texas, staging massacres at stops on the Southern Pacific Railroad line. Detectives got their first real break on January 22, 1912, when Felix Broussard, his wife and three children were hacked to death at Lake Charles. This time, the stalker left a note behind. It read: "When He maketh the Inquisition for Blood, He forgetteth not the cry of the humble — human five."

The text was lifted, more or less, from *Psalms* 9:12, and it focused official attention on the tiny "Sacrifice Church," a black sect led by Rev. King Harris, of New Orleans. Police informants spoke of links between the church and certain voodoo operators in the Crescent City, and authorities soon learned that Rev. Harris had delivered a sermon in Lafayette,

Louisiana, on November 26, 1911, mere hours before six members of the Norbert Randall family were slaughtered in their beds. That massacre had prompted the arrest of Clemmie Bernabet, and she surprised police in April 1912, with a confession to the early homicides. While Bernabet admitted sitting in on several meetings of the "Sacrifice Church," she insisted that the slayings were related to a voodoo charm — or *candja* — purchased from a local witch doctor. The charm reportedly insured Bernabet and certain unnamed friends that "we could do as we pleased and we would never be detected." For no apparent reason, they had chosen to test the magic by committing a series of axe murders. Police were understandably dubious, and Bernabet was never sent to trial.

The raids, meanwhile, continued, claiming another eight victims before the hacker made his first mistake, in San Antonio. In the predawn hours of August 16, 1912, the wife of mulatto James Dashiell woke to the pain of an axe shearing through her arm. Her screams put the killer to flight, and while she glimpsed him in the darkness, Mrs. Dashiell could offer no coherent description. Homicide investigators and potential victims waited anxiously for several weeks, until they finally decided that the murder spree was over. New defectors from the "Sacrifice Church" informed police that Rev. Harris preached a militant doctrine of racial purity, and they noted that one of Harris's favorite Bible texts was *Matthew* 3:10 — "And now also the axe is laid unto the root of the trees; therefore every tree which bringeth not forth good fruit is hewn down, and cast into the fire." It was a tantalizing lead, but there was still no solid evidence to link the preacher or his flock with any homicides. The gruesome case remains officially unsolved.

Salvi, John III: See "Pro-Life" Movement

Sand Creek Massacre: See Chivington, John

Schmidt, Hans

Late on the afternoon of Wednesday, September 6, 1913, a rope-bound parcel washed ashore at Woodcliff, New Jersey. When opened, it revealed the upper torso of a young woman, with the head and arms removed, wrapped in a pillow case which still had a manufacturer's label attached. That aside, without teeth or fingerprints, there was little hope of identifying the woman, described by medical examiners as 20 to 30 years of age.

On Sunday, the victim's legless lower torso was beached three miles downstream, at Weehawken. Again, the remains were wrapped in a pillowcase, this one embroidered with a stylish letter A. By the time a third parcel, containing one of the dead woman's legs, was dragged ashore at Keansburg, New Jersey, police were convinced that their victim had gone in the water somewhere along the New York City docks. If nothing else, it was a convenient way of passing the buck.

Detectives in New York went to work on the pillowcase, tracing it to a merchant on Eighth Avenue, who recalled making the sale to a young couple on August 25. Their address, on Broadhurst, was listed as the residence of one Hans Schmidt. Police who searched the flat found themselves in a makeshift butcher's shop, blood spattered everywhere. They also turned up documents identifying the victim as Anna Aumüller Schmidt, married six months earlier to Hans Schmidt, in a ceremony performed by a *Father* Hans Schmidt.

From Broadhurst Avenue, the trail led police to St. Boniface's Church, where Father Schmidt was assigned. They spoke to Father John Braun, who reluctantly untangled the web of deception. For starters, there was only one Hans Schmidt, formerly Braun's assistant priest, now working out of St. Joseph's Church in Harlem. Schmidt had fallen in love with one of his parishioners, and the rest was history, the marriage ceremony either a sham or flagrant violation of Father Schmidt's chastity vows.

Confronted by police in Harlem, Father Schmidt admitted killing Anna, but explained that the orders had come from Saint Elizabeth, his patron. "I received an instruction from on high," Schmidt explained, "to kill her and cut her up. Anna will be a sacrifice of blood and atonement, I was told by the voice." On those orders, he had slit her throat in bed, then dismembered Anna in the bathtub, taking time to drink some of her blood before he raped the corpse, then packaged her remains and dumped them off the Fort Lee Ferry.

Schmidt was clearly headed toward an insanity plea, but further investigation undermined the bid, when detectives turned up yet another flat — this one filled with equipment for printing counterfeit ten- and twenty-dollar bills. They also learned that Schmidt had tried, unsuccessfully, to insure his "sacrifice" for the sum of $5,000 before she was killed. A jury wasted no time in convicting Father Schmidt, and he soon became a burnt offering himself, in Sing Sing's electric chair.

Sekine, Michio: See Eto, Sachiko

Shamburger, Ronald Scott

From all appearances, 22-year-old Ronald Shamburger was the ideal "born-again" Christian. He attended Texas A&M, spent time at the Baptist Student Center on campus, and on September 29, 1994, he had picked up an application to the seminary, following his pastor's urging that he consider a career in the ministry.

Unknown to family and friends, however, Shamburger's righteous facade was coming apart at the seams. Two months earlier, in July 1994, he had been ousted from a church youth program for "questionable behavior" — and that vague accusation barely scratched the surface. In fact, "Christian" Ronald had been burglarizing homes for months around College Station, Texas, stealing cash and credit cards to fuel big-ticket shopping sprees. He often robbed the homes of individuals he knew, for extra thrills, and packed an automatic pistol ...just in case.

One of his favorite break-in targets was the home of Lori Ann Baker, the object of Shamburger's personal obsession since they dated briefly, two years earlier. Ronald invaded her house several times, amusing himself by fondling her lingerie. Lori was at home, asleep in her bed, when Shamburger paid another call on the night of September 29, but she woke and saw his face. Shamburger panicked, drew his gun, and shot her in the head.

From that point on, the deadly mishap turned bizarre. Ronald decided he could save himself by retrieving the bullet, so he fetched a pair of scissors and two steak knives, gouging away at the dead woman's skull. He was still operating when Lori's roommate, Victoria Kohler, returned and caught him in the act. Nearly berserk by now, Ron threw her to the floor and started grilling her: Was she a Christian? Had she accepted Jesus as her personal savior? Did she have a boyfriend? Could she identify Ron to police?

The last one was the clincher. Victoria told Shamburger the room was too dark for her to see his face, and he was foolish enough to believe her. Binding her with duct tape, Ronald finished digging his bullet out of Lori's brain, then forced

Victoria into the trunk of her own car, drove it several blocks away, and left her breathing, while he started back toward Lori's house. His car was there, and Ronald meant to burn the place, to wipe out any fingerprints he may have left.

Ronald set fire to Lori's bed all right, but he was fading in the stretch, his thoughts disjointed and chaotic. By the time he spied his car keys on the bed, beside her corpse, the flames forced him to flee the house. Outside, he sat down on the lawn with gun in hand and waited for the sirens, mumbling to himself.

The murder case was a slam-dunk. Shamburger could not raise $250,000 bond, so he remained in jail until his trial began, in October 1995. Jurors took a short half hour to convict him of first-degree murder, eight hours more to recommend a death sentence, which was promptly affirmed by the judge.

Singer, John

Yet another Mormon spin-off cult was led by John Singer, of Marion, Utah. An LDS fundamentalist who resented modern "corruption" in the church of his ancestors, Singer withdrew his seven children from public school in 1973, constructing his own one-room schoolhouse to provide a curriculum untainted by "worldly" immorality. School officials initially approved Singer's home-study plan, but misdemeanor charges were filed against him when he refused to submit his children for state-required progress tests. By year's end, Singer had been excommunicated from the Mormon Church, but his court case dragged on into 1978, with authorities pushing a strange double standard. On one hand, they finally approved his home-schooling program in 1978, but an arrest warrant was also issued on contempt charges stemming from the original complaint. (No bigamy charges were filed in October 1978, when Singer took his second wife and adopted her three children from a previous marriage.)

The tense situation came to a head on October 19, 1978, when police masquerading as newsmen descended on Singer's rural homestead. Distracted by his chaotic brood, the officers let Singer get the drop on them, withdrawing to "wait for the right time" to stage another raid. They saw their chance on January 18, 1979, invading Singer's property on snowmobiles to surprise their quarry, as he walked to a mailbox a quarter-mile from his house. When the smoke cleared, Singer had been shot to death "in self-defense" — a shotgun blast in the back — and his first wife was under arrest, their seven children delivered to juvenile authorities as wards of the state. (The children of his second wife were handed over to her ex-husband, whose custody order had been held in abeyance by the ten-month siege at Marion.) Belatedly a juvenile court ruled on January 27 that Singer's first wife should be allowed to teach her seven children at home, under the supervision of a private administrator. Despite that precaution, however, the children learned more than their simple "three R's," as authorities would discover ten years later.

Fanatic John Singer was long forgotten by most Mormons in 1988, when survivors of his clan announced that Singer would be resurrected on the ninth anniversary of his slaying by Utah police. If a return from the grave was not impressive enough, they declared, Saint John would also usher in the long-awaited millennium. To pave the way for his return, the cultists bombed a Mormon church at Marion, Utah, on January 16, leaving clues enough for lawmen to descend upon their nearby rural compound. Holed up in the makeshift fortress during 13 days of siege were Singer's widow Vickie, son-in-law Addam Swapp, his two wives (both Vickie's daughters), Swapp's brother Jonathan, John Timothy Singer, and nine children of various ages. The showdown ended with a burst of gunfire on January 28, leaving a state corrections officer dead and Addam Swapp gravely wounded. In May 1988, the Swapp brothers, Vickie Singer, and her son were all convicted on federal charges related to church bombing and the officer's death, with Addam Swapp drawing a prison term of 15 years. Seven months later, a state jury convicted the Swapps and John Timothy Singer on an additional charge of second-degree murder, effectively disposing of one bizarre cult.

Snell, Richard: See "Christian Identity" Movement

Sutcliffe, Peter William

A "harlot killer" who proved rather indiscriminate in choosing victims was Great Britain's Yorkshire Ripper, Peter Sutcliffe. While residing in apparent harmony with his beloved wife — herself a schizophrenic who spent time in institutions — Sutcliffe fancied himself "the street cleaner," waging a five-year messianic war against the female population of England's northern counties. With his ball peen hammer, chisel, and assorted other implements of slaughter, Yorkshire's ripper claimed a minimum of 13 victims killed and seven wounded. In addition to the documented body count, he is believed by some to be responsible for other unsolved murders on the European continent.

The roots of Sutcliffe's homicidal rage are difficult to trace. His family appears to have been torn by dark suspicions, on his father's part, of infidelity by Peter's mother, and the boy's opinion of all women may have suffered in an atmosphere of brooding doubt. As a young man, he found employment with a local mortuary and professed to hear the voice of God while digging graves — a circumstance that did not interfere with his "borrowing" of jewelry from the corpses. In his conversations, easily dismissed as "jokes" by his co-workers at the time, there is a hint of budding necrophilia, more disturbing than the strain of larceny. A favorite outing for the would-be ripper was a local wax museum, where he lingered by the hour over torsos that depicted the results of gross venereal disease. Before his marriage, Sutcliffe frequently expressed his fears of having caught "a dose" from contact with the prostitutes of Leeds and Birmingham.

Sutcliffe's first attacks on women, in July and August 1975, were unsuccessful in that both his victims managed to survive the crushing blows of hammers to their skulls, and the slashes he inflicted on their torsos after they were down. October was a better month for Peter: on the 29th he slaughtered prostitute Wilma McCann, in Leeds, and thus officially began the Ripper's reign of terror.

There seemed to be no schedule for the crimes. On January 20, 1976, housewife/hooker Emily Jackson was bludgeoned in Leeds, her prostrate body bearing 50 stab wounds. Sutcliffe did not strike again for 13 months, attacking Irene Richardson, another prostitute, again in Leeds. He moved to Bradford for the April butchery of Tina Atkinson, another prostitute, found murdered in her own apartment, mutilated after death.

On June 16, the Ripper struck again, but his selection of a victim made the slaying different, more appalling to the populace at large. At 16 years of age, Jane MacDonald was an "innocent," the perfect girl next door, cut down while strolling to a relative's house, almost within sight of home. Her murder put the Ripper on a different plane, immediately serving notice that no girl or woman in the northern counties was considered safe.

Maureen Long was assaulted on the streets of Bradford, in July, but she survived the blows that Sutcliffe rained upon her head. In October, he crossed the Pennines to murder Jean Jordan in Manchester, crushing her skull with 11 hammer strokes, stabbing her 24 times after death. When she had not been found within a week, he would return to move the body and slash it further, making its location more apparent to police.

In January 1978, Sutcliffe killed a prostitute named Helen Rytka in the town of Huddersfield. In April 1979, another "innocent," 19-year-old Josephine Whittaker, was butchered in Halifax. A civil servant, Marguerite Walls, was murdered at Pudsey in August, and 12 days later Sutcliffe slaughtered co-ed Barbara Leach, in Bradford.

In the middle of their manhunt, homicide investigators were bedeviled by a mocking tape and several letters from "the Ripper." Later, with their man in custody, they learned that all were hoaxes, perpetrated by another twisted mind that found vicarious release in toying with detectives. Countless hours were wasted by police and independent searchers, looking for a man whose penmanship and accent bore no resemblance to Sutcliffe's own. The charlatan responsible, suspected in two unrelated homicides, remains at large today.

The Ripper had two more near-misses in October and November, wounding his victims in the towns of Leeds and Huddersfield, respectively. Both would survive their wounds, and Sutcliffe took a year's vacation prior to killing co-ed Jacqueline Hill, at Leeds, in November 1980. The latest victim's mutilations were familiar to police, but Sutcliffe also stabbed her in the eye, unsettled by the corpse's "reproachful stare."

On January 2, 1981, police arrested Sutcliffe, with a prostitute, in one of several areas that been subject to surveillance through the manhunt. Even so, they almost let him slip the net by briefly stepping out of sight to urinate, then dropping the incriminating weapons that he carried underneath his jacket. At the station, Sutcliffe finally broke down after being confronted with the weapons he'd discarded, confessing everything, explaining that his choice of victims had been dictated by God. Detectives noted that their subject seemed relieved to have it all behind him. So he seemed to spectators in court, as well, when he received a term of life imprisonment for 13 homicides and various assaults. (Author David Yallop, in *Deliver Us From Evil*, links Sutcliffe to four additional murders and seven nonfatal assaults, including crimes in France and Sweden.) From Sutcliffe's truck, detectives retrieved a written statement that appeared to summarize the Ripper's twisted view of life:

> In this truck is a man whose latent genius, if unleashed, would rock the nation, whose dynamic energy would overpower those around him. Better let him sleep?

Swapp, Adam: See Singer, John

Taylor, Michael

Michael Taylor and his wife Christine were members of the Christian Fellowship in Ossett, England — an alternative sect which had divorced itself from the Church of England, preferring smallish gatherings in private homes, where members sang hymns, "testified," and spoke in "tongues." It all seemed harmless enough until October 2, 1974, when 31-year-old

Michael began telling his family and friends that he had glimpsed Satan. A day later, he was stopping neighbors on the street, kneeling before them to announce the imminent end of the world. That evening, at a Fellowship gathering, Taylor confessed that he had been seduced by the devil.

Prayers of exorcism were recited over Michael, but they clearly didn't take. Next morning, October 4, he ordered Christine to remove all crosses and Christian literature from their home. A sympathetic friend took the Taylors for a drive in the country on October 5, but that night found Michael violent and irrational. Father Peter Thomas, vicar of St.Thomasí Church in nearby Gawber, was summoned to perform an all-night exorcism, afterward claiming that he had driven a flock of 40 demons from Taylor's body and soul.

Unfortunately, Father Thomas must have missed one. Around 10:00 A.M. on October 6, Taylor attacked his wife bare-handed, ripping out her eyes and tongue, shredding the flesh of her face and leaving her to drown in her own blood. Momentarily sated, he strolled outside to catch some sun — stark naked but for stockings, smeared with blood, Christine's rings on his bloody fingers. A policeman stopped to ask him where the blood had come from, whereupon Taylor informed him, "It is the blood of Satan."

At trial, a battery of psychiatrists agreed that Michael Taylor was insane, perhaps entranced or "brainwashed" by the exorcism he had undergone the night before the murder. Absolved of criminal responsibility for Christine's death, he was consigned to Broadmoor asylum for treatment, rated sufficiently improved that he was cleared for unsupervised visits to his parents' home 18 months later.

"Temple of Love"

Hulon Mitchell, Jr. was an Oklahoma native, the oldest of 15 children in a Pentecostal family, born in 1935. Family members report that Mitchell regarded himself as divine from age three, with claims of mystic calling to "a distinct job" at age seven. After serving in the U.S. Air Force, he earned a bachelor's degree in psychology, but dropped out of law school in 1961 to pursue a religious career. Migrating to Chicago, he joined the Nation of Islam and renamed himself Hulon Shah. By 1967, there were rumors of sexual improprieties and the embezzlement of $50,000 from Muslim coffers, but Mitchell quit the sect before he was expelled. His next move took him to Atlanta, where he was reborn as "Father Michel," operating from a storefront church and preaching that whites are the root of all evil. Sale of "blessed prayer cloths" and similar scams enabled Mitchell to purchase a $75,000 home and two Cadillacs, but storm clouds were gathering once again. By the time his congregation got around to filing suit for fraud, in February 1978, "Father Michel" was long gone.

He surfaced in Miami, traveling as "Brother Moses Israel," attaching himself to the "Black Hebrew" movement, a.k.a. the "Hebrew Israelites." The movement, active in America since the late 19th century, presents a curious mirror image (or photographic negative) of **Christian Identity**, complete with racial bigotry and anti-Semitism, plus strict fundamentalist bans on abortion and any other form of birth control. Mitchell's sermons hailed the coming triumph of a "Great, Good, and Terrible Black God," while branding Caucasians as "the devil, Satan, serpent and beast." Jews were singled out for special condemnation, reviled for worshipping in the "synagogue of Satan." Before long, Mitchell had promoted himself from minister to deity, legally changing his name to "Yahweh Ben Yahweh" — literally "God, Son of God."

Disciples at Yahweh's ghetto "Temple of Love" followed the Black Muslim practice of shunning their "slave names," with all cult members adopting the surname "Israel." Submissive female cultists were sent out to beg on the streets, while Yahweh Ben Yahweh lived in baronial splendor, protected by an elite security unit dubbed the "Circle of Ten." From an estimated 150 disciples in October 1980, he claimed 9,000 in Miami by mid-decade, with temples in 35 cities across the continent. At home base, Yahweh billed himself as "the world's greatest attraction," ranting that "I am the Messiah. I am the word. I am incarnate." Such was Yahweh's economic and political strength, that Mayor Xavier Suarez proclaimed October 7, 1990 as "Yahweh Ben Yahweh Day" in Miami. One month later to the day, the "holy man" and 15 of his key subordinates were indicted on conspiracy and racketeering charges, for promoting what federal prosecutors called a "reign of terror" and an "era of extreme violence."

Though Yahweh/Mitchell would deny it, the trouble seemed to stem from his fascination with swords. He had begun to preach about them in the early spring of 1981, commanding each disciple to "go buy one and sharpen it up." Yahweh would later claim that he was *really* referring to Bibles, but if so, the faithful clearly missed his point. In fact, as indicated by substantive testimony at his trial, Yahweh's parishioners not only purchased swords, but felt they were expected to go out and use them on "white devils" to appease the self-styled son of God.

First, though, there was some housecleaning to do at home. Carlton Carey, a.k.a. "Misha Israel," served as the cult's bookkeeper before he grew disillusioned with Yahweh's financial scams, coming to regard the master as "a cheap crook and a swindler." Private doubts were bad enough, but Carey crossed the line when he led a group of defectors to found a competing sect. The rebels may have taken Yahweh's threat that "heads will roll" as a figure of speech, but they were sadly mistaken. Aston Green, alias "Elijah Israel," was the first to die, decapitated in November 1981, his headless corpse discarded in the Everglades. When Carey and associate Mildred Banks took their suspicions to police, their names were added to the death list, marked by machete-wielding night prowlers who left Carey dead and Banks gravely wounded. Back at the Temple of Love, meanwhile, discipline became increasingly severe, including brutal beatings for those who fell short of their panhandling quotas. In 1983, 22-year-old Leonard Dupree was beaten and kicked to death at the temple while Yahweh looked on, commanding all present to line up and "take a hit."

Outside the fold, Hebrew Israelites used their hardware and muscle to enforce Yahweh's will on the world at large, typically with an eye toward enhancing their leader's wealth and prestige. In May 1986, after some of Yahweh's street solicitors were roughed up by Miami dopers, a cult hit team stormed the offending neighborhood and firebombed several homes. Rumors of an internecine holy war filtered in from various parts of the country — a house bombed in Detroit, a stabbing in Albany, a heretic dismembered and left in a Chicago dumpster. In October 1986, a strike force of 75 Black Hebrews moved to evict tenants from a coveted Miami apartment complex, shooting and beheading two who dared to stand and fight. A suspect held on murder charges in that case identified himself as Neariah Israel, but his more familiar name was Robert Rozier. A former professional football player whose criminal activities and drug abuse had scuttled his career, Rozier was wanted by police in three states and Canada when he joined Yahweh's cult, in 1982. Four years later, the prospect of a date with the electric chair transformed him into Yahweh's worst enemy on earth.

It was Rozier/Israel who first blew the whistle on Yahweh's private army of "death angels," a term grimly reminiscent of the Black Muslim "Zebra" murders from a decade earlier. Said "angels" were recruited for a cult-within-a-cult, dubbed the Brotherhood by Yahweh, exhorted to "show thyselves approved" by murdering "white devils" and slicing an ear from each victim as a trophy of the hunt. Miami homicide detectives believe that 17 white victims, many of them homeless "street people," were dispatched in a series of "ear murders" committed by Hebrew Israelites, beginning in April 1986. Rozier himself pled guilty to four slayings, thus avoiding death row, and he later added two more victims to the tally, during unexpected courtroom testimony. According to his statements, Yahweh's order was specific: "Kill me a white devil and bring me an ear." On other occasions, Yahweh told the congregation at large, "Whoever does not want me to rule over them, those are my enemies. And if you are my enemy, you must die... I want to see your head come off personally. I want to see the blood seep from your vein, you know that jugular vein. I want to see it."

As his trial date loomed closer, Yahweh was reborn once again, dumping his Social Security number and changing his name to "God, Son of God." The trial itself dragged on for 16 weeks and featured 160 witnesses, but Robert Rozier was clearly the star of the show, describing an occasion when his hit team brought a drifter's ears to Yahweh, in September 1986. The son of God was so delighted, Rozier testified, that "We got the day off and went to the movies." Fifty other cult defectors took the stand to verify parts of Rozier's story, adding details of their own, but the jury's verdict, in May 1992, was a distinctly mixed bag. Seven defendants were ac-

panel deadlocked on two
piracy, but cleared on the
Yahweh himself was con-
failed to reach agreement
ugh to pack him off to jail
at November, on a single
net Reno grudgingly dis-
ding homicides.

ts of lethal terrorism have
out by zealots of one sect
olesale murder would ad-
alvation to the faithful. As
religious wars, it is im-
oll for religious terrorism,
suggests the scope of the

d, most Americans auto-
torn by endemic violence
litant Zionists of the Irgun
the 1930s and '40s, using
e British out of Palestine.
Zionist terrorists such as the Irgun and Stern Gang also helped drive many Arabs out of Palestine during the 1948 War, some of whom were forcibly expelled and some of whom fled in fear. The Israeli government, which was established in 1948, began confiscating these Arabs' "absentee property" and parceling it out to Jewish immigrants. These, and other Israeli policies, have obfuscated the restoration of peace in the region.

There have been terrorist acts perpetrated by both sides in this ongoing conflict. Arabs accuse the Israeli government of practicing "state terrorism," including military bombings of Arab villages, towns, and refugee camps in which civilians are killed, as well as acts of targeted assassination carried out by the Mossad, the Israeli intelligence service. Jewish individuals and groups, such as Kach and Kahane Choi, have also engaged in acts of terrorism on their own without Israeli authority.

For the past half-century, Arab Muslims have waged terrorist campaigns against Israel, through such groups as Hamas ("Islamic Resistance Movement"), Hizballah ("Party of God"), Palestine Islamic Jihad, Islamic Amal, and others. Fundamentalist Islamic governments in Libya, Iran, and Saudi Arabia, as well as the Ba'th-influenced governments of Iraq and Syria, are notorious for supporting global terrorist activities, which not only target Israeli agents, but also Americans, British — anyone, in fact, who is suspected of supporting Israel.

When not killing Jews, Muslim terrorists frequently turn on each other, with Sunnis battling Shi'ites, Shi'ites stalking Hanafis, and so on. Shi'ite terrorists, for instance, have waged sporadic guerrilla warfare against Hizballah since 1989. Egypt's government is constantly beset by Muslim fringe groups including the Islamic Brotherhood, the Egyptian Liberation Organization, the Islamic Group, and the Jihad Group (blamed for the assassination of President Anwar Sadat in 1981). In strife-torn Lebanon, Hizballah warriors skirmish with the Lebanese army, while conflict between Christian and Muslim militias has turned downtown Beirut into a shooting gallery. Iran, a staunchly fundamentalist nation, and Iraq have problems of their own. Iraq's Saddam Hussein and his regime have been a target of Pro-Iranian Iraqi terrorists from Al Dawa ("The Call") since 1980, and he returns the favor by harboring agents of Mujahedin-e Khalq, the main resistance movement opposing Iran's strict theocracy.

In Africa, Algeria has been renowned as a training ground for international terrorists since Muslim rebels expelled French colonial forces in 1962. At that, the government did not go far enough to satisfy Islamic fundamentalists, who have organized such groups as the Armed Islamic Group to strike at targets including tourists, native feminists, and foreign missionaries. Farther south, in Senegal, a small Catholic resistance movement based at Casamance struggles hopelessly against the nation's Islamic majority. In Uganda, on the other side of the continent, guerrillas of the Lord's Resistance Army clash with government troops and massacre refugees from the long civil war in neighboring Sudan.

Vast Asia has no shortage of terrorist movements inspired by religion of one kind or another, and India has probably suffered the most, with three-way carnage between Hindus, Sikhs, and Muslims raging virtually nonstop since 1947. Members of the Hindu fundamentalist group Rashtriya Swayamsevak Sang murdered Mahatma Gandhi in 1948, and remained active four decades later, despite an official ban on their organization. Sikh extremists (responsible for the assassination of Prime Minister Indira Gandhi in 1984 and the 1985 bombing of an Air-India flight that killed 329 persons) seek an independent state in the Punjab, as do Muslim rebels in Kashmir. A quasi-Hindu cult, the Path of Eternal Bliss, was officially banned in 1975, following a series of murders and bombings, but sporadic Hindu violence continues. Pakistan, separated from India as a Muslim-dominated state in 1947, has lately been the site of clan warfare between Sunni and Shi'ite Muslims, with 97 persons killed in the month of September 1996 alone. Tiny Bangladesh (formerly East Pakistan), is meanwhile on the verge of war with neighboring

Burma, over the repatriation of Islamic Arakanese/Royhinga rebels who have fled oppression in their Burmese homeland.

Another Asian hotbed of religious mayhem is Afghanistan, where peasant *mujahadeen* ("soldiers of God") resisted Soviet occupation throughout the 1980s. Despite the Muslim victory and installation of guerrilla leader Burhanuddin Rabbani as president in June 1992, fighting continued between Islamic moderates and fundamentalists. Organized government virtually ceased to exist in the mid-1990s, until Taliban zealots emerged victorious in September 1996 and imposed strict Muslim law on the country at large (including public beatings for any woman seen without a veil). When not abusing one another, Afghan Muslims train and support Islamic guerrillas in neighboring Tajikistan, rooting for a religious victory in their war against the pro-Russian government.

Elsewhere in Asia, the Christian government of the Philippines faces violent opposition from such Muslim factions as Abu Sayyaf and the Moro National Liberation Front, while Christian vigilantes oppose any move toward compromise and the creation of an independent Moro state. In Sri Lanka (formerly Ceylon), the dominant Buddhist majority is besieged by a welter of Hindu resistance groups, including the Tamil Tigers, the Tamil United Liberation Front, and the Eelam People's Revolutionary Liberation Front. By 1995, more than 35,000 persons had died in the ongoing civil war, including President Ranasinghe Premadasa, assassinated by a Tamil rebel in May 1993.

Europe, while presumably more "civilized" than Africa or Asia, has also endured its share of religious terrorism in modern times. Northern Ireland is a case in point, partitioned from the Irish Republic in 1920, after hundreds of years of conflict between Catholic natives and Protestant invaders. The Irish "Troubles" resumed in 1968, with a militant Catholic civil rights movement and armed Protestant resistance, and while the Provisional Irish Republican Army has espoused atheistic Marxism, its primary opponents (and targets) are still drawn from such Protestant vigilante groups as the Ulster Volunteer Force, the Loyalist Defense Volunteers, and the Shankill Butchers. In Spain, self-styled Warriors of Christ the King seek to install a neo-fascist government, while the Anti-Communist Apostolic Alliance, a staunchly Catholic group, terrorizes Basque and Catalan separatists. With the breakup of communist Yugoslavia in 1991, fierce three-way fighting erupted between Muslims, Serbs, and Croats in the new Republic of Bosnia and Herzegovina. Christian Serbs, in particular, utilized rape and murder against Muslims in a grisly program of "ethnic cleansing."

It should not be supposed that the American "melting pot" has been immune to religious terrorism, by any means. The 19th century witnessed brutal riots against Catholics, carried out by members of the so-called **"nativist" movement**, while later generations of Catholics and Jews faced deadly harassment from the **Ku Klux Klan**. Since 1980, widespread violence has been perpetrated by zealots of the racist **"Christian Identity"** sect, and by opponents of abortion in the sadly misnamed **"pro-life" movement**, with numerous **"gay bashing"** assaults directed at homosexuals. Despite much fear of Muslim terrorism from the Middle East, the only incident directly traceable to Islamic agents so far is the World Trade Center bombing of February 1993 (It's uncertain as to whether or not Rabbi Meir Kahane's 1990 assassination in New York City was the act of a Muslim terrorist.). Dozens of bombings, numerous assaults and at least two assassinations were also traced to the militant Jewish Defense League, founded in 1968 by Rabbi Meir Kahane. **[See also: Aum Shinrikyo; Black Hundreds]**

Theriault, Roch

Canada's version of Charles Manson was born May 16, 1947, one of seven children fathered by a poor house painter in Quebec. For fun around the house, he would recall, Roch Theriault, his father and two brothers would play a game called "Bone," in which they sat around the kitchen table, wearing heavy boots, and kicked each other's shins until somebody quit the game.

Raised Catholic, Theriault abandoned the church after he was ejected from the Aramis Club, a Catholic charitable group, because of "weird ideas" — including the notion that new initiates should wear portraits of Satan on their backs. Next, he signed up with the Seventh-Day Adventists, but they likewise failed to see his greatness and denied Theriault the leadership position he craved. Briefly hospitalized in his twenties, Roch emerged with a lifelong fascination for medicine, poring over medical texts, boring his friends with half-baked lectures on anatomy. By 1978, he was leading his own homeopathic cult, advocating "alternative medicine" and predicting the end of the world. With 17 disciples, Theriault moved to the Gaspe Peninsula, where he began calling himself Moses and assigned Biblical names to his disciples. On the side, he also started drinking heavily, seizing any excuse to "purify" his flock by "beating the devil out of them."

In March 1981, Theriault's followers left their children in the care of a new cult member, a 23-year-old escapee from a Quebec mental hospital. The drop-in loony chose that moment to go berserk, beating one of the children so badly that he suffered internal injuries. "Doctor" Theriault, stewed to the gills, decided to operate, and the child promptly died. Roch blamed the new arrival and castrated him as punish-

275

It was 1982 when word leaked out about weird goings-on at the commune, and police staged a raid, arresting Theriault and six other adults on a variety of charges. All pled guilty, with Roch drawing the most severe sentence. He served 18 months of a two-year term, reclaimed his "family," and moved them to rural Ontario, where they purchased 200 acres of woodland on the Burnt River.

Prison had been a revelation for Roch. Instead of Moses, he now told his flock that he "was like Abraham in the Bible," requiring sex from every woman in the group to help the cult proliferate. Each night, a different woman graced his bed, after long days of baking bread which they sold door-to-door. So industrious were they, in fact, that Roch's followers were dubbed the "Ant Hill Kids." As entertainment, Theriault commanded members of his cult to strip naked and fight for the amusement of their friends. Increasingly, his bouts of rage were fueled by alcohol, and Theriault became obsessed with his ability to cure most any ailment, usually by means of surgery *sans* anesthetic, using any tools at his disposal.

A flying squad of cops and social workers swept the new commune in 1985, rounding up 14 children — most of them fathered by Roch — and placing them in foster homes. From that time on, authorities would seize each infant shortly after birth; the mothers stubbornly refused to abandon Theriault, even when it meant forsaking their children forever.

With the kids gone, Roch lost any vestige of restraint. He grew a beard of Biblical dimensions, donned a robe and mock-gold crown, "operating" on his disciples at the drop of a hat. A woman who complained of toothache had eight teeth ripped from her mouth. A male disciple's swollen testicle was crudely amputated.

And the worst was yet to come.

And the worst was yet to come.

Cultist Solange Boilard had borne three children by her guru, earning sufficient trust that Roch called her his "governor," but it was not enough to save her on the night of September 28, 1988, when he flew into a drunken fit of rage. Theriault first choked Solange to near-unconsciousness, as a means of convincing her "that her every breath belonged to him," then he decided that she needed "treatment" for some imaginary illness. Stretching her out on a table, Roch beat the woman senseless, then opened her abdomen with a knife, extracted her intestine, severed part of it, and pushed the rest back in, ordering someone from the audience to suture the wound. Solange died the next day, tormented by peritonitis, but Theriault was convinced that he could raise her from the dead. His method was bizarre, to say the least: Roch ordered one of his flunkies to saw off the top of the dead woman's skull, after which he masturbated onto her exposed brain, convinced that his "essence" would revive the corpse.

Surprisingly enough, the tactic failed, but Roch was not discouraged. Even after Solange was buried, he kept digging her up, expecting signs of life. Frantic disciples finally convinced Theriault to cremate the body, but not before he extracted part of one rib, which he wore around his neck, suspended on a leather thong.

Eleven months would pass before authorities learned of the murder, informed by another "patient" whose healthy arm Theriault had severed below the elbow. This time, the victim survived to reach a hospital, and she spun a grisly tale for the police. Arrested for murder in October 1989, Roch sat in jail for over three years before his trial convened, in January 1993. There, in lieu of taking his chances with a jury, Theriault pled guilty on January 18, admitting that he was responsible for "traumatizing, mutilating and inflicting suffering on

onment, with a stipulation of no parole for at least the first ten years.

Vollmer, Ralph: See Nuske, Matthew

Watson, John Selby

A child of London, born in 1804, John Watson graduated from Trinity College in Dublin, then entered the Anglican clergy. Ordained as a deacon at Cambridge, at age 35, he was soon inducted as a priest, and rose to the office of curate at Langportil two years later. By age 40, he had become headmaster at the Stockwell Grammar School, in Surrey, and there finally married his college sweetheart, Anne Armstrong, in December 1844. When not busy with his headmaster's duties, Watson spent most of his time translating Greek classics into English.

In 1870, after a quarter-century at Stockwell Grammar, declining enrollment and tuitions led to his dismissal as headmaster. The Watsons moved to Chelsfield, in Kent, where Watson was visibly depressed. Rumors circulated that he was also impotent, and that Anne was none too happy with the fact.

When Watson's servant girl arrived to fix dinner on the evening of October 8, 1871, Rev. Watson informed her that his wife would be gone "for two or three days." In fact, she his wife would be gone "for two or three days." In fact, she was stashed in a guest room, skull crushed by a brutal pistol-whipping. Three days later, Watson swallowed poison, leaving a suicide note that explained the killing of his wife as "a fit of rage," but a servant found him still breathing, and medical help arrived in time to save his life.

Watson's murder trial opened at the Old Bailey, in London, on January 10, 1872. He pled insanity, but a battery of doctors disagreed, and jurors deliberated 90 minutes before convicting him of murder. Even then, they recommended mercy, based on Watson's age, and he was sentenced to life imprisonment. The killer reverend lasted 12 years in confinement, before he suffered a fall in his cell and died of the resulting injuries.

Witchcraft: See Capital Punishment and Inquisition

Women's Health-Care Clinic Murders: See "Pro-Life" Movement

Yahweh Ben Yahweh: See "Temple of Love"

Bibliography

Anderson, Scott. *The 4 O'clock Murders*. New York: Doubleday, 1993.

Barkun, Michael. *Religion and the Racist Right*. Chapel Hill, NC: University of North Carolina Press, 1994.

Bennett, David. *The Party of Fear*. New York: Vintage, 1995.

Bishop, Patrick, and Eamonn Mallie. *The Provisional IRA*. London: Corgi Books, 1988.

Boyd, Andrew. *Holy War in Belfast*. Belfast: Pretani Press, 1969.

Boyle, James. *Killer Cults*. New York: St. Martin's Press, 1995.

Burghardt, Tom. "Neo-Nazis Salute the Anti-Abortion Zealots." *Covert Action Quarterly*, Spring 1995.

Chalmers, David. *Hooded Americanism*. Durham, NC: Duke University Press, 1981.

Coates, James. *Armed and Dangerous*. New York: Hill & Wang, 1987.

Coogan, Tim Pat. *The IRA*. Glasgow: Fontana/Collins, 1987.

Dobson, Christopher, and Ronald Payne. *The Terrorists*. New York: Facts on File, 1982.

Downing, Taylor (ed). *The Troubles*. London: Thames Macdonald, 1980.

D'Souza, Dinesh. *The End of Racism*. New York: The Free Press, 1995.

Earley, Pete. *Prophet of Death*. New York: William Morrow, 1991.

Ellerbe, Helen. *The Dark Side of Christian History*. San Rafael, CA: Morningstar Books, 1995.

Freedberg, Sydney. *Brother Love*. New York: Pantheon Books, 1994.

Friedly, Michael. *Malcolm X: The Assassination*. New York: Carroll & Graf, 1992.

Gaute, J.H.H., and Robin Odell. *Murder Whereabouts*. London: Harrap, 1986.

Gaute, J.H.H., and Robin Odell. *The New Murderers' Who's Who*. New York: International Polygonics, 1989.

Haining, Peter. *Black Magic and Witchcraft*. New York: Bantam, 1972.

Hofstadter, Richard, and Michael Wallace (eds). *American Violence: A Documentary History*. New York: Alfred A. Knopf, 1970.

Hogg, Gary. *Cannibalism and Human Sacrifice*. Secaucus, NJ: Citadel, 1966.

Holms, John Pynchon, and Tom Burke. *Terrorism*. New York: Pinnacle Books, 1994.

Hubner, John, and Lindsey Gruson. *Monkey on a Stick*. New York: Onyx, 1988.

Humes, Edward. *Buried Secrets*. New York: Dutton, 1991.

Karl, Jonathan. *The Right To Bear Arms*. New York: Harper Paperbacks, 1995.

Kilroy, Jim, and Bob Stewart. *Sacrifice*. Dallas: Word Publishing, 1990.

Kohn, George. *Dictionary of Wars*. New York: Anchor Books, 1986.

Lane, Brian, and Wilfred Greg. *The Encyclopedia of Serial Killers*. London: Headline, 1992.

Lincoln, C. Eric. *The Black Muslims in America*. Grand Rapids, MI: William B. Eerdmans, 1994.

Lindsey, Robert. *A Gathering of Saints*. New York: Dell, 1988.

Linedecker, Clifford. *Hell Ranch*. Austin, TX: Diamond Books, 1989.

Lyons, Arthur. *Satan Wants You*. New York: Mysterious Press, 1988.

Massengill, Reed. *Portrait of a Racist*. New York: St. Martin's Press, 1994.

McConnell, Brian. *Holy Killers*. London: Headline Books, 1995.

Myers, Gustavus. *History of Bigotry in the United States*. New York: Capricorn Books, 1960.

Naifeh, Steven, and Gregory Smith. *The Mormon Murders*. New York: Onyx, 1989.

Newton, Michael. *Bad Girls Do It!* Port Townsend, WA: Loompanics Unlimited, 1993.

Newton, Michael. *Hunting Humans*. Port Townsend, WA: Loompanics Unlimited, 1990.

Newton, Michael. *Raising Hell*. New York: Avon, 1993.

Newton, Michael. "Season of the Witch." *Gauntlet, Vol. 1*, No. 8, 1994.

Newton, Michael. "Written in Blood: A History of Human Sacrifice." *The Journal of Psychohistory*, Fall 1996.

Newton, Michael, and Judy Ann Newton. *The Ku Klux Klan*. New York: Garland, 1991.

Newton, Michael, and Judy Ann Newton. *Racial and Religious Violence in America*. New York: Garland, 1991.

Oke, Isaiah. *Blood Secrets*. Buffalo, NY: Prometheus Books, 1989.

Provost, Gary. *Across the Border*. New York: Pocket Books, 1989.

Reynolds, Richard. *Cry for War*. San Francisco: Squibob Press, 1987.

Ridgeway, James. *Blood in the Face*. New York: Thunder's Mouth Press, 1990.

Rosie, George. *The Directory of International Terrorism*. Edinburgh: Mainstream Publishing, 1986.

Schutze, Jim. *Cauldron of Blood*. New York: Avon, 1989.

Singer, Margaret. *Cults in Our Midst*. San Francisco: Jossey-Bass Publishers, 1995.

Smith. Brent. *Terrorism in America*. Albany: State University of New York Press, 1994.

Sterling, Claire. *The Terror Network.* New York: Berkley, 1982.

Stern, Kenneth. *A Force Upon the Plain*. New York: Simon & Schuster, 1996.

Tierney, Patrick. *The Highest Altar.* New York: Viking, 1989.

Wade, Wyn Craig. *The Fiery Cross*. New York: Simon and Schuster, 1987.